Table of Contents

This book is dedicated to two dear friends
without whom it would not have been possible:
Karen Underhill and Jim Blandy.

Foreword

The most well-known organizational models of getting things done—whether it's building a house, producing a motion picture, or writing software—tend to concern the prediction of and commitment to specific outcomes, mitigating risk to the plan, and correcting surprises along the way. In such models, innovation is seen to happen at the moment of inspiration of the idea—and the remaining 99% of the effort is perspiration, to paraphrase Edison. Say it along with me: "Yeah, right." This view looks at innovation as a very solitary sport; we want to talk about Steve Jobs as the guy behind the iPod, rather than the mix of good engineers and product marketing types who collaborated with Steve to find the right sweet-spot combination of features and fashion.

We also want to talk about Linus Torvalds as the guy responsible for Linux, but that's even less close to the truth than the Jobs/iPod example. Linus' brilliance is not in creating an unprecedented technology innovation, nor in plotting the perfect road map for the Linux kernel, nor in having a full-time staff of his own to assign work to. The brilliance inside Linus is his ability to orchestrate the aggregated interests of thousands of other developers, all individually scratching their own itch (or that of their employer), and thereby making a product renowned for reliability, performance, and the features people need. Linus' role is like that of an air traffic controller—watching the skies fill with ideas, prototypes based on those ideas, and serious production-quality code implementing the best of those ideas—then deciding when that work is mature enough to land at the airport known as Linus' official kernel source code repository.

It's been said that humility is the most underrated force in the world today. Successful open source leaders demonstrate this over and over by driving for consensus on major ideas, making it clear their own ideas are open to challenge, and being as transparent as possible. Building a sense of empowerment amongst the developers is more important than meeting ship dates with specific features, and more important than creating zero-defect software. The Apache Software Foundation, for example, believes that its first order of business is creating healthy software developer communities focused on solving common problems; good software is a simply an emergent result.

In fact it couldn't happen any other way, and here's why. The Open Source Definition is a list of terms that are requirements of any license claiming to be an open source license, and any project claiming to be an open source project must have such a license. One of the key themes of the OSD is "the right to fork": the right to create a derivative work and redistribute it to other people under the terms of the same license, *without* the approval of the original developers. This doesn't happen often; most of the time, when someone fixes a bug or adds a minor feature, they usually offer it back to the original developers, and if the project is well run, that ends up in a subsequent release. But when it needs to happen—when the original developers have moved on to other things, or worse, become difficult to work with—the right to fork acts as an essential device to carry a project forward.

Among many other benefits, this rule means that leadership in an open source community comes not from leverage or control, but from finding common interests and expertly managing what is volunteered. Open source projects don't compete for "market share"—for dollars from the user base—because there aren't any. Instead, they compete for developer mind share and heart share, and that's not going to flow to a leader who's obstinate, unresponsive to the user community, or technically unsophisticated.

Those who see open source as a bunch of zero-price software created by impossibly altruistic amateurs don't get this at all. The rest of the world, though, is starting to clue in to the idea that the software industry doesn't have to be a zero-sum game, and that letting go of a little control and ownership might actually result in something grander in return. This notion is larger than just software. Professor Eric von Hippel at MIT has charted a history of interesting experiments and patterns in the domain of "user-led innovation"—companies who have experimented with involving their customers in the design of follow-up products; or delivering toolkits rather than finished works, allowing customers to create new uses or solve more complicated problems. The Wikipedia is a huge example of participatory creation that sounds like it should be an unmanageable chaos, but instead has developed a reputation for being more complete, up-to-date, and balanced than any series you could buy and put on your bookshelf.

These successes don't just happen by magically pressing the "Be More Open" button on the keyboard. There is a universe of best practice and lore that before now has been largely an oral tradition, picked up by sitting on a good project mailing list for years and learning the patterns of communication and process.

Karl has done the software development world a tremendous favor by finally capturing much of that in this book. While the software engineering world is much more comfortable with the concepts of open source, software developer communities, and unpredictable outcomes than they were before, there are still not enough leaders with Karl's grasp of the nuances that make all the difference. With this book, that can change.

—*Brian Behlendorf*
Apache Software Foundation and CollabNet

Preface

Why Write This Book?

At parties, people no longer give me a blank stare when I tell them I write free software. "Oh, yes, open source—like Linux?" they say. I nod eagerly in agreement. "Yes, exactly! That's what I do." It's nice not to be completely on the fringe anymore. In the past, the next question was usually fairly predictable: "How do you make money doing that?" To answer, I'd summarize the economics of open source: that there are organizations in whose interest it is to have certain software exist, but that they don't need to sell copies, they just want to make sure the software is available and maintained, as a tool instead of a commodity.

Lately, however, the next question has not always been about money. The business case for open source software[1] is no longer so mysterious, and many non-programmers already understand—or at least are not surprised—that there are people employed at it full time. Instead, the question I have been hearing more and more often is *"Oh, how does that work?"*

I didn't have a satisfactory answer ready, and the harder I tried to come up with one, the more I realized how complex a topic it really is. Running a free software project is not exactly like running a business (imagine having to constantly negotiate the nature

---

1   The terms "open source" and "free" are essentially synonymous in this context; they are discussed more in the section "Free Versus Open Source" in Chapter 1.

of your product with a group of volunteers, most of whom you've never met!). Nor, for various reasons, is it exactly like running a traditional non-profit organization, nor a government. It has similarities to all these things, but I have slowly come to the conclusion that free software is *sui generis*. There are many things with which it can be usefully compared, but none with which it can be equated. Indeed, even the assumption that free software projects can be "run" is a stretch. A free software project can be *started*, and it can be influenced by interested parties, often quite strongly. But its assets cannot be made the property of any single owner, and as long as there are people somewhere—anywhere—interested in continuing it, it cannot be unilaterally shut down. Everyone has infinite power; everyone has no power. It makes for an interesting dynamic.

That is why I wanted to write this book. Free software projects have evolved a distinct culture, an ethos in which the liberty to make the software do anything one wants is a central tenet, and yet the result of this liberty is not a scattering of individuals each going their own separate way with the code, but enthusiastic collaboration. Indeed, competence at cooperation itself is one of the most highly valued skills in free software. To manage these projects is to engage in a kind of hypertrophied cooperation, where one's ability not only to work with others but to come up with new ways of working together can result in tangible benefits to the software. This book attempts to describe the techniques by which this may be done. It is by no means complete, but it is at least a beginning.

Good free software is a worthy goal in itself, and I hope that readers who come looking for ways to achieve it will be satisfied with what they find here. But beyond that I also hope to convey something of the sheer pleasure to be had from working with a motivated team of open source developers, and from interacting with users in the wonderfully direct way that open source encourages. Participating in a successful free software project is *fun*, and ultimately that's what keeps the whole system going.

Who Should Read This Book?

This book is meant for software developers and managers who are considering starting an open source project, or who have started one and are wondering what to do now. It should also be helpful for people who just want to participate in an open source project but have never done so before.

The reader need not be a programmer, but should know basic software engineering concepts such as source code, compilers, and patches.

Prior experience with open source software, as either a user or a developer, is not necessary. Those who have worked in free software projects before will probably find at least some parts of the book a bit obvious, and may want to skip those sections. Because there's such a potentially wide range of audience experience, I've made an effort to label sections clearly, and to say when something can be skipped by those already familiar with the material.

How to Use This Book

This book consists of nine chapters and four appendixes:

Chapter 1, *Introduction*
> A brief history of free software, and an overview of the open source world today.

Chapter 2, *Getting Started*
> How to get an open source project off on the right foot, including gathering developers, choosing a license, and announcing the project.

Chapter 3, *Technical Infrastructure*
> An in-depth look at the tools a project needs to function smoothly, including communications, version control, and bug tracking software.

Chapter 4, *Social and Political Infrastructure*
> How to set up formal and informal political structures to enable project members to work together and achieve consensus on important issues.

Chapter 5, *Money*
> Why and how to have a commercial relationship with an open source project.

Chapter 6, *Communications*
> A guide to productive conduct in project forums, covering both the social and technical aspects of communications.

Chapter 7, *Packaging, Releasing, and Daily Development*
> How to manage regular releases of open source software, without disrupting the development cycles of the volunteer participants.

Chapter 8, *Managing Volunteers*
> Understanding why volunteer developers do what they do, and treating them in such a way that they keep doing it.

Chapter 9, *Licenses, Copyrights, and Patents*
> How to evaluate and choose free software licenses, including an in-depth examination of license compatibility issues.

Appendix A, *Free Version Control Systems*
> A list of open source version control systems, for projects just starting out.

Appendix B, *Free Bug Trackers*
> Likewise, a list of open source bug trackers.

Appendix C, *Why Should I Care What Color the Bikeshed Is?*
> An oft-cited screed by Poul-Henning Kamp about the dangers of group decision-making and open source discussion lists.

Appendix D, *Example Instructions for Reporting Bugs*

An example that shows how an open source project can use bug reporting instructions to gradually teach certain users about the development procedures the project follows.

Sources

Much of the raw material for this book came from five years of working with the Subversion project (*http://subversion.tigris.org/*). Subversion is an open source version control system, written from scratch, and intended to replace CVS as the de facto version control system of choice in the open source community. The project was started by my employer, CollabNet (*http://www.collab.net/*), in early 2000, and thank goodness CollabNet understood right from the start how to run it as a truly collaborative, distributed effort. We got a lot of volunteer developer buy-in early on; today there are 50-some developers on the project, of whom only a few are CollabNet employees.

Subversion is in many ways a classic example of an open source project, and I ended up drawing on it more heavily than I originally expected. This was partly a matter of convenience: whenever I needed an example of a particular phenomenon, I could usually call one up from Subversion right off the top of my head. But it was also a matter of verification. Although I am involved in other free software projects to varying degrees, and talk to friends and acquaintances involved in many more, one quickly realizes when writing for print that all assertions need to be fact-checked. I didn't want to make statements about events in other projects based only on what I could read in their public mailing list archives. If someone were to try that with Subversion, I knew, she'd be right about half the time and wrong the other half. So when drawing inspiration or examples from a project with which I didn't have direct experience, I tried to first talk to an informant there, someone I could trust to explain what was really going on.

Subversion has been my job for the last 5 years, but I've been involved in free software for 12. Other projects that influenced this book include:

- The GNU Emacs text editor project at the Free Software Foundation, in which I maintain a few small packages.

- Concurrent Versions System (CVS), which I worked on intensely in 1994–1995 with Jim Blandy, but have been involved with only intermittently since.

- The collection of open source projects known as the Apache Software Foundation, especially the Apache Portable Runtime (APR) and Apache HTTP Server.

- OpenOffice.org, the Berkeley Database from Sleepycat, and MySQL Database; I have not been involved with these projects personally, but have observed them and, in some cases, talked to people there.

- GDB, the GNU Debugger (likewise).
- The Debian Project (likewise).

This is not a complete list, of course. Like most open source programmers, I keep loose tabs on many different projects, just to have a sense of the general state of things. I won't name all of them here, but they are mentioned in the text where appropriate.

Conventions

The following conventions are used in this book:

Italic

> Used for file and directory names, for URLs, and for emphasis when introducing a new term.

`Constant width`

> Used for code examples.

`Constant width italic`

> In some code examples, indicates an element (e.g., a filename) that you supply.

Comments and Questions

Please address comments and questions concerning this book to the publisher:

> O'Reilly Media, Inc.
> 1005 Gravenstein Highway North
> Sebastopol, CA 95472
> (800) 998-9938 (in the United States or Canada)
> (707) 829-0515 (international or local)
> (707) 829-0104 (fax)

We have a web page for this book, where we list errata, examples, and any additional information. You can access this page at:

> *http://www.oreilly.com/catalog/producingoss*

To comment or ask technical questions about this book, send email to:

> *bookquestions@oreilly.com*

For more information about our books, conferences, Resource Centers, and the O'Reilly Network, see our web site at:

> *http://www.oreilly.com*

Safari Enabled

 When you see a Safari® Enabled icon on the cover of your favorite technology book, it means the book is available online through the O'Reilly Network Safari Bookshelf.

Safari offers a solution that's better than e-books. It's a virtual library that lets you easily search thousands of top technology books, cut and paste code samples, download chapters, and find quick answers when you need the most accurate, current information. Try it for free at *http://safari.oreilly.com*.

Acknowledgments

This book took four times longer to write than I thought it would, and for much of that time felt rather like i had a grand piano suspended above my head wherever I went. Without help from many people, I would not have been able to complete it while staying sane.

Andy Oram, my editor at O'Reilly, was a writer's dream. Aside from knowing the field intimately (he suggested many of the topics), he has the rare gift of knowing what one meant to say and helping one find the right way to say it. It has been an honor to work with him. Thanks also to Chuck Toporek for steering this proposal to Andy right away.

Brian Fitzpatrick reviewed almost all of the material as I wrote it, which not only made the book better, but kept me writing when I wanted to be anywhere in the world but in front of the computer. Ben Collins-Sussman and Mike Pilato also checked up on progress, and were always happy to discuss—sometimes at length—whatever topic I was trying to cover that week. They also noticed when I slowed down, and gently nagged when necessary. Thanks, guys.

Biella Coleman was writing her dissertation at the same time as I was writing this book. She knows what it means to sit down and write every day, and provided an inspiring example as well as a sympathetic ear. She also has a fascinating anthropologist's-eye view of the free software movement, giving both ideas and references that I was able use in the book. Alex Golub—another anthropologist with one foot in the free software world, and also finishing his dissertation at the same time—was exceptionally supportive early on, which helped a great deal.

Micah Anderson somehow never seemed too oppressed by his own writing gig, which was inspiring in a sick, envy-generating sort of way, but he was ever ready with friendship, conversation, and (on at least one occasion) technical support. Thanks, Micah!

Jon Trowbridge and Sander Striker gave both encouragement and concrete help—their broad experience in free software provided material I couldn't have gotten any other way.

Thanks to Greg Stein not only for friendship and well-timed encouragement, but for showing the Subversion project how important regular code review is in building a programming community. Thanks also to Brian Behlendorf, who tactfully drummed into our heads the importance of having discussions publicly; I hope that principle is reflected throughout this book.

Thanks to Benjamin "Mako" Hill and Seth Schoen, for various conversations about free software and its politics; to Zack Urlocker and Louis Suarez-Potts for taking time out of their busy schedules to be interviewed; to Shane on the Slashcode list for allowing his post to be quoted; and to Haggen So for his enormously helpful comparison of canned hosting sites.

Thanks to Alla Dekhtyar, Polina, and Sonya for their unflagging and patient encouragement. I'm very glad that I will no longer have to end (or rather, try unsuccessfully to end) our evenings early to go home and work on "The Book."

Thanks to Jack Repenning for friendship, conversation, and a stubborn refusal to ever accept an easy wrong analysis when a harder right one is available. I hope that some of his long experience with both software development and the software industry rubbed off on this book.

CollabNet was exceptionally generous in allowing me a flexible schedule to write, and didn't complain when it went on far longer than originally planned. I don't know all the intricacies of how management arrives at such decisions, but I suspect Sandhya Klute, and later Mahesh Murthy, had something to do with it—my thanks to them both.

The entire Subversion development team has been an inspiration for the past five years, and much of what is in this book I learned from working with them. I won't thank them all by name here, because there are too many, but I implore any reader who runs into a Subversion committer to immediately buy that committer the drink of his choice—I certainly plan to.

Many times I ranted to Rachel Scollon about the state of the book; she was always willing to listen, and somehow managed to make the problems seem smaller than before we talked. That helped a lot—thanks.

Thanks (again) to Noel Taylor, who must surely have wondered why I wanted to write another book given how much I complained the last time, but whose friendship and leadership of Golosá helped keep music and good fellowship in my life even in the busiest times. Thanks also to Matthew Dean and Dorothea Samtleben, friends and long-suffering musical partners, who were very understanding as my excuses for not practicing piled up. Megan Jennings was constantly supportive, and genuinely interested in the topic even though it was unfamiliar to her—a great tonic for an insecure writer. Thanks, pal!

I had four knowledgeable and diligent reviewers for this book: Yoav Shapira, Andrew Stellman, Davanum Srinivas, and Ben Hyde. If I had been able to incorporate all of their excellent suggestions, this would be a better book. As it was, time constraints forced me to pick and choose, but the improvements were still significant. Any errors that remain are entirely my own.

My parents, Frances and Henry, were wonderfully supportive as always, and as this book is less technical than the previous one, I hope they'll find it somewhat more readable.

Finally, I would like to thank the dedicatees, Karen Underhill and Jim Blandy. Karen's friendship and understanding have meant everything to me, not only during the writing of this book but for the last seven years. I simply would not have finished without her help. Likewise for Jim, a true friend and a hacker's hacker, who first taught me about free software, much as a bird might teach an airplane about flying.

Disclaimer

The thoughts and opinions expressed in this book are my own. They do not necessarily represent the views of CollabNet or of the Subversion project.

## CHAPTER 1

Introduction

Most free software projects fail.

We tend not to hear very much about the failures. Only successful projects attract attention, and there are so many free software projects in total[1] that even though only a small percentage succeed, the result is still a lot of visible projects. We also don't hear about the failures because failure is not an event. There is no single moment when a project ceases to be viable; people just sort of drift away and stop working on it. There may be a moment when a final change is made to the project, but those who made it usually didn't know at the time that it was the last one. There is not even a clear definition of when a project is expired. Is it when it hasn't been actively worked on for six months? When its user base stops growing, without having exceeded the developer base? What if the developers of one project abandon it because they realized they were duplicating the work of another—and what if they join that other project, then expand it to include much of their earlier effort? Did the first project end, or just change homes?

Because of such complexities, it's impossible to put a precise number on the failure rate. But anecdotal evidence from over a decade in open source, some casting around on SourceForge.net, and a little Googling all point to the same conclusion: the rate is

---

1   SourceForge.net, one popular hosting site, had 79,225 projects registered as of mid-April 2004. This is nowhere near the total number of free software projects on the Internet, of course; it's just the number that chose to use SourceForge.

extremely high, probably on the order of 90-95%. The number climbs higher if you include surviving but dysfunctional projects: those which *are* producing running code, but which are not pleasant places to be, or are not making progress as quickly or as dependably as they could.

This book is about avoiding failure. It examines not only how to do things right, but how to do them wrong, so you can recognize and correct problems early. My hope is that after reading it, you will have a repertory of techniques not just for avoiding common pitfalls of open source development, but also for dealing with the growth and maintenance of a successful project. Success is not a zero-sum game, and this book is not about winning or getting ahead of the competition. Indeed, an important part of running an open source project is working smoothly with other, related projects. In the long run, every successful project contributes to the well-being of the overall, worldwide body of free software.

It would be tempting to say that free software projects fail for the same sorts of reasons proprietary software projects do. Certainly, free software has no monopoly on unrealistic requirements, vague specifications, poor resource management, insufficient design phases, or any of the other hobgoblins already well known to the software industry. There is a huge body of writing on these topics, and I will try not to duplicate it in this book. Instead, I will attempt to describe the problems peculiar to free software. When a free software project runs aground, it is often because the developers (or the managers) did not appreciate the unique problems of open source software development, even though they might have been quite prepared for the better-known difficulties of closed-source development.

One of the most common mistakes is unrealistic expectations about the benefits of open source itself. An open license does not guarantee that hordes of active developers will suddenly volunteer their time to your project, nor does open-sourcing a troubled project automatically cure its ills. In fact, quite the opposite: opening up a project can add whole new sets of complexities, and cost *more* in the short term than simply keeping it in-house. Opening up means arranging the code to be comprehensible to complete strangers, setting up a development web site and email lists, and often writing documentation for the first time. All this is a lot of work. And of course, if any interested developers *do* show up, there is the added burden of answering their questions for a while before seeing any benefit from their presence. As developer Jamie Zawinski said about the troubled early days of the Mozilla project:

> Open source does work, but it is most definitely not a panacea. If there's a cautionary tale here, it is that you can't take a dying project, sprinkle it with the

magic pixie dust of "open source," and have everything magically work out. Software is hard. The issues aren't that simple. (from *http://www.jwz.org/gruntle/ nomo.html*)

A related mistake is that of skimping on presentation and packaging, figuring that these can always be done later, when the project is well under way. Presentation and packaging comprise a wide range of tasks, all revolving around the theme of reducing the barrier to entry. Making the project inviting to the uninitiated means writing user and developer documentation, setting up a project web site that's informative to newcomers, automating as much of the software's compilation and installation as possible, etc. Many programmers unfortunately treat this work as being of secondary importance to the code itself. There are a couple of reasons for this. First, it can feel like busywork, because its benefits are most visible to those least familiar with the project, and vice versa. After all, the people who develop the code don't really need the packaging. They already know how to install, administer, and use the software, because they wrote it. Second, the skills required to do presentation and packaging well are often completely different from those required to write code. People tend to focus on what they're good at, even if it might serve the project better to spend a little time on something that suits them less. Chapter 2 discusses presentation and packaging in detail, and explains why it's crucial that they be a priority from the very start of the project.

Next comes the fallacy that little or no project management is required in open source, or conversely, that the same management practices used for in-house development will work equally well on an open source project. Management in an open source project isn't always very visible, but in the successful projects, it's usually happening behind the scenes in some form or another. A small thought experiment suffices to show why. An open source project consists of a random collection of programmers—already a notoriously independent-minded category—who have most likely never met each other, and who may each have different personal goals in working on the project. The thought experiment is simply to imagine what would happen to such a group *without* management. Barring miracles, it would collapse or drift apart very quickly. Things won't simply run themselves, much as we might wish otherwise. But the management, though it may be quite active, is often informal, subtle, and low-key. The only thing keeping a development group together is their shared belief that they can do more in concert than individually. Thus the goal of management is mostly to ensure that they continue to believe this, by setting standards for communications, by making sure useful developers don't get marginalized due to personal idiosyncrasies, and in general by making the project a place developers want to keep coming back to. Specific techniques for doing this are discussed throughout the rest of this book.

Finally, there is a general category of problems that may be called "failures of cultural navigation." Ten years ago, even five, it would have been premature to talk about a global culture of free software, but not anymore. A recognizable culture has slowly emerged, and while it is certainly not monolithic—it is at least as prone to internal dissent and factionalism as any geographically bound culture—it does have a basically consistent core. Most successful open source projects exhibit some or all of the characteristics of this core. They reward certain types of behaviors, and punish others; they create an atmosphere that encourages unplanned participation, sometimes at the expense of central coordination; they have concepts of rudeness and politeness that can differ substantially from those prevalent elsewhere. Most importantly, longtime participants have generally internalized these standards, so that they share a rough consensus about expected conduct. Unsuccessful projects usually deviate in significant ways from this core, albeit unintentionally, and often do not have a consensus about what constitutes reasonable default behavior. This means that when problems arise, the situation can quickly deteriorate, as the participants lack an already established stock of cultural reflexes to fall back on for resolving differences.

This book is a practical guide, not an anthropological study or a history. However, a working knowledge of the origins of today's free software culture is an essential foundation for any practical advice. A person who understands the culture can travel far and wide in the open source world, encountering many local variations in custom and dialect, yet still be able to participate comfortably and effectively everywhere. In contrast, a person who does not understand the culture will find the process of organizing or participating in a project difficult and full of surprises. Since the number of people developing free software is still growing by leaps and bounds, there are many people in that latter category—this is largely a culture of recent immigrants, and will continue to be so for some time. If you think you might be one of them, the next section provides background for discussions you'll encounter later, both in this book and on the Internet. (On the other hand, if you've been working with open source for a while, you may already know a lot of its history, so feel free to skip the next section.)

History

Software sharing has been around as long as software itself. In the early days of computers, manufacturers felt that competitive advantages were to be had mainly in hardware innovation, and therefore didn't pay much attention to software as a business asset. Many of the customers for these early machines were scientists or technicians, who were able to modify and extend the software shipped with the machine themselves. Customers sometimes distributed their patches back not only to the manufacturer, but to other owners of similar machines. The manufacturers often tolerated and even encouraged this: in their eyes, improvements to the software, from whatever source, just made the machine more attractive to other potential customers.

Although this early period resembled today's free software culture in many ways, it differed in two crucial respects. First, there was as yet little standardization of hardware—it was a time of flourishing innovation in computer design, but the diversity of computing architectures meant that everything was incompatible with everything else. Thus, software written for one machine would generally not work on another. Programmers tended to acquire expertise in a particular architecture or family of architectures (whereas today they would be more likely to acquire expertise in a programming language or family of languages, confident that their expertise will be transferable to whatever computing hardware they happen to find themselves working with). Because a person's expertise tended to be specific to one kind of computer, their accumulation of expertise had the effect of making that computer more attractive to them and their colleagues. It was therefore in the manufacturer's interests for machine-specific code and knowledge to spread as widely as possible.

Second, there was no Internet. Though there were fewer legal restrictions on sharing than today, there were more technical ones: the means of getting data from place to place were inconvenient and cumbersome, relatively speaking. There were some small, local networks, good for sharing information among employees at the same research lab or company. But there remained barriers to overcome if one wanted to share with everyone, no matter where they were. These barriers *were* overcome in many cases. Sometimes different groups made contact with each other independently, sending disks or tapes through land mail, and sometimes the manufacturers themselves served as central clearing houses for patches. It also helped that many of the early computer developers worked at universities, where publishing one's knowledge was expected. But the physical realities of data transmission meant there was always an impedance to sharing, an impedance proportional to the distance (real or organizational) that the software had to travel. Widespread, frictionless sharing, as we know it today, was not possible.

The Rise of Proprietary Software and Free Software

As the industry matured, several interrelated changes occurred simultaneously. The wild diversity of hardware designs gradually gave way to a few clear winners—winners through superior technology, superior marketing, or some combination of the two. At the same time, and not entirely coincidentally, the development of so-called "high level" programming languages meant that one could write a program once, in one language, and have it automatically translated ("compiled") to run on different kinds of computers. The implications of this were not lost on the hardware manufacturers: a customer could now undertake a major software engineering effort without necessarily locking themselves into one particular computer architecture. When this was combined with the gradual narrowing of performance differences between various computers, as the less efficient designs were weeded out, a manufacturer that treated its hardware as its only asset could look forward to a future of declining profit margins. Raw computing power was becoming a fungible good, while software was becoming the differentiator. Selling software, or at least treating it as an integral part of hardware sales, began to look like a good strategy.

This meant that manufacturers had to start enforcing the copyrights on their code more strictly. If users simply continued to share and modify code freely among themselves, they might independently reimplement some of the improvements now being sold as "added value" by the supplier. Worse, shared code could get into the hands of competitors. The irony is that all this was happening around the time the Internet was getting off the ground. Just when truly unobstructed software sharing was finally becoming technically possible, changes in the computer business made it economically undesirable, at least from the point of view of any single company. The suppliers clamped down, either denying users access to the code that ran their machines, or insisting on non-disclosure agreements that made effective sharing impossible.

Conscious resistance

As the world of unrestricted code swapping slowly faded away, a counterreaction crystallized in the mind of at least one programmer. Richard Stallman worked in the Artificial Intelligence Lab at the Massachusetts Institute of Technology in the 1970s and early '80s, during what turned out to be a golden age and a golden location for code sharing. The AI Lab had a strong "hacker ethic,"[2] and people were not only encouraged but expected to share whatever improvements they made to the system. As Stallman wrote later:

> We did not call our software "free software", because that term did not yet exist; but that is what it was. Whenever people from another university or a company wanted to port and use a program, we gladly let them. If you saw someone using

---

2   Stallman uses the word "hacker" in the sense of "someone who loves to program and enjoys being clever about it," not the relatively new meaning of "someone who breaks into computers."

an unfamiliar and interesting program, you could always ask to see the source code, so that you could read it, change it, or cannibalize parts of it to make a new program. (from *http://www.gnu.org/gnu/thegnuproject.html*)

This Edenic community collapsed around Stallman shortly after 1980, when the changes that had been happening in the rest of the industry finally caught up with the AI Lab. A startup company hired away many of the Lab's programmers to work on an operating system similar to what they had been working on at the Lab, only now under an exclusive license. At the same time, the AI Lab acquired new equipment that came with a proprietary operating system.

Stallman saw the larger pattern in what was happening:

> The modern computers of the era, such as the VAX or the 68020, had their own operating systems, but none of them were free software: you had to sign a non-disclosure agreement even to get an executable copy.

> This meant that the first step in using a computer was to promise not to help your neighbor. A cooperating community was forbidden. The rule made by the owners of proprietary software was, "If you share with your neighbor, you are a pirate. If you want any changes, beg us to make them."

By some quirk of personality, he decided to resist the trend. Instead of continuing to work at the now-decimated AI Lab, or taking a job writing code at one of the new companies, where the results of his work would be kept locked in a box, he resigned from the Lab and started the GNU Project and the Free Software Foundation (FSF). The goal of GNU[3] was to develop a completely free and open computer operating system and body of application software, in which users would never be prevented from hacking or from sharing their modifications. He was, in essence, setting out to recreate what had been destroyed at the AI Lab, but on a worldwide scale and without the vulnerabilities that had made the AI Lab's culture susceptible to disintegration.

In addition to working on the new operating system, Stallman devised a copyright license whose terms guaranteed that his code would be perpetually free. The GNU General Public License (GPL) is a clever piece of legal judo: it says that the code may be copied and modified without restriction, and that both copies and derivative works (i.e., modified versions) must be distributed under the same license as the original, with no additional restrictions. In effect, it uses copyright law to achieve an effect opposite to that of traditional copyright: instead of limiting the software's distribution, it prevents *anyone*, even the author, from limiting it. For Stallman, this was

---

3   It stands for "GNU's Not Unix," and the "GNU" in that expansion stands for...the same thing.

better than simply putting his code into the public domain. If it were in the public domain, any particular copy of it could be incorporated into a proprietary program (as has also been known to happen to code under permissive copyright licenses). While such incorporation wouldn't in any way diminish the original code's continued availability, it would have meant that Stallman's efforts could benefit the enemy—proprietary software. The GPL can be thought of as a form of protectionism for free software, because it prevents non-free software from taking full advantage of GPLed code. The GPL and its relationship to other free software licenses are discussed in detail in Chapter 9.

With the help of many programmers, some of whom shared Stallman's ideology and some of whom simply wanted to see a lot of free code available, the GNU Project began releasing free replacements for many of the most critical components of an operating system. Because of the now-widespread standardization in computer hardware and software, it was possible to use the GNU replacements on otherwise non-free systems, and many people did. The GNU text editor (Emacs) and C compiler (GCC) were particularly successful, gaining large and loyal followings not on ideological grounds, but simply on their technical merits. By about 1990, GNU had produced most of a free operating system, except for the kernel—the part that the machine actually boots up, and that is responsible for managing memory, disk, and other system resources.

Unfortunately, the GNU project had chosen a kernel design that turned out to be harder to implement than expected. The ensuing delay prevented the Free Software Foundation from making the first release of an entirely free operating system. The final piece was put into place instead by Linus Torvalds, a Finnish computer science student who, with the help of volunteers around the world, had completed a free kernel using a more conservative design. He named it Linux, and when it was combined with the existing GNU programs, the result was a completely free operating system. For the first time, you could boot up your computer and do work without using any proprietary software.[4]

Much of the software on this new operating system was not produced by the GNU project. In fact, GNU wasn't even the only group working on producing a free operating system (for example, the code that eventually became NetBSD and FreeBSD

---

4   Technically, Linux was not the first. A free operating system for IBM-compatible computers, called 386BSD, had come out shortly before Linux. However, it was a lot harder to get 386BSD up and running. Linux made such a splash not only because it was free, but because it actually had a high chance of booting your computer when you installed it.

was already under development by this time). The importance of the Free Software Foundation was not only in the code they wrote, but in their political rhetoric. By talking about free software as a cause instead of a convenience, they made it difficult for programmers *not* to have a political consciousness about it. Even those who disagreed with the FSF had to engage the issue, if only to stake out a different position. The FSF's effectiveness as propagandists lay in tying their code to a message, by means of the GPL and other texts. As their code spread widely, that message spread as well.

Accidental resistance

There were many other things going on in the nascent free software scene, however, and few were as explictly ideological as Stallman's GNU Project. One of the most important was the Berkeley Software Distribution (BSD), a gradual reimplementation of the Unix operating system—which up until the late 1970s had been a loosely proprietary research project at AT&T—by programmers at the University of California at Berkeley. The BSD group did not make any overt political statements about the need for programmers to band together and share with one another, but they *practiced* the idea with flair and enthusiasm, by coordinating a massive distributed development effort in which the Unix command-line utilities and code libraries, and eventually the operating system kernel itself, were rewritten from scratch mostly by volunteers. The BSD project became a prime example of non-ideological free software development, and also served as a training ground for many developers who would go on to remain active in the open source world.

Another crucible of cooperative development was the X Window System, a free, network-transparent graphical computing environment, developed at MIT in the mid-1980s in partnership with hardware vendors who had a common interest in being able to offer their customers a windowing system. Far from opposing proprietary software, the X license deliberately allowed proprietary extensions on top of the free core—each member of the consortium wanted the chance to enhance the default X distribution, and thereby gain a competitive advantage over the other members. X Windows[5] itself was free software, but mainly as a way to level the playing field between competing business interests, not out of some desire to end the dominance of proprietary software. Yet another example, predating the GNU project by a few years, was TeX, Donald Knuth's free, publishing-quality typesetting system. He released it under a license that allowed anyone to modify and distribute the code, but

---

5   They prefer it to be called the "X Window System," but in practice, people usually call it "X Windows," because three words is just too cumbersome.

not to call the result "TeX" unless it passed a very strict set of compatibility tests (this is an example of the "trademark-protecting" class of free licenses, discussed more in Chapter 9). Knuth wasn't taking a stand one way or the other on the question of free-versus-proprietary software, he just needed a better typesetting system in order to complete his *real* goal—a book on computer programming—and saw no reason not to release his system to the world when done.

Without listing every project and every license, it's safe to say that by the late 80s, there was a lot of free software available under a wide variety of licenses. The diversity of licenses reflected a corresponding diversity of motivations. Even some of the programers who chose the GNU GPL were much less ideologically driven than the GNU project itself. Although they enjoyed working on free software, many developers did not consider proprietary software a social evil. There were people who felt a moral impulse to rid the world of "software hoarding" (Stallman's term for non-free software), but others were motivated more by technical excitement, or by the pleasure of working with like-minded collaborators, or even by a simple human desire for glory. Yet by and large these disparate motivations did not interact in destructive ways. This is partly because software, unlike other creative forms like prose or the visual arts, must pass semi-objective tests in order to be considered successful: it must run, and be reasonably free of bugs. This gives all participants in a project a kind of automatic common ground, a reason and a framework for working together without worrying too much about qualifications beyond the technical.

Developers had another reason to stick together as well: it turned out that the free software world was producing some very high-quality code. In some cases, it was demonstrably technically superior to the nearest non-free alternative; in others, it was at least comparable, and of course it always cost less. While only a few people might have been motivated to run free software on strictly philosophical grounds, a great many people were happy to run it because it did a better job. And of those who used it, some percentage were always willing to donate their time and skills to help maintain and improve the software.

This tendency to produce good code was certainly not universal, but it was happening with increasing frequency in free software projects around the world. Businesses that depended heavily on software gradually began to take notice. Many of them discovered that they were already using free software in day-to-day operations, and simply hadn't known it (upper management isn't always aware of everything the IT department does). Corporations began to take a more active and public role in free software projects, contributing time and equipment, and sometimes even directly funding the development of free programs. Such investments could, in the best scenarios, repay themselves many times over. The sponsor only pays a small number of expert programmers to devote themselves to the project full time, but reaps the benefits of *everyone's* contributions, including work from unpaid volunteers and from programmers being paid by other corporations.

Free Versus Open Source

As the corporate world gave more and more attention to free software, programmers were faced with new issues of presentation. One was the word "free" itself. On first hearing the term "free software," many people mistakenly think it means just "zero-cost software." It's true that all free software is zero-cost,[6] but not all zero-cost software is free. For example, during the battle of the browsers in the 1990s, both Netscape and Microsoft gave away their competing web browsers at no charge, in a scramble to gain market share. Neither browser was free in the "free software" sense. You couldn't get the source code, and even if you could, you didn't have the right to modify or redistribute it.[7] The only thing you could do was download an executable and run it. The browsers were no more free than shrink-wrapped software bought in a store; they merely had a lower price.

This confusion over the word "free" is due entirely to an unfortunate ambiguity in the English language. Most other tongues distinguish low prices from liberty (the distinction between *gratis* and *libre* is immediately clear to speakers of Romance languages, for example). But English's position as the de facto bridge language of the Internet means that a problem with English is, to some degree, a problem for everyone. The misunderstanding around the word "free" was so prevalent that free software programmers eventually evolved a standard formula in response: "It's *free* as in *freedom*—think *free speech*, not *free beer*." Still, having to explain it over and over is tiring. Many programmers felt, with some justification, that the ambiguous word "free" was hampering the public's understanding of this software.

But the problem went deeper than that. The word "free" carried with it an inescapable moral connotation: if freedom was an end in itself, it didn't matter whether free software also happened to be better, or more profitable for certain businesses in certain circumstances. Those were merely pleasant side effects of a motive that was, at bottom, neither technical nor mercantile, but moral. Furthermore, the "free as in

---

6   One may charge a fee for giving out copies of free software, but since one cannot stop the recipients from offering it at no charge afterwards, the price is effectively driven to zero immediately.

7   The source code to Netscape Navigator *was* eventually released under an open source license, in 1998, and became the foundation for the Mozilla web browser. See *http://www.mozilla.org/*.

freedom" position forced a glaring inconsistency on corporations who wanted to support particular free programs in one aspect of their business, but continue marketing proprietary software in others.

These dilemmas came to a community that was already poised for an identity crisis. The programmers who actually *write* free software have never been of one mind about the overall goal, if any, of the free software movement. Even to say that opinions run from one extreme to the other would be misleading, in that it would falsely imply a linear range where there is instead a multidimensional scattering. However, two broad categories of belief can be distinguished, if we are willing to ignore subtleties for the moment. One group takes Stallman's view, that the freedom to share and modify is the most important thing, and that therefore if you stop talking about freedom, you've left out the core issue. Others feel that the software itself is the most important argument in its favor, and are uncomfortable with proclaiming proprietary software inherently bad. Some, but not all, free software programmers believe that the author (or employer, in the case of paid work) *should* have the right to control the terms of distribution, and that no moral judgement need be attached to the choice of particular terms.

For a long time, these differences did not need to be carefully examined or articulated, but free software's burgeoning success in the business world made the issue unavoidable. In 1998, the term *open source* was created as an alternative to "free", by a coalition of programmers who eventually became The Open Source Initiative (OSI).[8] The OSI felt not only that "free software" was potentially confusing, but that the word "free" was just one symptom of a general problem: that the movement needed a marketing program to pitch it to the corporate world, and that talk of morals and the social benefits of sharing would never fly in corporate boardrooms. In their own words:

> The Open Source Initiative is a marketing program for free software. It's a pitch for "free software" on solid pragmatic grounds rather than ideological tub-thumping. The winning substance has not changed, the losing attitude and symbolism have. ...

> The case that needs to be made to most techies isn't about the concept of open source, but the name. Why not call it, as we traditionally have, free software?

> One direct reason is that the term "free software" is easily misunderstood in ways that lead to conflict....

---

8   OSI's web home is *http://www.opensource.org/*.

But the real reason for the re-labeling is a marketing one. We're trying to pitch our concept to the corporate world now. We have a winning product, but our positioning, in the past, has been awful. The term "free software" has been mis-understood by business persons, who mistake the desire to share with anti-com-mercialism, or worse, theft.

Mainstream corporate CEOs and CTOs will never buy "free software." But if we take the very same tradition, the same people, and the same free-software licenses and change the label to "open source"? That, they'll buy.

Some hackers find this hard to believe, but that's because they're techies who think in concrete, substantial terms and don't understand how important image is when you're selling something.

In marketing, appearance is reality. The appearance that we're willing to climb down off the barricades and work with the corporate world counts for as much as the reality of our behavior, our convictions, and our software.

(from *http://www.opensource.org/advocacy/faq.php* and *http://www.opensource.org/advocacy/case_for_hackers.php#marketing*)

The tips of many icebergs of controversy are visible in that text. It refers to "our con-victions" but smartly avoids spelling out exactly what those convictions are. For some, it might be the conviction that code developed according to an open process will be better code; for others, it might be the conviction that all information should be shared. There's the use of the word "theft" to refer (presumably) to illegal copy-ing—a usage that many object to, on the grounds that it's not theft if the original possessor still has the item afterwards. There's the tantalizing hint that the free soft-ware movement might be mistakenly accused of anti-commercialism, but it leaves carefully unexamined the question of whether such an accusation would have any basis in fact.

None of which is to say that the OSI's web site is inconsistent or misleading. It's not. Rather, it is an example of exactly what the OSI claims had been missing from the free software movement: good marketing, where "good" means "viable in the busi-ness world." The Open Source Initiative gave a lot of people exactly what they had been looking for—a vocabulary for talking about free software as a development methodology and business strategy, instead of as a moral crusade.

The appearance of the Open Source Initiative changed the landscape of free soft-ware. It formalized a dichotomy that had long been unnamed, and in doing so forced the movement to acknowledge that it had internal politics as well as external. The effect today is that both sides have had to find common ground, since most projects include programmers from both camps, as well as participants who don't fit any clear category. This doesn't mean people never talk about moral motivations—lapses in the traditional "hacker ethic" are sometimes called out, for example. But it is rare for a free software/open source developer to openly question the basic motivations of others in a project. The contribution trumps the contributor. If someone writes good code, you don't ask them whether they do it for moral reasons, or because their employer paid them to, or because they're building up their resumé, or whatever. You evaluate the contribution on technical grounds, and respond on technical grounds. Even explicitly political organizations like the Debian project, whose goal is to offer a 100% free (that is, "free as in freedom") computing environment, are fairly relaxed about integrating with non-free code and cooperating with programmers who don't share exactly the same goals.

The Situation Today

When running a free software project, you won't need to talk about such weighty philosophical matters on a daily basis. Programmers will not insist that everyone else in the project agree with their views on all things (those who do insist on this quickly find themselves unable to work on any project). But you do need to be aware that the question of "free" versus "open source" exists, partly to avoid saying things that might be inimical to some of the participants, and partly because understanding developers' motivations is the best way—in some sense, the *only* way—to manage a project.

Free software is a culture by choice. To operate successfully in it, you have to understand why people choose to be in it in the first place. Coercive techniques don't work. If people are unhappy in one project, they will just wander off to another one. Free software is remarkable even among volunteer communities for its lightness of investment. Most of the people involved have never actually met the other participants face-to-face, and simply donate bits of time whenever they feel like it. The normal conduits by which humans bond with each other and form lasting groups are narrowed down to a tiny channel: the written word, carried over electronic wires. Because of this, it can take a long time for a cohesive and dedicated group to form. Conversely, it's quite easy for a project to lose a potential volunteer in the first five minutes of acquaintanceship. If a project doesn't make a good first impression, newcomers rarely give it a second chance.

The transience, or rather the *potential* transience, of relationships is perhaps the single most daunting task facing a new project. What will persuade all these people to stick together long enough to produce something useful? The answer to that question is complex enough to occupy the rest of this book, but if it had to be expressed in one sentence, it would be this:

> People should feel that their connection to a project, and influence over it, is directly proportional to their contributions.

No class of developers, or potential developers, should ever feel discounted or discriminated against for non-technical reasons. Clearly, projects with corporate sponsorship and/or salaried developers need to be especially careful in this regard, as Chapter 5 discusses in detail. Of course, this doesn't mean that if there's no corporate sponsorship then you have nothing to worry about. Money is merely one of many factors that can affect the success of a project. There are also questions of what language to choose, what license, what development process, precisely what kind of infrastructure to set up, how to publicize the project's inception effectively, and much more. Starting a project out on the right foot is the topic of the next chapter.

## CHAPTER 2

Getting Started

The classic model of how free software projects get started was supplied by Eric Raymond, in a now-famous paper on open source processes entitled "The Cathedral and the Bazaar." He wrote:

> Every good work of software starts by scratching a developer's personal itch. (from *http://www.catb.org/~esr/writings/cathedral-bazaar/*)

Note that Raymond wasn't saying that open source projects happen only when some individual gets an itch. Rather, he was saying that *good* software results when the programmer has a personal interest in seeing the problem solved; the relevance of this to free software was that a personal itch happened to be the most frequent motivation for starting a free software project.

This is still how most free projects are started, but less so now than in 1997, when Raymond wrote those words. Today, we have the phenomenon of organizations—including for-profit corporations—starting large, centrally-managed open source projects from scratch. The lone programmer, banging out some code to solve a local problem and then realizing the result has wider applicability, is still the source of much new free software, but is not the only story.

Raymond's point is still insightful, however. The essential condition is that the producers of the software have a direct interest in its success, because they use it themselves. If the software doesn't do what it's supposed to do, the person or organization producing it will feel the dissatisfaction in their daily work. For example, the

OpenAdapter project (*http://www.openadapter.org/*), which was started by investment bank Dresdner Kleinwort Wasserstein as an open source framework for integrating disparate financial information systems, can hardly be said to scratch any individual programmer's personal itch. It scratches an institutional itch. But that itch arises directly from the experiences of the institution and its partners, and therefore if the project fails to relieve them, they will know. This arrangement produces good software because the feedback loop flows in the right direction. The program isn't being written to be sold to someone else so they can solve *their* problem. It's being written to solve one's *own* problem, and then shared with everyone, much as though the problem were a disease and the software were medicine whose distribution is meant to completely eradicate the epidemic.

This chapter is about how to introduce a new free software project to the world, but many of its recommendations would sound familiar to a health organization distributing medicine. The goals are very similar: you want to make it clear what the medicine does, get it into the hands of the right people, and make sure that those who receive it know how to use it. But with software, you also want to entice some of the recipients into joining the ongoing research effort to improve the medicine.

Free software distribution is a twofold task. The software needs to acquire users, and to acquire developers. These two needs are not necessarily in conflict, but they do add some complexity to a project's initial presentation. Some information is useful for both audiences, some is useful only for one or the other. Both kinds of information should subscribe to the principle of scaled presentation; that is, the degree of detail presented at each stage should correspond directly to the amount of time and effort put in by the reader. More effort should always equal more reward. When the two do not correlate tightly, people may quickly lose faith and stop investing effort.

The corollary to this is that *appearances matter*. Programmers, in particular, often don't like to believe this. Their love of substance over form is almost a point of professional pride. It's no accident that so many programmers exhibit an antipathy for marketing and public relations work, nor that professional graphic designers are often horrified at what programmers come up with on their own.

This is a pity, because there are situations where form *is* substance, and project presentation is one of them. For example, the very first thing a visitor learns about a project is what its web site looks like. This information is absorbed before any of the actual content on the site is comprehended—before any of the text has been read or links clicked on. However unjust it may be, people cannot stop themselves from forming an immediate first impression. The site's appearance signals whether care was taken in organizing the project's presentation. Humans have extremely sensitive antennae for detecting the investment of care. Most of us can tell in one glance whether a web site was thrown together quickly or was given serious thought. This is the first piece of information your project puts out, and the impression it creates will carry over to the rest of the project by association.

Thus, while much of this chapter talks about the content your project should start out with, remember that its look and feel matters too. Because the project web site has to work for two different types of visitors—users and developers—special attention must be paid to clarity and directedness. Although this is not the place for a general treatise on web design, one principle is important enough to deserve mention, particularly when the site serves multiple (if overlapping) audiences: people should have a rough idea where a link goes before clicking on it. For example, it should be obvious *from looking at the links* to user documentation that they lead to user documentation, and not to, say, developer documentation. Running a project is partly about supplying information, but it's also about supplying comfort. The mere presence of certain standard offerings, in expected places, reassures users and developers who are deciding whether they want to get involved. It says that this project has its act together, has anticipated the questions people will ask, and has made an effort to answer them in a way that requires minimal exertion on the part of the asker. By giving off this aura of preparedness, the project sends out a message: "Your time will not be wasted if you get involved," which is exactly what people need to hear.

First, Look Around

Before starting an open source project, there is one important caveat:

Always look around to see if there's an existing project that does what you want. The chances are pretty good that whatever problem you want solved now, someone else wanted solved before you. If they did solve it, and released their code under a free license, then there's no reason for you to reinvent the wheel today. There are exceptions, of course: if you want to start a project as an educational experience, pre-existing code won't help; or maybe the project you have in mind is so specialized that you know there is zero chance anyone else has done it. But generally, there's no point in not looking, and the payoff can be huge. If the usual Internet search engines don't turn up anything, try searching on *http://freshmeat.net/* (an open source project news site, about which more will be said later), on *http://www.sourceforge.net/*, and in the Free Software Foundation's directory of free software at *http://directory.fsf.org/*.

Even if you don't find exactly what you were looking for, you might find something so close that it makes more sense to join that project and add functionality than to start from scratch yourself.

Starting from What You Have

You've looked around, found that nothing out there really fits your needs, and decided to start a new project.

What now?

The hardest part about launching a free software project is transforming a private vision into a public one. You or your organization may know perfectly well what you want, but expressing that goal comprehensibly to the world is a fair amount of work. It is essential, however, that you take the time to do it. You and the other founders must decide what the project is really about—that is, decide its limitations, what it won't do as well as what it will—and write up a mission statement. This part is usually not too hard, though it can sometimes reveal unspoken assumptions and even disagreements about the nature of the project, which is fine: better to resolve those now than later. The next step is to package up the project for public consumption, and this is, basically, pure drudgery.

What makes it so laborious is that it consists mainly of organizing and documenting things everyone already knows—"everyone," that is, who's been involved in the project so far. Thus, for the people doing the work, there is no immediate benefit. They do not need a *README* file giving an overview of the project, nor a design document or user manual. They do not need a carefully arranged code tree conforming to the informal but widespread standards of software source distributions. Whatever way the source code is arranged is fine for them, because they're already accustomed to it anyway, and if the code runs at all, they know how to use it. It doesn't even matter, for them, if the fundamental architectural assumptions of the project remain undocumented; they're already familiar with that too.

Newcomers, on the other hand, need these things. Fortunately, they don't need them all at once. It's not necessary for you to provide every possible resource before taking a project public. In a perfect world, perhaps, every new open source project would start out life with a thorough design document, a complete user manual (with special markings for features planned but not yet implemented), beautifully and portably packaged code, capable of running on any computing platform, and so on. In reality, taking care of all these loose ends would be prohibitively time-consuming, and anyway, it's work that one can reasonably hope volunteers will help with once the project is under way.

What *is* necessary, however, is that enough investment be put into presentation that newcomers can get past the initial obstacle of unfamiliarity. Think of it as the first step in a bootstrapping process, to bring the project to a kind of minimum activation energy. I've heard this threshold called the *hacktivation energy*: the amount of energy a newcomer must put in before she starts getting something back. The lower a project's hacktivation energy, the better. Your first task is bring the hacktivation energy down to a level that encourages people to get involved.

Each of the following subsections describes one important aspect of starting a new project. They are presented roughly in the order that a new visitor would encounter them, though, of course, the order in which you actually implement them might be different. You can treat them as a checklist. When starting a project, just go down the list and make sure you've got each item covered, or at least that you're comfortable with the potential consequences if you've left one out.

Choose a Good Name

Put yourself in the shoes of someone who's just heard about your project, perhaps by having stumbled across it while searching for software to solve some problem. The first thing they'll encounter is the project's name.

A good name will not automatically make your project successful, and a bad name will not doom it—well, a *really* bad name probably could do that, but we start from the assumption that no one here is actively trying to make their project fail. However, a bad name can slow down adoption of the project, either because people don't take it seriously, or because they simply have trouble remembering it.

A good name:

- Gives some idea what the project does, or at least is related in an obvious way, such that if one knows the name and knows what the project does, the name will come quickly to mind thereafter.

- Is easy to remember. Here, there is no getting around the fact that English has become the default language of the Internet: "easy to remember" means "easy for someone who can read English to remember." Names that are puns dependent on native-speaker pronunciation, for example, will be opaque to the many non-native English readers out there. If the pun is particularly compelling and memorable, it may still be worth it; just keep in mind that many people seeing the name will not hear it in their head the way a native speaker would.

- Is not the same as some other project's name, and does not infringe on any trademarks. This is just good manners, as well as good legal sense. You don't want to create identity confusion. It's hard enough to keep track of everything that's available on the Net already, without different things have the same name.

  The resources mentioned earlier in "First, Look Around" are useful in discovering whether another project already has the name you're thinking of. Free trademark searches are available at *http://www.nameprotect.org/* and *http://www.uspto.gov/*.

- If possible, is available as a domain name in the *.com*, *.net*, and *.org* top-level domains. You should pick one, probably *.org*, to advertise as the official home site for the project; the other two should forward there and are simply to prevent third parties from creating identity confusion around the project's name. Even if you intend to host the project at some other site (see "Canned Hosting"), you can still register project-specific domains and forward them to the hosting site. It helps users a lot to have a simple URL to remember.

Have a Clear Mission Statement

Once they've found the project's web site, the next thing people will look for is a quick description, a mission statement, so they can decide (within 30 seconds) whether or not they're interested in learning more. This should be prominently placed on the front page, preferably right under the project's name.

The mission statement should be concrete, limiting, and above all, short. Here's an example of a good one, from *http://www.openoffice.org/*:

> To create, as a community, the leading international office suite that will run on all major platforms and provide access to all functionality and data through open-component based APIs and an XML-based file format.

In just a few words, they've hit all the high points, largely by drawing on the reader's prior knowledge. By saying "*as a community,*" they signal that no one corporation will dominate development; "*international*" means that the software will allow people to work in multiple languages and locales; "*all major platforms*" means it will be portable to Unix, Macintosh, and Windows. The rest signals that open interfaces and easily understandable file formats are an important part of the goal. They don't come right out and say that they're trying to be a free alternative to Microsoft Office, but most people can probably read between the lines. Although this mission statement looks broad at first glance, in fact it is quite circumscribed: the words "*office suite*" mean something very concrete to those familiar with such software. Again, the reader's presumed prior knowledge (in this case probably from MS Office) is used to keep the mission statement concise.

The nature of a mission statement depends partly on who is writing it, not just on the software it describes. For example, it makes sense for OpenOffice.org to use the words "*as a community*" because the project was started, and is still largely sponsored, by Sun Microsystems. By including those words, Sun indicates its sensitivity to worries that it might try to dominate the development process. With this sort of thing, merely demonstrating awareness of the *potential* for a problem goes a long way toward avoiding the problem entirely. On the other hand, projects that aren't sponsored by a single corporation probably don't need such language; after all, development by community is the norm, so there would ordinarily be no reason to list it as part of the mission.

State that the Project Is Free

Those who remain interested after reading the mission statement will next want to see more details, perhaps some user or developer documentation, and eventually will want to download something. But before any of that, they'll need to be sure it's open source.

The front page must make it unambiguously clear that the project is open source. This may seem obvious, but you would be surprised how many projects forget to do it. I have seen free software project web sites where the front page not only did not say which particular free license the software was distributed under, but did not even state outright that the software was free at all. Sometimes the crucial bit of information was relegated to the Downloads page, or the Developers page, or some other place that required one more mouse click to get to. In extreme cases, the license was not given anywhere on the web site at all—the only way to find it was to download the software and look inside.

Don't make this mistake. Such an omission can lose many potential developers and users. State up front, right below the mission statement, that the project is "free software" or "open source software," and give the exact license. A quick guide to choosing a license is given in "Choosing a License and Applying It," later in this chapter, and licensing issues are discussed in detail in Chapter 9.

At this point, our hypothetical visitor has determined—probably in a minute or less—that she's interested in spending, say, at least five more minutes investigating this project. The next sections describe what she should encounter in those five minutes.

Features and Requirements List

There should be a brief list of the features the software supports (if something isn't completed yet, you can still list it, but put "*planned*" or "*in progress*" next to it), and the kind of computing environment required to run the software. Think of the features/requirements list as what you would give to someone asking for a quick summary of the software. It is often just a logical expansion of the mission statement. For example, the mission statement might say:

> To create a full-text indexer and search engine with a rich API, for use by programmers in providing search services for large collections of text files.

The features and requirements list would give the details, clarifying the mission statement's scope.

Features:

- Searches plain text, HTML, and XML
- Word or phrase searching
- (planned) Fuzzy matching
- (planned) Incremental updating of indexes
- (planned) Indexing of remote web sites

Requirements:

- Python 2.2 or higher
- Enough disk space to hold the indexes (approximately twice original data size)

With this information, readers can quickly get a feel for whether this software has any hope of working for them, and they can consider getting involved as developers too.

Development Status

People always want to know how a project is doing. For new projects, they want to know the gap between the project's promise and current reality. For mature projects, they want to know how actively it is maintained, how often it puts out new releases, how responsive it is likely to be to bug reports, etc.

To answer these questions, you should provide a development status page, listing the project's near-term goals and needs (for example, it might be looking for developers with a particular kind of expertise). The page can also give a history of past releases, with feature lists, so visitors can get an idea of how the project defines "progress" and how quickly it makes progress according to that definition.

Don't be afraid of looking unready, and don't give in to the temptation to hype the development status. Everyone knows that software evolves by stages; there's no shame in saying "This is alpha software with known bugs. It runs, and works at least some of the time, but use at your own risk." Such language won't scare away the kinds of developers you need at that stage. As for users, one of the worst things a project can do is attract users before the software is ready for them. A reputation for instability or bugginess is very hard to shake, once acquired. Conservativism pays off in the long run; it's always better for the software to be *more* stable than the user expected than less, and pleasant surprises produce the best kind of word-of-mouth.

Alpha and Beta

The term *alpha* usually means a first release, with which users can get real work done and which has all the intended functionality, but which also has known bugs. The main purpose of alpha software is to generate feedback, so the developers know what to work on. The next stage, *beta*, means the software has had all the serious bugs fixed, but has not yet been tested enough to certify for release. The purpose of beta software is to either become the official release, assuming no bugs are found, or provide detailed feedback to the developers so they can reach the official release quickly. The difference between alpha and beta is very much a matter of judgment.

Downloads

The software should be downloadable as source code in standard formats. When a project is first getting started, binary (executable) packages are not necessary, unless the software has such complicated build requirements or dependencies that merely getting it to run would be a lot of work for most people. (But if this is the case, the project is going to have a hard time attracting developers anyway!)

The distribution mechanism should be as convenient, standard, and low-overhead as possible. If you were trying to eradicate a disease, you wouldn't distribute the medicine in such a way that it requires a non-standard syringe size to administer. Likewise, software should conform to standard build and installation methods; the more it deviates from the standards, the more potential users and developers will give up and go away confused.

That sounds obvious, but many projects don't bother to standardize their installation procedures until very late in the game, telling themselves they can do it any time: *"We'll sort all that stuff out when the code is closer to being ready."* What they don't realize is that by putting off the boring work of finishing the build and installation procedures, they are actually making the code take longer to get ready—because they discourage developers who might otherwise have contributed to the code. Most insidiously, they don't *know* they're losing all those developers, because the process is an accumulation of non-events: someone visits a web site, downloads the software, tries to build it, fails, gives up and goes away. Who will ever know it happened, except the person themselves? No one working on the project will realize that someone's interest and good will have been silently squandered.

Boring work with a high payoff should always be done early, and significantly lowering the project's barrier to entry through good packaging brings a very high payoff.

When you release a downloadable package, it is vital that you give a unique version number to the release, so that people can compare any two releases and know which supersedes the other. A detailed discussion of version numbering can be found in "Release Numbering" in Chapter 7.

The details of standardizing build and installation procedures are covered in "Packaging." in Chapter 7.

Version Control and Bug Tracker Access

Downloading source packages is fine for those who just want to install and use the software, but it's not enough for those who want to debug or add new features. Nightly source snapshots can help, but they're still not fine-grained enough for a thriving development community. People need real-time access to the latest sources, and the way to give them that is to use a version control system. The presence of anonymously accessible version controlled sources is a sign—to both users and developers—that this project is making an effort to give people what they need to participate. If you can't offer version control right away, then put up a sign saying you intend to set it up soon. Version control infrastructure is discussed in detail in "Version Control" in Chapter 3.

The same goes for the project's bug tracker. The importance of a bug tracking system lies not only in its usefulness to developers, but in what it signifies for project observers. For many people, an accessible bug database is one of the strongest signs that a project should be taken seriously. Furthermore, the higher the number of bugs in the database, the better the project looks. This might seem counterintuitive, but remember that the number of bugs recorded really depends on three things: the absolute number of bugs present in the software, the number of users using the software, and the convenience with which those users can register new bugs. Of these three factors, the latter two are more significant than the first. Any software of sufficient size and complexity has an essentially arbitrary number of bugs waiting to be discovered. The real question is, how well will the project do at recording and prioritizing those bugs? A project with a large and well-maintained bug database (meaning bugs are responded to promptly, duplicate bugs are unified, etc.) therefore makes a better impression than a project with no bug database, or a nearly empty database.

Of course, if your project is just getting started, then the bug database will contain very few bugs, and there's not much you can do about that. But if the status page emphasizes the project's youth, and if people looking at the bug database can see that most filings have taken place recently, they can extrapolate from that the project still has a healthy *rate* of filings, and they will not be unduly alarmed by the low absolute number of bugs recorded.

Note that bug trackers are often used to track not only software bugs, but enhancement requests, documentation changes, pending tasks, and more. The details of running a bug tracker are covered in "Bug Tracker" in Chapter 3, so I won't go into them here. The important thing from a presentation point of view is just to *have* a bug tracker, and to make sure that fact is visible from the front page of the project.

Communications Channels

Visitors usually want to know how to reach the human beings involved with the project. Provide the addresses of mailing lists, chat rooms, and IRC channels, and any other forums where others involved with the software can be reached. Make it clear that you and the other authors of the project are subscribed to these mailing lists, so people see there's a way to give feedback that will reach the developers. Your presence on the lists does not imply a commitment to answer all questions or implement all feature requests. In the long run, most users will probably never join the forums anyway, but they will be comforted to know that they *could* if they ever needed to.

In the early stages of a project, there's no need to have separate user and developer forums. It's much better to have everyone involved with the software talking together, in one "room." Among early adopters, the distinction between developer and user is often fuzzy; to the extent that the distinction can be made, the ratio of developers to users is usually much higher in the early days of the project than later on. While you can't assume that every early adopter is a programmer who wants to hack on the software, you can assume that they are at least interested in following development discussions and in getting a sense of the project's direction.

As this chapter is only about getting a project started, it's enough merely to say that these communications forums need to exist. Later, in "Handling Growth" in Chapter 6, we'll examine where and how to set up such forums, the ways in which they might need moderation or other management, and how to separate user forums from developer forums, when the time comes, without creating an unbridgeable gulf.

Developer Guidelines

If someone is considering contributing to the project, he'll look for developer guidelines. Developer guidelines are not so much technical as social: they explain how the developers interact with each other and with the users, and ultimately how things get done.

This topic is covered in detail in "Writing It All Down" in Chapter 4, but the basic elements of developer guidelines are:

- Pointers to forums for interaction with other developers
- Instructions on how to report bugs and submit patches
- Some indication of *how* development is usually done—is the project a benevolent dictatorship, a democracy, or something else

No pejorative sense is intended by "dictatorship," by the way. It's perfectly okay to run a tyranny where one particular developer has veto power over all changes. Many successful projects work this way. The important thing is that the project come right out and say so. A tyranny pretending to be a democracy will turn people off; a tyranny that says it's a tyranny will do fine as long as the tyrant is competent and trusted.

See *http://svn.collab.net/repos/svn/trunk/HACKING* for an example of particularly thorough developer guidelines, or *http://www.openoffice.org/dev_docs/guidelines.html* for broader guidelines that focus more on governance and the spirit of participation and less on technical matters.

The separate issue of providing a programmer's introduction to the software is discussed in "Developer documentation" later in this chapter.

Documentation

Documentation is essential. There needs to be *something* for people to read, even if it's rudimentary and incomplete. This falls squarely into the "drudgery" category referred to earlier, and is often the first area where a new open source project falls down. Coming up with a mission statement and feature list, choosing a license, summarizing development status—these are all relatively small tasks, which can be definitively completed and usually need not be returned to once done. Documentation, on the other hand, is never really finished, which may be one reason people sometimes delay starting it at all.

The most insidious thing is that documentation's utility to those writing it is the reverse of its utility to those who will read it. The most important documentation for initial users is the basics: how to quickly set up the software, an overview of how it works, perhaps some guides to doing common tasks. Yet these are exactly the things the *writers* of the documentation know all too well—so well that it can be difficult for them to see things from the reader's point of view, and to laboriously spell out the steps that (to the writers) seem so obvious as to be unworthy of mention.

There's no magic solution to this problem. Someone just needs to sit down and write the stuff, and then run it by typical new users to test its quality. Use a simple, easy-to-edit format such as HTML, plain text, texinfo, or some variant of XML—something that's convenient for lightweight, quick improvements on the spur of the moment. This is not only to remove any overhead that might impede the original writers from making incremental improvements, but also for those who join the project later and want to work on the documentation.

One way to ensure basic initial documentation gets done is to limit its scope in advance. That way, writing it at least won't feel like an open-ended task. A good rule of thumb is that it should meet the following minimal criteria:

- Tell the reader clearly how much technical expertise she's expected to have.

- Describe clearly and thoroughly how to set up the software, and somewhere near the beginning of the documentation, tell the user how to run some sort of diagnostic test or simple command to confirm that they've set things up correctly. Startup documentation is in some ways more important than actual usage documentation. The more effort someone has invested in installing and getting started with the software, the more persistent she'll be in figuring out advanced functionality that's not well-documented. When people abandon a project, they abandon early; therefore, it's the earliest stages, like installation, that need the most support.

- Give one tutorial-style example of how to do a common task. Obviously, many examples for many tasks would be even better, but if time is limited, pick one task and walk through it thoroughly. Once someone sees that the software *can* be used for one thing, they'll start to explore what else it can do on their own—and, if you're lucky, start filling in the documentation themselves. Which brings us to the next point...

- Label the areas where the documentation is known to be incomplete. By showing the readers that you are aware of its deficiencies, you align yourself with their point of view. Your empathy reassures them that they don't face a struggle to convince the project of what's important. These labels needn't represent promises to fill in the gaps by any particular date —it's equally legitimate to treat them as open requests for volunteer help.

The last point is of wider importance, actually, and can be applied to the entire project, not just the documentation. An accurate accounting of known deficiencies is the norm in the open source world. You don't have to exaggerate the project's shortcomings, just identify them scrupulously and dispassionately when the context calls for it (whether in the documentation, in the bug tracking database, or on a mailing list discussion). No one will treat this as defeatism on the part of the project, nor as a commitment to solve the problems by a certain date, unless the project makes such a commitment explicitly. Since anyone who uses the software will discover the deficiencies for themselves, it's much better for them to be psychologically prepared— then the project will look like it has a solid knowledge of how it's doing.

Availability of documentation

Documentation should be available from two places: online (directly from the web site), *and* in the downloadable distribution of the software (see "Packaging" in Chapter 7). It needs to be online, in browseable form, because people often read documentation *before* downloading software for the first time, as a way of helping them decide whether to download at all. But it should also accompany the software, on the principle that downloading should supply (i.e., make locally accessible) everything one needs to use the package.

For online documentation, make sure that there is a link that brings up the *entire* documentation in one HTML page (put a note like "monolithic" or "all-in-one" or "single large page" next to the link, so people know that it might take a while to load). This is useful because people often want to search for a specific word or phrase across the entire documentation. Generally, they already know what they're looking for, they just can't remember what section it's in. For such people, nothing is more frustrating than encountering one HTML page for the table of contents, then a different page for the introduction, then a different page for installation instructions, etc. When the pages are broken up like that, their browser's search function is useless. The separate-page style is useful for those who already know what section they need,

Maintaining an FAQ

An *FAQ* ("Frequently Asked Questions" document) can be one of the best investments a project makes in terms of educational payoff. FAQs are highly tuned to
the questions users and developers actually ask—as opposed to the questions
you might have *expected* them to ask—and therefore, a well-maintained FAQ
tends to give those who consult it exactly what they're looking for. The FAQ is
often the first place users look when they encounter a problem, often even in
preference to the official manual, and it's probably the document in your project
most likely to be linked to from other sites.

Unfortunately, you cannot make the FAQ at the start of the project. Good FAQs
are not written, they are grown. They are by definition reactive documents,
evolving over time in response to people's day-to-day usage of the software. Since
it's impossible to correctly anticipate the questions people will ask, it is impossible to sit down and write a useful FAQ from scratch.

Therefore, don't waste your time trying to. You may, however, find it useful to
set up a mostly blank FAQ template, so there will be an obvious place for people
to contribute questions and answers after the project is under way. At this stage,
the most important property is not completeness, but convenience: if the FAQ is
easy to add to, people will add to it. (Proper FAQ maintenance is a non-trivial
and intriguing problem, and is discussed more in "FAQ Manager" in Chapter 8.)

---

or who want to read the entire documentation from front to back in sequence. But
this is *not* the most common way documentation is accessed. Far more often, someone who is basically familiar with the software is coming back to search for a specific
word or phrase. To fail to provide them with a single, searchable document would
only make their lives harder.

Developer documentation

Developer documentation is written to help programmers understand the code, so
they can repair and extend it. This is somewhat different from the *developer guidelines* discussed earlier, which are more social than technical. Developer guidelines tell
programmers how to get along with each other; developer documentation tells them
how to get along with the code itself. The two are often packaged together in one
document for convenience (as with the *http://svn.collab.net/repos/svn/trunk/HACKING*
example given earlier), but they don't have to be.

Although developer documentation can be very helpful, there's no reason to delay a release to do it. As long as the original authors are available (and willing) to answer questions about the code, that's enough to start with. In fact, having to answer the same questions over and over is a common motivation for writing documentation. But even before it's written, determined contributors will still manage to find their way around the code. The force that drives people to spend time learning a code base is that the code does something useful for them. If people have faith in that, they will take the time to figure things out; if they don't have that faith, no amount of developer documentation will get or keep them.

So if you have time to write documentation for only one audience, write it for users. All user documentation is, in effect, developer documentation as well; any programmer who's going to work on a piece of software will need to be familiar with how to use it. Later, when you see programmers asking the same questions over and over, take the time to write up some separate documents just for them.

Some projects use wikis for their initial documentation, or even as their primary documentation. In my experience, this really works only if the wiki is actively edited by a few people who agree on how the documentation is to be organized and what sort of "voice" it should have. See "Wikis" in Chapter 3 for more.

Example Output and Screenshots

If the project involves a graphical user interface, or if it produces graphical or otherwise distinctive output, put some samples up on the project web site. In the case of interface, this means screenshots; for output, it might be screenshots or just files. Both cater to people's need for instant gratification: a single screenshot can be more convincing than paragraphs of descriptive text and mailing list chatter, because a screenshot is inarguable proof that the software *works*. It may be buggy, it may be hard to install, it may be incompletely documented, but that screenshot is still proof that if one puts in enough effort, one can get it to run.

There are many other things you could put on the project web site, if you have the time, or if for one reason or another they are especially appropriate: a news page, a project history page, a related links page, a site-search feature, a donations link, etc. None of these are necessities at startup time, but keep them in mind for the future.

Canned Hosting

There are a few sites that provide free hosting and infrastructure for open source projects: a web area, version control, a bug tracker, a download area, chat forums, regular backups, etc. The details vary from site to site, but the same basic services are offered at all of them. By using one of these sites, you get a lot for free; what you give up, obviously, is fine-grained control over the user experience. The hosting service decides what software the site runs, and may control or at least influence the look and feel of the project's web pages.

See "Canned Hosting" in Chapter 3 for a more detailed discussion of the advantages and disadvantages of canned hosting, and a list of sites that offer it.

Choosing a License and Applying It

This section is intended to be a very quick, very rough guide to choosing a license. Read Chapter 9 to understand the detailed legal implications of the different licenses, and how the license you choose can affect people's ability to mix your software with other free software.

There are a great many free software licenses to choose from. Most of them we needn't consider here, as they were written to satisfy the particular legal needs of some corporation or person, and wouldn't be appropriate for your project. We will restrict ourselves to just the most commonly used licenses; in most cases, you will want to choose one of them.

The "Do Anything" Licenses

If you're comfortable with your project's code potentially being used in proprietary programs, then use an *MIT/X-style* license. It is the simplest of several minimal licenses that do little more than assert nominal copyright (without actually restricting copying) and specify that the code comes with no warranty. See "The MIT/X Window System License" in Chapter 9 for details.

The GPL

If you don't want your code to be used in proprietary programs, use the GNU General Public License (*http://www.gnu.org/licenses/gpl.html*). The GPL is probably the most widely recognized free software license in the world today. This is in itself a big advantage, since many potential users and contributors will already be familiar with it, and therefore won't have to spend extra time to read and understand your license. See "The GNU General Public License" in Chapter 9 for details.

How to Apply a License to Your Software

Once you've chosen a license, you should state it on the project's front page. You don't need to include the actual text of the license there; just give the name of the license, and make it link to the full license text on another page.

This tells the public what license you *intend* the software to be released under, but it's not sufficient for legal purposes. For that, the software itself must contain the license. The standard way to do this is to put the full license text in a file called *COPYING* (or *LICENSE*), and then put a short notice at the top of each source file, naming the copyright date, holder, and license, and saying where to find the full text of the license.

There are many variations on this pattern, so we'll look at just one example here. The GNU GPL says to put a notice like this at the top of each source file:

```
Copyright (C) <year>   <name of author>

This program is free software; you can redistribute it and/or modify
it under the terms of the GNU General Public License as published by
the Free Software Foundation; either version 2 of the License, or
(at your option) any later version.

This program is distributed in the hope that it will be useful,
but WITHOUT ANY WARRANTY; without even the implied warranty of
MERCHANTABILITY or FITNESS FOR A PARTICULAR PURPOSE.  See the
GNU General Public License for more details.

You should have received a copy of the GNU General Public License
along with this program; if not, write to the Free Software
Foundation, Inc., 59 Temple Place, Suite 330, Boston, MA  02111-1307  USA
```

It does not say specifically that the copy of the license you received along with the program is in the file *COPYING*, but that's where it's usually put. (You could change the above notice to state that directly.) This template also gives a geographical address from which to request a copy of the license. Another common method is to give a link to a web page containing the license. Just use your judgement and point to wherever you feel the most permanent copy of the license is maintained, which might simply be somewhere on your project's web site. In general, the notice you put in each source file does not have to look exactly like the one above, as long as it starts with the same notice of copyright holder and date, states the name of the license, and makes it clear where to view the full license.

Setting the Tone

So far we've covered one-time tasks you do during project setup: picking a license, arranging the initial web site, etc. But the most important aspects of starting a new project are dynamic. Choosing a mailing list address is easy; ensuring that the list's conversations remain on-topic and productive is another matter entirely. If the project is being opened up after years of closed, in-house development, its development processes will change, and you will have to prepare the existing developers for that change.

The first steps are the hardest, because precedents and expectations for future conduct have not yet been set. Stability in a project does not come from formal policies, but from a shared, hard-to-pin-down collective wisdom that develops over time. There are often written rules as well, but they tend to be essentially a distillation of the intangible, ever-evolving agreements that really guide the project. The written policies do not define the project's culture so much as describe it, and even then only approximately.

There are a few reasons why things work out this way. Growth and high turnover are not as damaging to the accumulation of social norms as one might think. As long as change does not happen *too* quickly, there is time for new arrivals to learn how things are done, and after they learn, they will help reinforce those ways themselves. Consider how children's songs survive the centuries. There are children today singing roughly the same rhymes as children did hundreds of years ago, even though there are no children alive now who were alive then. Younger children hear the songs sung by older ones, and when they are older, they in turn will sing them in front of other younger ones. The children are not engaging in a conscious program of transmission, of course, but the reason the songs survive is nonetheless that they are transmitted regularly and repeatedly. The time scale of free software projects may not be measured in centuries (we don't know yet), but the dynamics of transmission are much the same. The turnover rate is faster, however, and must be compensated for by a more active and deliberate transmission effort.

This effort is aided by the fact that people generally show up expecting and looking for social norms. That's just how humans are built. In any group unified by a common endeavor, people who join instinctively search for behaviors that will mark them as part of the group. The goal of setting precedents early is to make those "in-group" behaviors be ones that are useful to the project; once established, they will be largely self-perpetuating.

Following are some examples of specific things you can do to set good precedents. They're not meant as an exhaustive list, just as illustrations of the idea that setting a collaborative mood early helps a project tremendously. Physically, every developer may be working alone in a room by themselves, but you can do a lot to make them *feel* like they're all working together in the same room. The more they feel this way, the more time they'll want to spend on the project. I chose these particular examples because they came up in the Subversion project (*http://subversion.tigris.org/*), which I participated in and observed from its very beginning. But they're not unique to Subversion; situations like these will come up in most open source projects, and should be seen as opportunities to start things off on the right foot.

Avoid Private Discussions

Even after you've taken the project public, you and the other founders will often find yourselves wanting to settle difficult questions by private communications among an inner circle. This is especially true in the early days of the project, when there are so many important decisions to make, and, usually, few volunteers qualified to make them. All the obvious disadvantages of public list discussions will loom palpably in front of you: the delay inherent in email conversations, the need to leave sufficient time for consensus to form, the hassle of dealing with naive volunteers who think they understand all the issues but actually don't (every project has these; sometimes they're next year's star contributors, sometimes they stay naive forever), the person who can't understand why you only want to solve problem X when it's obviously a subset of larger problem Y, and so on. The temptation to make decisions behind closed doors and present them as *faits accomplis*, or at least as the firm recommendations of a united and influential voting block, will be great indeed.

Don't do it.

As slow and cumbersome as public discussions can be, they're almost always preferable in the long run. Making important decisions in private is like spraying contributor repellent on your project. No serious volunteer would stick around for long in an environment where a secret council makes all the big decisions. Furthermore, public discussion has beneficial side effects that will last beyond whatever ephemeral technical question was at issue:

- The discussion will help train and educate new developers. You never know how many eyes are watching the conversation; even if most people don't participate, many may be tracking silently, gleaning information about the software.

- The discussion will train *you* in the art of explaining technical issues to people who are not as familiar with the software as you are. This is a skill that requires practice, and you can't get that practice by talking to people who already know what you know.

- The discussion and its conclusions will be available in public archives forever after, enabling future discussions to avoid retracing the same steps. See "Conspicuous Use of Archives in Chapter 6."

Finally, there is the possibility that someone on the list may make a real contribution to the conversation, by coming up with an idea you never anticipated. It's hard to say how likely this is; it just depends on the complexity of the code and degree of specialization required. But if anecdotal evidence may be permitted, I would hazard that this is more likely than one would intuitively expect. In the Subversion project, we (the founders) believed we faced a deep and complex set of problems, which we had been thinking about hard for several months, and we frankly doubted that anyone on the newly created mailing list was likely to make a real contribution to the discussion. So we took the lazy route and started batting some technical ideas back and forth in private emails, until an observer of the project[1] caught wind of what was happening and asked for the discussion to be moved to the public list. Rolling our eyes a bit, we did—and were stunned by the number of insightful comments and suggestions that quickly resulted. In many cases people offered ideas that had never even occurred to us. It turned out there were some *very* smart people on that list; they'd just been waiting for the right bait. It's true that the ensuing discussions took longer than they would have if we had kept the conversation private, but they were so much more productive that it was well worth the extra time.

Without descending into hand-waving generalizations like "the group is always smarter than the individual" (we've all met enough groups to know better), it must be acknowledged that there are certain activities at which groups excel. Massive peer review is one of them; generating large numbers of ideas quickly is another. The

---

1 We haven't gotten to the section on crediting yet, but just to practice what I'll later preach: the observer's name was Brian Behlendorf, and it was he who pointed out the general importance of keeping all discussions public unless there was a specific need for privacy.

quality of the ideas depends on the quality of the thinking that went into them, of course, but you won't know what kinds of thinkers are out there until you stimulate them with a challenging problem.

Naturally, there are some discussions that must be had privately; throughout this book we'll see examples of those. But the guiding principle should always be: *If there's no reason for it to be private, it should be public.*

Making this happen requires action. It's not enough merely to ensure that all your own posts go to the public list. You also have to nudge other people's unnecessarily private conversations to the list too. If someone tries to start a private discussion, and there's no reason for it to be private, then it is incumbent on you to open the appropriate meta-discussion immediately. Don't even comment on the original topic until you've either successfully steered the conversation to a public place, or ascertained that privacy really was needed. If you do this consistently, people will catch on pretty quickly and start to use the public forums by default.

Nip Rudeness in the Bud

From the very start of your project's public existence, you should maintain a zero-tolerance policy toward rude or insulting behavior in its forums. Zero-tolerance does not mean technical enforcement per se. You don't have to remove people from the mailing list when they flame another subscriber, or take away their commit access because they made derogatory comments. (In theory, you might eventually have to resort to such actions, but only after all other avenues have failed—which, by definition, isn't the case at the start of the project.) Zero-tolerance simply means never letting bad behavior slide by unnoticed. For example, when someone posts a technical comment mixed together with an *ad hominem* attack on some other developer in the project, it is imperative that your response address the *ad hominem* attack *first*, as a separate issue unto itself, and only afterward move on to the technical content.

It is unfortunately very easy, and all too typical, for constructive discussions to lapse into destructive flame wars. People will say things in email that they would never say face-to-face. The topics of discussion only amplify this effect: in technical issues, people often feel there is a single right answer to most questions, and that disagreement with that answer can be explained only by ignorance or stupidity. It's a short distance from calling someone's technical proposal stupid to calling the person themselves stupid. In fact, it's often hard to tell where technical debate leaves off and character attack begins, which is one reason why drastic responses or punishments are not a good idea. Instead, when you think you see it happening, make a post that stresses the importance of keeping the discussion friendly, without accusing anyone of being deliberately poisonous. Such "Nice Police" posts do have an unfortunate tendency to sound like a kindergarten teacher lecturing a class on good behavior:

> First, let's please cut down on the (potentially) ad hominem comments; for example, calling J's design for the security layer "naive and ignorant of the basic principles of computer security." That may be true or it may not, but in either case it's no way to have the discussion. J made his proposal in good faith. If it has deficiencies, point them out, and we'll fix them or get a new design. I'm sure M meant no personal insult to J, but the phrasing was unfortunate, and we try to keep things constructive around here.
>
> Now, on to the proposal. I think M was right in saying that...

As stilted as such responses sound, they have a noticeable effect. If you consistently call out bad behavior, but don't demand an apology or acknowledgment from the offending party, then you leave people free to cool down and show their better side by behaving more decorously next time—and they will. One of the secrets of doing this successfully is to never make the meta-discussion the main topic. It should always be an aside, a brief preface to the main portion of your response. Point out in passing that "we don't do things that way around here," but then move on to the real content, so that you're giving people something on-topic to respond to. If someone protests that they didn't deserve your rebuke, simply refuse to be drawn into an argument about it. Either don't respond (if you think they're just letting off steam and don't require a response), or say you're sorry if you overreacted and that it's hard to detect nuance in email, then get back to the main topic. Never, ever insist on an acknowledgment, whether public or private, from someone that they behaved inappropriately. If they choose of their own volition to post an apology, that's great, but demanding that they do so will only cause resentment.

The overall goal is to make good etiquette be seen as one of the "in-group" behaviors. This helps the project, because developers can be driven away (even from projects they like and want to support) by flame wars. You may not even know that they were driven away; someone might lurk on the mailing list, see that it takes a thick skin to participate in the project, and decide against getting involved at all. Keeping forums friendly is a long-term survival strategy, and it's easier to do when the project is still small. Once it's part of the culture, you won't have to be the only person promoting it. It will be maintained by everyone.

Practice Conspicuous Code Review

One of the best ways to foster a productive development community is to get people looking at each others' code. Some technical infrastructure is required to do this effectively—in particular, commit emails must be turned on; see "Commit emails" in Chapter 3 for more details. The effect of commit emails is that every time someone commits a change to the source code, an email goes out showing the log message and diffs for the change. *Code review* is the practice of reviewing commit emails as they come in, looking for bugs and possible improvements.[2]

Code review serves several purposes simultaneously. It's the most obvious example of peer review in the open source world, and directly helps to maintain software quality. Every bug that ships in a piece of software got there by being committed and not detected; therefore, the more eyes watch commits, the fewer bugs will ship. But code review also serves an indirect purpose: it confirms to people that what they do matters, because one obviously wouldn't take time to review a commit unless one cared about its effect. People do their best work when they know that others will take the time to evaluate it.

Reviews should be public. Even on occasions when I have been sitting in the same physical room with developers, and one of us has made a commit, we take care not to do the review verbally in the room, but to send it to the development mailing list instead. Everyone benefits from seeing the review happen. People follow the commentary and sometimes find flaws in it, and even when they don't, it still reminds them that review is an expected, regular activity, like washing the dishes or mowing the lawn.

In the Subversion project, we did not at first make a regular practice of code review. There was no guarantee that every commit would be reviewed, though one might sometimes look over a change if one was particularly interested in that area of the code. Bugs slipped in that really could and should have been caught. A developer named Greg Stein, who knew the value of code review from past work, decided that he was going to set an example by reviewing every line of *every single commit* that went into the code repository. Each commit anyone made was soon followed by an email to the developer's list from Greg, dissecting the commit, analyzing possible problems, and occasionally praising a clever bit of code. Right away, he was catching bugs and non-optimal coding practices that would otherwise have slipped by without ever being noticed. Pointedly, he never complained about being the only person reviewing every commit, even though it took a fair amount of his time, but he did sing the praises of code review whenever he had the chance. Pretty soon, other people, myself included,

---

2   This is how code review is usually done in open source projects, at any rate. In more centralized projects, "code review" can also mean multiple people sitting down together and going over printouts of source code, looking for specific problems and patterns.

started reviewing commits regularly too. What was our motivation? It wasn't that Greg had consciously shamed us into it. But he had proven that reviewing code was a valuable way to spend time, and that one could contribute as much to the project by reviewing others' changes as by writing new code. Once he demonstrated that, it became expected behavior, to the point where any commit that didn't get some reaction would cause the committer to worry, and even ask on the list whether anyone had a chance to review it yet. Later, Greg got a job that didn't leave him as much time for Subversion, and had to stop doing regular reviews. But by then, the habit was so ingrained for the rest of us as to seem that it had been going on since time immemorial.

Start doing reviews from very first commit. The sorts of problems that are easiest to catch by reviewing diffs are security vulnerabilities, memory leaks, insufficient comments or API documentation, off-by-one errors, caller/callee discipline mismatches, and other problems that require a minimum of surrounding context to spot. However, even larger-scale issues such as failure to abstract repeated patterns to a single location become spottable after one has been doing reviews regularly, because the memory of past diffs informs the review of present diffs.

Don't worry that you might not find anything to comment on, or that you don't know enough about every area of the code. There will usually be something to say about almost every commit; even where you don't find anything to question, you may find something to praise. The important thing is to make it clear to every committer that what they do is seen and understood. Of course, code review does not absolve programmers of the responsibility to review and test their changes before committing; no one should depend on code review to catch things she ought to have caught on her own.

When Opening a Formerly Closed Project, Be Sensitive to the Magnitude of the Change

If you're opening up an existing project, one that already has active developers accustomed to working in a closed-source environment, make sure everyone understands that a big change is coming—and make sure that you understand how it's going to feel from their point of view.

Try to imagine how the situation looks to them: formerly, all code and design decisions were made with a group of other programmers who knew the software more or less equally well, who all received the same pressures from the same management, and who all know each others' strengths and weaknesses. Now you're asking them to expose their code to the scrutiny of random strangers, who will form judgements based only on the code, with no awareness of what business pressures may have forced certain decisions. These strangers will ask lots of questions, questions that jolt the existing developers into realizing that the documentation they slaved so hard over is *still* inadequate (this is inevitable). To top it all off, the newcomers are unknown, faceless entities. If one of your developers already feels insecure about his skills, imagine how that will be exacerbated when newcomers point out flaws in code he wrote, and worse, do so in front of his colleagues. Unless you have a team of perfect coders, this is unavoidable—in fact, it will probably happen to all of them at first. This is not because they're bad programmers; it's just that any program above a certain size has bugs, and peer review will spot some of those bugs (see "Practice Conspicuous Code Review" earlier in this chapter). At the same time, the newcomers themselves won't be subject to much peer review at first, since they can't contribute code until they're more familiar with the project. To your developers, it may feel like all the criticism is incoming, never outgoing. Thus, there is the danger of a siege mentality taking hold among the old hands.

The best way to prevent this is to warn everyone about what's coming, explain it, tell them that the initial discomfort is perfectly normal, and reassure them that it's going to get better. Some of these warnings should take place privately, before the project is opened. But you may also find it helpful to remind people on the public lists that this is a new way of development for the project, and that it will take some time to adjust. The very best thing you can do is lead by example. If you don't see your developers answering enough newbie questions, then just telling them to answer more isn't going to help. They may not have a good sense of what warrants a response and what doesn't yet, or it could be that they don't have a feel for how to prioritize coding work against the new burden of external communications. The way to get them to participate is to participate yourself. Be on the public mailing lists, and make sure to answer some questions there. When you don't have the expertise to field a question, then visibly hand it off to a developer who does—and watch to make sure she follows up with an answer, or at least a response. It will naturally be tempting for the longtime developers to lapse into private discussions, since that's what they're used to. Make sure you're subscribed to the internal mailing lists on which this might happen, so you can ask that such discussions be moved to the public lists right away.

There are other, longer-term concerns with opening up formerly closed projects. Chapter 5 explores techniques for mixing paid and unpaid developers successfully, and Chapter 9 discusses the necessity of legal diligence when opening up a private code base that may contain software written or "owned" by other parties.

Announcing

Once the project is presentable—not perfect, just presentable—you're ready to announce it to the world. This is actually a very simple process: go to *http://freshmeat. net/*, click on Submit in the top navigation bar, and fill out a form announcing your new project. Freshmeat is the place everyone watches for new project announcements. You only have to catch a few eyes there for news of your project to spread by word of mouth.

If you know of mailing lists or newsgroups where an announcement of your project would be on-topic and of interest, then post there, but be careful to make exactly *one* post per forum, and to direct people to your project's own forums for follow-up discussion (by setting the *Reply-to* header). The posts should be short and get right to the point:

```
To: discuss@lists.example.org
Subject: [ANN] Scanley full-text indexer project
Reply-to: dev@scanley.org

This is a one-time post to announce the creation of the Scanley
project, an open source full-text indexer and search engine with a
rich API, for use by programmers in providing search services for
large collections of text files.  Scanley is now running code, is
under active development, and is looking for both developers and
testers.

Home page: http://www.scanley.org/

Features:
    - Searches plain text, HTML, and XML
    - Word or phrase searching
    - (planned) Fuzzy matching
    - (planned) Incremental updating of indexes
    - (planned) Indexing of remote web sites

Requirements:
    - Python 2.2 or higher
    - Enough disk space to hold the indexes (approximately twice
      original data size)

For more information, please come to scanley.org.

Thank you,
-J. Random
```

(See "Publicity" in Chapter 6 for advice on announcing further releases and other project events.)

There is an ongoing debate in the free software world about whether it is necessary to begin with running code, or whether a project can benefit from being opened even during the design/discussion stage. I used to think starting with running code was the most important factor, that it was what separated successful projects from toys, and that serious developers would be attracted only to software that did something concrete already.

This turned out not to be the case. In the Subversion project, we started with a design document, a core of interested and well-connected developers, a lot of fanfare, and *no* running code at all. To my complete surprise, the project acquired active participants right from the beginning, and by the time we did have something running, there were quite a few volunteer developers already deeply involved. Subversion is not the only example; the Mozilla project was also launched without running code, and is now a successful and popular web browser.

In the face of such evidence, I have to back away from the assertion that running code is absolutely necessary for launching a project. Running code is still the best foundation for success, and a good rule of thumb would be to wait until you have it before announcing your project. However, there may be circumstances where announcing earlier makes sense. I do think that at least a well-developed design document, or else some sort of code framework, is necessary—of course it may be revised based on public feedback, but there has to be something concrete, something more tangible than just good intentions, for people to sink their teeth into.

Whenever you announce, don't expect a horde of volunteers to join the project immediately afterward. Usually, the result of announcing is that you get a few casual inquiries, a few more people join your mailing lists, and aside from that, everything continues pretty much as before. But over time, you will notice a gradual increase in participation from both new code contributors and users. Announcement is merely the planting of a seed. It can take a long time for the news to spread. If the project consistently rewards those who get involved, the news *will* spread, though, because people want to share when they've found something good. If all goes well, the dynamics of exponential communications networks will slowly transform the project into a complex community, where you don't necessarily know everyone's name and can no longer follow every single conversation. The next chapters are about working in that environment.

## CHAPTER 3

Technical Infrastructure

Free software projects rely on technologies that support the selective capture and integration of information. The more skilled you are at using these technologies, and at persuading others to use them, the more successful your project will be. This only becomes more true as the project grows. Good information management is what prevents open source projects from collapsing under the weight of Brooks' Law,[1] which states that adding manpower to a late software project makes it later. Fred Brooks observed that the complexity of a project increases as the *square* of the number of participants. When only a few people are involved, everyone can easily talk to everyone else, but when hundreds of people are involved, it is no longer possible for each person to remain constantly aware of what everyone else is doing. If good free software project management is about making everyone feel like they're all working together in the same room, the obvious question is: what happens when everyone in a crowded room tries to talk at once?

This problem is not new. In non-metaphorical crowded rooms, the solution is *parliamentary procedure*: formal guidelines for how to have real-time discussions in large groups, how to make sure important dissents are not lost in floods of "me-too" comments, how to form subcommittees, how to recognize when decisions are made, etc. An important part of parliamentary procedure is specifying how the group interacts

---

1   From *The Mythical Man Month* by Frederick P. Brooks (Addison-Wesley Professional, 1995). See *http://en.wikipedia.org/wiki/The_Mythical_Man-Month* and *http://en.wikipedia.org/wiki/Brooks_Law*.

with its information management system. Some remarks are made "for the record," others are not. The record itself is subject to direct manipulation, and is understood to be not a literal transcript of what occurred, but a representation of what the group is willing to *agree* occurred. The record is not monolithic, but takes different forms for different purposes. It comprises the minutes of individual meetings, the complete collection of all minutes of all meetings, summaries, agendas and their annotations, committee reports, reports from correspondents not present, lists of action items, etc.

Because the Internet is not really a room, we don't have to worry about replicating those parts of parliamentary procedure that keep some people quiet while others are speaking. But when it comes to information management techniques, well-run open source projects are parliamentary procedure on steroids. Since almost all communication in open source projects happens in writing, elaborate systems have evolved for routing and labeling data appropriately; for minimizing repetitions so as to avoid spurious divergences; for storing and retrieving data; for correcting bad or obsolete information; and for associating disparate bits of information with each other as new connections are observed. Active participants in open source projects internalize many of these techniques, and will often perform complex manual tasks to ensure that information is routed correctly. But the whole endeavor ultimately depends on sophisticated software support. As much as possible, the communications media themselves should do the routing, labeling, and recording, and should make the information available to humans in the most convenient way possible. In practice, of course, humans will still need to intervene at many points in the process, and it's important that the software make such interventions convenient too. But in general, if the humans take care to label and route information accurately on its first entry into the system, then the software should be configured to make as much use of that metadata as possible.

The advice in this chapter is intensely practical, based on experiences with specific software and usage patterns. But the point is not just to teach a particular collection of techniques. It is also to demonstrate, by means of many small examples, the overall attitude that will best encourage good information management in your project. This attitude will involve a combination of technical skills and people skills. The technical skills are essential because information management software always requires configuration, plus a certain amount of ongoing maintenance and tweaking as new needs arise (for example, see the discussion of how to handle project growth in "Prefiltering the Bug Tracker" later in this chapter). The people skills are necessary because the human community also requires maintenance: it's not always immediately obvious how to use these tools to full advantage, and in some cases projects have conflicting conventions (for example, see the discussion of setting *Reply-to* headers on outgoing mailing list posts, in "Mailing Lists" later in this chapter). Everyone involved with the project will need to be encouraged, at the right times and in the right ways, to do their part to keep the project's information well organized. The more involved the contributor, the more complex and specialized the techniques he can be expected to learn.

Information management has no cut-and-dried solution. There are too many variables. You may finally get everything configured just the way you want it, and have most of the community participating, but then project growth will make some of those practices unscalable. Or project growth may stabilize, and the developer and user communities settle into a comfortable relationship with the technical infrastructure, but then someone will come along and invent a whole new information management service, and pretty soon newcomers will be asking why your project doesn't use it—for example, this is happening now to a lot of free software projects that predate the invention of the wiki (see *http://en.wikipedia.org/wiki/Wiki*). Many questions are matters of judgement, involving trade-offs between the convenience of those producing information and the convenience of those consuming it, or between the time required to configure information management software and the benefit it brings to the project.

Beware of the temptation to over-automate, that is, to automate things that really require human attention. Technical infrastructure is important, but what makes a free software project work is care—and intelligent expression of that care—by the humans involved. The technical infrastructure is mainly about giving humans convenient ways to do that.

What a Project Needs

Most open source projects offer at least a minimum, standard set of tools for managing information:

Web site
> Primarily a centralized, one-way conduit of information from the project out to the public. The web site may also serve as an administrative interface for other project tools.

Mailing lists
> Usually the most active communications forum in the project, and the "medium of record."

Version control
> Enables developers to manage code changes conveniently, including reverting and "change porting." Enables everyone to watch what's happening to the code.

Bug tracking
> Enables developers to keep track of what they're working on, coordinate with each other, and plan releases. Enables everyone to query the status of bugs and record information (e.g., reproduction recipes) about particular bugs. Can be used for tracking not only bugs, but also tasks, releases, new features, etc.

Real-time chat
> A place for quick, lightweight discussions and question/answer exchanges. Not always archived completely.

Each tool in this set addresses a distinct need, but their functions are also interrelated, and the tools must be made to work together. Below we will examine how they can do so, and more importantly, how to get people to use them. The web site is not discussed until the end, since it acts more as glue for the other components than as a tool unto itself.

You may be able to avoid a lot of the headache of choosing and configuring these tools by using a *canned hosting* site: a server that offers prepackaged, templatized web areas with all the accompanying tools needed to run a free software project. See "Canned Hosting" later in this chapter for a discussion of the advantages and disadvantages of canned hosting.

Mailing Lists

Mailing lists are the bread and butter of project communications. If a user is exposed to any forum besides the web pages, it is most likely to be one of the project's mailing lists. But before she experiences the mailing list itself, she will experience the mailing list interface—that is, the mechanism by which she joins ("subscribes to") the list. This brings us to Rule #1 of mailing lists:

> Don't try to manage mailing lists by hand—get list management software.

It will be tempting to put this off. Setting up mailing list management software might seem like overkill at first. Managing small, low-traffic lists by hand will seem seductively easy: you just set up a subscription address that forwards to you, and when someone mails it, you add (or remove) their email address in some text file that holds all the addresses on the list. What could be simpler?

The trick is that good mailing list management—which is what people have come to expect—is not simple at all. It's not just about subscribing and unsubscribing users when they request. It's also about moderating to prevent spam, offering the mailing list in digest versus message-by-message form, providing standard list and project information by means of auto-responders, and various other things. A human being monitoring a subscription address can supply only a bare minimum of functionality, and even then not as reliably and promptly as software could.

Modern list management software usually offers at least the following features:

Both email- and web-based subscription
> When a user subscribes to a list, she should *promptly* get an automated welcome message in reply, telling her what she has subscribed to, how to interact further with the mailing list software, and (most importantly) how to unsubscribe. This automatic reply can be customized to contain project-specific information, of course, such as the project's web site, FAQ location, etc.

Subscription in either digest mode or message-by-message mode
> In digest mode, the subscriber receives one email per day, containing all the list activity for that day. For people who are following a list loosely, without participating, digest mode is often preferable, because it allows them to scan all the subjects at once and avoid the distraction of emails coming in at random times.

Moderation features
> To "moderate" is to check posts to make sure they are a) not spam, and b) on topic, before they go out to the entire list. Moderation necessarily involves humans, but software can do a lot to make it easier. There is more said about moderation later in "Filtering posts."

Administrative interface
> Among other things, this enables an administrator to go in and remove obsolete addresses easily. This can become urgent when a recipient's address starts sending automatic "I am no longer at this address" replies back to the list in response to every list post. (Some mailing list software can even detect this by itself and unsubscribe the person automatically.)

Header manipulation
> Many people have sophisticated filtering and replying rules set up in their mail-readers. Mailing list software can add and manipulate certain standard headers for these people to take advantage of (more details follow).

Archiving

All posts to the managed lists are stored and made available on the web; alternatively, some mailing list software offers special interfaces for plugging in an external archiving tool such as MHonArc (*http://www.mhonarc.org/*). As "Conspicuous Use of Archives" discusses in Chapter 6, archiving is crucial.

The point of all this is merely to emphasize that mailing list management is a complex problem that has been given a lot of thought, and mostly been solved. You certainly don't need to become an expert in it. But you should be aware that there's always room to learn more, and that list management will occupy your attention from time to time in the course of running a free software project. Next, we'll examine a few of the most common mailing list configuration issues.

Spam Prevention

Between when this sentence is written and when it is published, the Internet-wide spam problem will probably double in severity—or at least it will feel that way. There was a time, not so long ago, when one could run a mailing list without taking any spam-prevention measures at all. The occasional stray post would still show up, but infrequently enough to be only a low-level annoyance. That era is gone forever. Today, a mailing list that takes no spam prevention measures will quickly be submerged in junk emails, to the point of unusability. Spam prevention is mandatory.

We divide spam prevention into two categories: preventing spam posts from appearing on your mailing lists, and preventing your mailing list from being a source of new email addresses for spammers' harvesters. The former is more important, so we examine it first.

Filtering posts

There are three basic techniques for preventing spam posts, and most mailing list software offers all three. They are best used in tandem:

Auto-allow postings only from list subscribers. This is effective as far as it goes, and also involves very little administrative overhead, since it's usually just a matter of changing a setting in the mailing list software's configuration. But note that posts that aren't automatically approved must not be simply discarded. Instead, they should be passed along for moderation, for two reasons. First, you want to allow non-subscribers to post. A person with a question or suggestion should not need to subscribe to a mailing list just to make a single post there. Second, even subscribers may sometimes post from an address other than the one by which they're subscribed. Email addresses are not a reliable method of identifying people, and shouldn't be treated as such.

Filter posts through spam-filtering software. If the mailing list software makes it possible (most do), you can have posts filtered by spam-filtering software. Automatic spam-filtering is not perfect, and never will be, since there is a never-ending arms race between spammers and filter writers. However, it can greatly reduce the amount of spam that gets through to the moderation queue, and since the longer that queue is, the more time humans must spend examining it, any amount of automated filtering is beneficial.

There is not space here for detailed instructions on setting up spam filters. You will have to consult your mailing list software's documentation for that (see "Software" later in this chapter). List software often comes with some built-in spam prevention features, but you may want to add some third-party filters. I've had good experiences with these two: SpamAssassin (*http://spamassassin.apache. org/*) and SpamProbe (*http://spamprobe.sourceforge.net/*). This is not a comment on the many other open source spam filters out there, some of which are apparently also quite good. I just happen to have used those two myself and been satisfied with them.

Moderation. For mails that aren't automatically allowed by virtue of being from a list subscriber, and that make it through the spam filtering software, if any, the last stage is *moderation*: the mail is routed to a special address, where a human examines it and confirms or rejects it.

Confirming a post takes one of two forms: you can accept the post just this once, or you can tell the list software to allow this and all future posts from the same sender. You almost always want to do the latter, in order to reduce the future moderation burden. Details on how to confirm vary from system to system, but it's usually a matter of replying to a special address with the command "accept" (meaning accept just this one post) or "allow" (allow this and future posts).

Rejecting is usually done by simply ignoring the moderation mail. If the list software never receives confirmation that something is a valid post, then it won't pass that post on to the list, so simply dropping the moderation mail achieves the desired effect. Sometimes you also have the option of responding with a "reject" or "deny" command, to automatically disapprove future mails from the same sender without even running them through moderation. There is rarely any point doing this, since moderation is mostly about spam prevention, and spammers tend not to send from the same address twice anyway.

Be sure to use moderation *only* for filtering out spams and clearly off-topic messages, such as when someone accidentally posts to the wrong mailing list. The moderation system will usually give you a way to respond directly to the sender, but don't use that method to answer questions that really belong on the mailing list itself, even if you know the answer off the top of your head. To do so would deprive the project's community of an accurate picture of what sorts of questions people are asking, and deprive them of a chance to answer questions themselves and/or see answers from others. Mailing list moderation is strictly about keeping the list free of junk and off-topic emails, nothing more.

Address hiding in archives

To prevent your mailing lists from being a source of addresses for spammers, a common technique is for the archives to obscure people's email addresses, for example by replacing:

> *jrandom@somedomain.com*

with:

> *jrandom_AT_somedomain.com*

or:

> *jrandomNOSPAM@somedomain.com*

or some similarly obvious (to a human) encoding. Since spam address harvesters often work by crawling through web pages—including your mailing list's online archives—and looking for sequences containing "@", encoding the addresses is a way of making people's email addresses invisible or useless to spammers. This does nothing to prevent spam from being sent to the mailing list itself, of course, but it does avoid increasing the amount of spam sent directly to list users' personal addresses.

Address hiding can be controversial. Some people like it a lot, and will be surprised if your archives don't do it automatically. Other people think it's too much of an inconvenience (because humans also have to translate the addresses back before using them). Sometimes people assert that it's ineffective, because a harvester could in theory compensate for any consistent encoding pattern. However, note that there is empirical evidence that address hiding *is* effective; see *http://www.cdt.org/speech/spam/030319spamreport.shtml*.

Ideally, the list management software would leave the choice up to each individual subscriber, either through a special yes/no header or a setting in that subscriber's list account preferences. However, I don't know of any software that offers per-subscriber or per-post choice in the matter, so for now the list manager must make a decision for everyone (assuming the archiver offers the feature at all, which is not always the case). I lean very mildly toward turning address hiding on. Some people are very careful to avoid posting their email addresses on web pages or anywhere else a spam harvester might see it, and they would be disappointed to have all that care thrown away by a mailing list archive; meanwhile, the inconvenience address hiding imposes on archive users is very slight, since it's trivial to transform an obscured address back to a valid one if you need to reach the person. But keep in mind that, in the end, it's still an arms race: by the time you read this, harvesters might well have evolved to the point where they can recognize most common forms of hiding, and we'll have to think of something else.

Identification and Header Management

List subscribers often want to put mails from the list into a project-specific folder, separate from their other mail. Their mail-reading software can do this automatically by examining the mail's *headers*. The headers are the fields at the top of the mail that indicate the sender, recipient, subject, date, and various other things about the message. Certain headers are well known and effectively mandatory:

```
From: ...
To: ...
Subject: ...
Date: ...
```

Others are optional, though still quite standard. For example, emails are not strictly required to have the

```
Reply-to: sender@email.address.here
```

header, but most do, because it gives recipients a foolproof way to reach the author (it is especially useful when the author had to send from an address other than the one to which replies should be directed).

Some mail-reading software offers an easy-to-use interface for filing mails based on patterns in the Subject header. This leads people to request that the mailing list add an automatic prefix to all Subjects, so they can set their readers to look for that prefix and automatically file the mails in the right folder. The idea is that the original author would write:

```
Subject: Making the 2.5 release.
```

but the mail would show up on the list looking like this:

```
Subject: [discuss@lists.example.org] Making the 2.5 release.
```

Although most list management software offers the option to do this, I strongly recommend against turning the option on. The problem it solves can easily be solved in much less obtrusive ways, and the cost of eating space in the Subject field is far too high. Experienced mailing list users typically scan the Subjects of the day's incoming list mail to decide what to read and/or respond to. Prepending the list's name to the Subject can push the right side of the Subject off the screen, rendering it invisible. This obscures information that people depend on to decide what mails to open, thus reducing the overall functionality of the mailing list for everyone.

Instead of munging the Subject header, teach your users to take advantage of the other standard headers, starting with the To header, which should say the mailing list's name:

```
To: <discuss@lists.example.org>
```

Any mail reader that can filter on Subject should be able to filter on To just as easily.

There are a few other optional-but-standard headers expected for mailing lists. Filtering on these is even more reliable than using the "To" or "Cc" headers, since these headers are added to each post by the mailing list management software itself, so some users may be counting on their presence:

```
list-help: <mailto:discuss-help@lists.example.org>
list-unsubscribe: <mailto:discuss-unsubscribe@lists.example.org>
list-post: <mailto:discuss@lists.example.org>
Delivered-To: mailing list discuss@lists.example.org
Mailing-List: contact discuss-help@lists.example.org; run by ezmlm
```

For the most part, they are self-explanatory. See *http://www.nisto.com/listspec/list-manager-intro.html*, for more explanation, or if you need the really detailed, formal specification, see *http://www.faqs.org/rfcs/rfc2369.html*.

Notice how these headers imply that if you have a mailing list named "list", you also have administrative addresses "list-help" and "list-unsubscribe" available. In addition to these, it is normal to have "list-subscribe" for joining and "list-owner" for reaching the list administrators. Depending on the list management software you use, these and/or various other administrative addresses may be set up; the documentation will have details. Usually a complete explanation of all these special addresses is mailed to each new user as part of an automated "welcome mail" on subscribing. You yourself will probably get a copy of this welcome mail. If you don't, then ask someone else for a copy, so you know what your users are seeing when they join the list. Keep the copy handy so you can answer questions about the mailing list functions, or better yet, put it on a web page somewhere. That way when people lose their own copy of the instructions and post to ask "How do I unsubscribe from this list?", you can just hand them the URL.

Some mailing list software offers an option to append unsubscription instructions to the bottom of every post. If that option is available, turn it on. It causes only a couple of extra lines per message, in a harmless location, and it can save you a lot of time, by cutting down on the number of people who mail you—or worse, mail the list!—asking how to unsubscribe.

The Great Reply-to Debate

In the Chapter 2 section "Avoid Private Discussions," I stressed the importance of making sure discussions stay in public forums, and talked about how active measures are sometimes needed to prevent conversations from trailing off into private email threads. This chapter is all about setting up project communications software to do as much of the work for you as possible. Therefore, if the mailing list management software offers a way to automatically cause discussions to stay on the list, you would think turning that feature on would be the obvious choice.

Well, not quite. There is such a feature, but it has some pretty severe disadvantages. The question of whether or not to use it is one of the hottest debates in mailing list management—admittedly, not a controversy that's likely to make the evening news in your city, but it can flare up from time to time in free software projects. Below, I will describe the feature, give the major arguments on both sides, and make the best recommendation I can.

The feature itself is very simple: the mailing list software can, if you wish, automatically set the Reply-to header on every post to redirect replies to the mailing list. That is, no matter what the original sender puts in the Reply-to header (or even if they don't include one at all), by the time the list subscribers see the post, the header will contain the list address:

```
Reply-to: discuss@lists.example.org
```

On its face, this seems like a good thing. Because virtually all mail-reading software pays attention to the Reply-to header, now when anyone responds to a post, their response will be automatically addressed to the entire list, not just to the sender of the message being responded to. Of course, the responder can still manually change where the message goes, but the important thing is that *by default* replies are directed to the list. It's a perfect example of using technology to encourage collaboration.

Unfortunately, there are some disadvantages. The first is known as the *Can't Find My Way Back Home* problem: sometimes the original sender will put their "real" email address in the Reply-to field, because for one reason or another they send email from a different address from where they receive it. People who always read and send from the same location don't have this problem, and may be surprised that it even exists. But for those who have unusual email configurations, or who cannot control how the From address on their mails looks (perhaps because they send from work and do not have any influence over the IT department), using Reply-to may be the only way they have to ensure that responses reach them. When such a person posts to a mailing list that he's not subscribed to, his setting of Reply-to becomes essential information. If the list software overwrites it, he may never see the responses to his post.

The second disadvantage has to do with expectations, and in my opinion is the most powerful argument against Reply-to munging. Most experienced mail users are accustomed to two basic methods of replying: *reply-to-all* and *reply-to-author*. All modern mail-reading software has separate keys for these two actions. Users know that to reply to everyone (that is, including the list), they should choose reply-to-all, and to reply privately to the author, they should choose reply-to-author. Although you want to encourage people to reply to the list whenever possible, there are certainly circumstances where a private reply is the responder's prerogative—for example, they may want to say something confidential to the author of the original message, something that would be inappropriate on the public list.

Now consider what happens when the list has overridden the original sender's Reply-to. The responder hits the reply-to-author key, expecting to send a private message back to the original author. Because that's the expected behavior, he may not bother to look carefully at the recipient address in the new message. He composes his private, confidential message, one which perhaps says embarrassing things about someone on the list, and hits the send key. Unexpectedly, a few hours later his message appears *on the mailing list!* True, in theory he should have looked carefully at the recipient field, and should not have assumed anything about the Reply-to header. But authors almost always set Reply-to to their own personal address (or rather, their mail software sets it for them), and many longtime email users have come to expect that. In fact, when a person deliberately sets Reply-to to some other address, such as the list, he usually makes a point of mentioning this in the body of the message, so people won't be surprised at what happens when they reply.

Because of the possibly severe consequences of this unexpected behavior, my own preference is to configure list management software to never touch the Reply-to header. This is one instance where using technology to encourage collaboration has, it seems to me, potentially dangerous side-effects. However, there are also some powerful arguments on the other side of this debate. Whichever way you choose, you will occasionally get people posting to your list asking why you didn't choose the other way. Since this is not something you ever want as the main topic of discussion on your list, it might be good to have a canned response ready, of the sort that's more likely to stop discussion than encourage it. Make sure you do *not* insist that your decision, whichever it is, is obviously the only right and sensible one (even if you think that's the case). Instead, point out that this is a very old debate, there are good arguments on both sides, no choice is going to satisfy all users, and therefore you just made the best decision you could. Politely ask that the subject not be revisited unless someone has something genuinely new to say, then stay out of the thread and hope it dies a natural death.

Someone may suggest a vote to choose one way or the other. You can do that if you want, but I personally do not feel that counting heads is a satisfactory solution in this case. The penalty for someone who is surprised by the behavior is so huge (accidentally sending a private mail to a public list), and the inconvenience for everyone else is fairly slight (occasionally having to remind someone to respond to the whole list instead of just to you), that it's not clear that the majority, even though they are the majority, should be able to put the minority at such risk.

I have not addressed all aspects of this issue here, just the ones that seemed of overriding importance. For a full discussion, see these two canonical documents, which are the ones people always cite when they're having this debate:

"Leave Reply-to alone," by Chip Rosenthal
  http://www.unicom.com/pw/reply-to-harmful.html

"Set Reply-to to list," by Simon Hill
  http://www.metasystema.net/essays/reply-to.mhtml

Despite the mild preference indicated above, I do not feel there is a "right" answer to this question, and happily participate in many lists that *do* set Reply-to. The most important thing you can do is settle on one way or the other early, and try not to get entangled in debates about it after that.

Two fantasies

Someday, someone will get the bright idea to implement a *reply-to-list* key in a mailreader. It would use some of the custom list headers mentioned earlier to figure out the address of the mailing list, and then address the reply directly to the list only, leaving off any other recipient addresses, since most are probably subscribed to the list anyway. Eventually, other mail readers will pick up the feature, and this whole debate will go away. (Actually, the *http://www.mutt.org/* Mutt mail reader does offer this feature. Now, if only others would copy it.)

An even better solution would be for Reply-to munging to be a per-subscriber preference. Those who want the list set to Reply-to munged (either on others' posts or on their own posts) could ask for that, and those who don't would ask for Reply-to in order to be left alone. However, I don't know of any list management software that offers this on a per-subscriber basis. For now, we seem to be stuck with a global setting.

Archiving

The technical details of setting up mailing list archiving are specific to the software that's running the list, and are beyond the scope of this book. When choosing or configuring an archiver, consider these qualities:

Prompt updating

People will often want to refer to an archived post made within the last hour or two. If possible, the archiver should archive each post instantaneously, so that by the time a post appears on the mailing list, it's already present in the archives. If that option isn't available, then at least try to set the archiver to update itself every hour or so. (By default, some archivers run their update processes once per night, but in practice that's far too much lag time for an active mailing list.)

Referential stability

Once a message is archived at a particular URL, it should remain accessible at that exact same URL forever, or as close to forever as possible. Even if the archives are rebuilt, restored from backup, or otherwise fixed, any URLs that have already been made publicly available should remain the same. Stable references make it possible for Internet search engines to index the archives, which is a major boon to users looking for answers. Stable references are also important because mailing list posts and threads are often linked to from the bug tracker (see "Bug Tracker" later in this chapter) or from other project documents.

Ideally, mailing list software would include a message's archive URL, or at least the message-specific portion of the URL, in a header when it distributes the message to recipients. That way people who have a copy of the message would be able to know to its archive location without having to actually visit the archives, which would be helpful because any operation that involves one's web browser is automatically time-consuming. Whether any mailing list software actually offers this feature, I don't know; unfortunately, the ones I have used do not. However, it's something to look for (or, if you write mailing list software, it's a feature to consider implementing, please).

Backups

It should be reasonably obvious how to back up the archives, and the restoration recipe should not be too difficult. In other words, don't treat your archiver as a black box. You (or someone in your project) should know where it's storing the messages, and how to regenerate the actual archive pages from the message store if it should ever become necessary. Those archives are precious data—a project that loses them loses a good part of its collective memory.

Thread support

It should be possible to go from any individual message to the *thread* (group of related messages) that the original message is part of. Each thread should have its own URL too, separate from the URLs of the individual messages in the thread.

Searchability

An archiver that doesn't support searching—on the bodies of messages, as well as on authors and subjects—is close to useless. Note that some archivers support searching by simply farming the work out to an external search engine such as Google (*http://www.google.com/*). This is acceptable, but direct search support is usually more fine-tuned, because it allows the searcher to specify that the match must appear in a subject line versus the body, for example.

The above is just a technical checklist to help you evaluate and set up an archiver. Getting people to actually *use* the archiver to the project's advantage is discussed in later chapters, in particular the section "Conspicuous Use of Archives." in Chapter 6.

Software

Here are some open source tools for doing list management and archiving. If the site where you're hosting your project already has a default setup, then you may not ever have to decide on a tool at all. But if you must install one yourself, these are some possibilities. The ones I have actually used are Mailman, Ezmlm, MHonArc, and Hypermail, but that doesn't mean the others aren't good too (and of course, there are probably other tools out there that I just didn't happen to find, so don't take this as a complete list).

Mailing list management software:

Mailman

http://www.list.org/. Has built-in archiver and hooks for plugging in external archivers.

SmartList

http://www.procmail.org/. To be used with the Procmail mail processing system.

Ecartis

> *http://www.ecartis.org/*

ListProc

> *http://listproc.sourceforge.net/*

Ezmlm

> *http://cr.yp.to/ezmlm.html*. To work with the Qmail mail delivery system (*http://cr. yp.to/qmail.html*).

Dada

> *http://mojo.skazat.com/*. Despite the web site's bizarre attempts to hide the fact, this is free software, released under the GNU General Public License. It also has a built-in archiver.

Mailing list archiving software:

MHonArc

> *http://www.mhonarc.org/*

Hypermail

> *http://www.hypermail.org/*

Lurker

> *http://sourceforge.net/projects/lurker*

Procmail

> *http://www.procmail.org/*. Companion software to SmartList, this is a general mail processing system that can, apparently, be configured as an archiver.

Version Control

A *version control system* (or *revision control system*) is a combination of technologies and practices for tracking and controlling changes to a project's files, in particular to source code, documentation, and web pages. If you have never used version control before, the first thing you should do is go find someone who has, and get them to join your project. These days, everyone will expect at least your project's source code to be under version control, and probably will not take the project seriously if it doesn't use version control with at least minimal competence.

The reason version control is so universal is that it helps with virtually every aspect of running a project: interdeveloper communications, release management, bug management, code stability and experimental development efforts, and attribution and authorization of changes by particular developers. The version control system provides a central coordinating force among all of these areas. The core of version control is *change management*: identifying each discrete change made to the project's files, annotating each change with metadata like the change's date and author, and then replaying these facts to whoever asks, in whatever way they ask. It is a communications mechanism where a change is the basic unit of information.

This section does not discuss all aspects of using a version control system. It's so all-encompassing that it must be addressed topically throughout the book. Here, we will concentrate on choosing and setting up a version control system in a way that will foster cooperative development down the road.

Version Control Vocabulary

This book cannot teach you how to use version control if you've never used it before, but it would be impossible to discuss the subject without a few key terms. These terms are useful independently of any particular version control system: they are the basic nouns and verbs of networked collaboration, and will be used generically throughout the rest of this book. Even if there were no version control systems in the world, the problem of change management would remain, and these words give us a language for talking about that problem concisely.

Commit

> To make a change to the project; more formally, to store a change in the version control database in such a way that it can be incorporated into future releases of the project. "Commit" can be used as a verb or a noun. As a noun, it is essentially synonymous with "change." For example: "I just committed a fix for the server crash bug people have been reporting on Mac OS X. Jay, could you please review the commit and check that I'm not misusing the allocator there?"

Log message

> A bit of commentary attached to each commit, describing the nature and purpose of the commit. Log messages are among the most important documents in any project: they are the bridge between the highly technical language of individual code changes and the more user-oriented language of features, bug fixes, and project progress. Later in this section, we'll look at ways to distribute log messages to the appropriate audiences; also, "Codifying Tradition" in Chapter 6 discusses ways to encourage contributors to write concise and useful log messages.

Update

> To ask that others' changes (commits) be incorporated into your local copy of the project; that is, to bring your copy "up-to-date." This is a very common operation;

most developers update their code several times a day, so that they know they're running roughly the same thing the other developers are running, and so that if they see a bug, they can be pretty sure it hasn't been fixed already. For example: "Hey, I noticed the indexing code is always dropping the last byte. Is this a new bug?" "Yes, but it was fixed last week—try updating, it should go away."

Repository

A database in which changes are stored. Some version control systems are centralized: there is a single, master repository, which stores all changes to the project. Others are decentralized: each developer has her own repository, and changes can be swapped back and forth between repositories arbitrarily. The version control system keeps track of dependencies between changes, and when it's time to make a release, a particular set of changes is approved for that release. The question of whether centralized or decentralized is better is one of the enduring holy wars of software development; try not to fall into the trap of arguing about it on your project lists.

Checkout

The process of obtaining a copy of the project from a repository. A checkout usually produces a directory tree called a "working copy" (see the next entry), from which changes may be committed back to the original repository. In some decentralized version control systems, each working copy is itself a repository, and changes can be pushed out to (or pulled into) any repository that's willing to accept them.

Working copy

A developer's private directory tree containing the project's source code files, and possibly its web pages or other documents. A working copy also contains a little bit of metadata managed by the version control system, telling the working copy what repository it comes from, what "revisions" (see the next entry) of the files are present, etc. Generally, each developer has his own working copy, in which he makes and tests changes, and from which he commits.

Revision, change, changeset

A revision is usually one specific incarnation of a particular file or directory. For example, if the project starts out with revision 6 of file F, and then someone commits a change to F, this produces revision 7 of F. Some systems also use the terms "revision," "change," or "changeset" to refer to a set of changes committed together as one conceptual unit.

These terms occasionally have distinct technical meanings in different version control systems, but the general idea is always the same: they give a way to speak precisely about exact points in time in the history of a file or a set of files (say, immediately before and after a bug is fixed). For example: "Oh yes, she fixed that in revision 10" or "She fixed that in revision 10 of foo.c."

When one talks about a file or collection of files without specifying a particular revision, it is generally assumed that one means the most recent revision(s) available.

Diff

A textual representation of a change. A diff shows which lines were changed and how, plus a few lines of surrounding context on either side. A developer who is already familiar with some code can usually read a diff against that code and understand what the change did, and even spot bugs.

Tag

A label for a particular collection of files at specified revisions. Tags are usually used to preserve interesting snapshots of the project. For example, a tag is usually made for each public release, so that one can obtain, directly from the version control system, the exact set of files/revisions comprising that release. Common tag names are things like `Release_1_0`, `Delivery_00456`, etc.

Branch

A copy of the project kept under version control but isolated, so that changes made to the branch don't affect the rest of the project and vice versa, except when changes are deliberately merged from one side to the other (see the next entry). Branches are also known as "lines of development." Even when a project has no explicit branches, development is still considered to be happening on the "main branch" also known as the "main line" or "trunk."

Branches offer a way to isolate different lines of development from each other. For example, a branch can be used for experimental development that would be too destabilizing for the main trunk. Or conversely, a branch can be used as a place to stabilize a new release. During the release process, regular development would continue uninterrupted in the main branch of the repository; meanwhile, on the release branch, no changes are allowed except those approved by the release managers. This way, making a release needn't interfere with ongoing development work. See "Use branches to avoid bottlenecks" later in this chapter for a more detailed discussion of branching.

Merge (a.k.a. port)

To move a change from one branch to another. This includes merging from the main trunk to some other branch, or vice versa. In fact, those are the most common kinds of merges; it is rare to port a change between two non-main branches. See "Singularity of information" for more about this kind of merging.

Merge has a second, related meaning: it is what the version control system does when it sees that two people have changed the same file but in non-overlapping ways. Since the two changes don't interfere with each other, when one of the people updates his copy of the file (already containing his own changes), the other person's changes will be automatically merged in. This is very common, especially on projects where multiple people are hacking on the same code. When two different changes *do* overlap, the result is a "conflict"; see the next entry.

Conflict

What happens when two people try to make different changes to the same place in the code. All version control systems automatically detect conflicts, and notify at least one of the humans involved that their changes conflict with someone else's. It is then up to that human to *resolve* the conflict, and to communicate that resolution to the version control system.

Lock

A way to declare an exclusive intent to change a particular file or directory. For example, "I can't commit any changes to the web pages right now. It seems Alfred has them all locked while he fixes their background images." Not all version control systems even offer the ability to lock, and of those that do, not all require the locking feature to be used. This is because parallel, simultaneous development is the norm, and locking people out of files is (usually) contrary to this ideal.

Version control systems that require locking to make commits are said to use the *lock-modify-unlock* model. Those that do not are said to use the *copy-modify-merge* model. An excellent in-depth explanation and comparison of the two models may be found at *http://svnbook.red-bean.com/svnbook-1.0/ch02s02.html*. In general, the copy-modify-merge model is better for open source development, and all the version control systems discussed in this book support that model.

Choosing a Version Control System

As of this writing, the version control system of choice in the free software world is the Concurrent Versions System, or *CVS* (*http://www.nongnu.org/cvs*). CVS has been around for a long time. Most experienced developers are already familiar with it, it

Version Versus Revision

The word *version* is sometimes used as a synonym for "revision," but I will not use it that way in this book, because it is too easily confused with "version" in the sense of a version of a piece of software—that is, the release or edition number, as in "Version 1.0". However, since the phrase "version control" is already standard, I will continue to use it as a synonym for "revision control" and "change control."

does more or less what you need, and since it's the default, you won't end up in any long debates about whether or not it was the right choice. CVS has some disadvantages, however. It doesn't provide an easy way to refer to multi-file changes; it doesn't allow you to rename or copy files under version control (so if you need to reorganize your code tree after starting the project, it can be a real pain); it has poor merging support; it doesn't handle large files or binary files very well; and some operations are slow when large numbers of files are involved.

None of CVS's flaws is fatal, and it is still quite popular. However, in the last few years a number of new version control systems have appeared, and free software projects are beginning to try them out. Appendix A lists all the ones I know of. As that list makes clear, deciding on a version control system could easily become a life-long research project. Possibly you will be spared the decision because it will be made for you by your hosting site. But if you must choose, consult with your other developers, ask around to see what people have experience with, then pick one and run with it. Any stable, production-ready version control system will do; you don't have to worry too much about making a drastically wrong decision. If you simply can't make up your mind, then go with CVS. It's still the standard, and will probably continue to be so for a few years. Also, many of the other systems support one-way conversion from CVS, so you can change your mind later anyway.

Using the Version Control System

The recommendations in this section are not targeted toward a particular version control system, and should be simple to implement in any of them. Consult your specific system's documentation for details.

Version everything

Keep not only your project's source code under version control, but also its web pages, documentation, FAQ, design notes, and anything else that people might want to edit. Keep them right next to the source code, in the same repository tree. Any piece of information worth writing down is worth versioning—that is, any piece of information that could change. Things that don't change should be archived, not versioned. For example, an email, once posted, does not change; therefore, versioning it wouldn't make sense (unless it becomes part of some larger, evolving document).

The reason versioning everything together in one place is important is so people have to learn only one mechanism for submitting changes. Often a contributor will start out making edits to the web pages or documentation, and move to small code contributions later, for example. When the project uses the same system for all kinds of submissions, people have to learn the ropes only once. Versioning everything together also means that new features can be committed together with their documentation updates, that branching the code will branch the documentation too, etc.

Don't keep *generated files* under version control. They are not truly editable data, since they are produced programmatically from other files. For example, some build systems create *configure* based on the template *configure.in*. To make a change to the *configure*, one would edit *configure.in* and then regenerate; thus, only the template *configure.in* is an "editable file." Always version only the templates. If you version the result files as well, people will inevitably forget to regenerate when they commit a change to a template, and the resulting inconsistencies will cause no end of confusion.

The rule that all editable data should be kept under version control has one unfortunate exception: the bug tracker. Bug databases hold plenty of editable data, but for technical reasons generally cannot store that data in the main version control system. (Some trackers have primitive versioning features of their own, however, independent of the project's main repository.)

Browseability

The project's repository should be browseable on the Web. This means not only the ability to see the latest revisions of the project's files, but to go back in time and look at earlier revisions, view the differences between revisions, read log messages for selected changes, etc.

Browseability is important because it is a lightweight portal to project data. If the repository cannot be viewed through a web browser, then someone wanting to inspect a particular file (say, to see if a certain bug fix had made it into the code) would first have to install version control client software locally, which could turn her simple query from a two-minute task into a half-hour or longer task.

Browseability also implies canonical URLs for viewing specific revisions of files, and for viewing the latest revision at any given time. This can be very useful in technical discussions or when pointing people to documentation. For example, instead of saying "For tips on debugging the server, see the HACKING file in the top of your working copy," one can say "For tips on debugging the server, see *http://svn.collab.net/repos/svn/trunk/HACKING*," giving a URL that always points to the latest revision of the HACKING file. The URL is better because it is completely unambiguous, and avoids the question of whether the addressee has an up-to-date working copy.

Some version control systems come with built-in repository-browsing mechanisms, while others rely on third-party tools to do it. Three such tools are ViewCVS (*http://viewcvs.sourceforge.net/*), CVSWeb (*http://www.freebsd.org/projects/cvsweb.html*), and WebSVN (*http://websvn.tigris.org/*). The first works with both CVS and Subversion, the second with CVS only, and the third with Subversion only.

Commit emails

Every commit to the repository should generate an email showing who made the change, when they made it, what files and directories changed, and how they changed. The email should go to a special mailing list devoted to commit emails, separate from the mailing lists to which humans post. Developers and other interested parties should be encouraged to subscribe to the commits list, as it is the most effective way to keep up with what's happening in the project at the code level. Aside from the obvious technical benefits of peer review (see "Practice Conspicuous Code Review" in Chapter 2), commit emails help create a sense of community, because they establish a shared environment in which people can react to events (commits) that they know are visible to others as well.

The specifics of setting up commit emails will vary depending on your version control system, but usually there's a script or other packaged facility for doing it. If you're having trouble finding it, try looking for documentation on *hooks*, specifically a *post-commit hook*, also called the *loginfo hook* in CVS. Post-commit hooks are a general means of launching automated tasks in response to commits. The hook is triggered by an individual commit, is fed all the information about that commit, and is then free to use that information to do anything—for example, to send out an email.

With prepackaged commit email systems, you may want to modify some of the default behaviors:

- Some commit mailers don't include the actual diffs in the email, but instead provide a URL to view the change on the web using the repository browsing system. While it's good to provide the URL, so the change can be referred to later, it is also *very* important that the commit email include the diffs themselves. Reading email is already part of people's routine, so if the content of the change is visible right there in the commit email, developers will review the commit on the spot, without leaving their mail reader. If they have to click on a URL to review the change, most won't do it, because that requires a new action instead of a continuation of what they were already doing. Furthermore, if the reviewer wants to ask something about the change, it's vastly easier to hit reply-with-text and simply annotate the quoted diff than it is to visit a web page and laboriously cut-and-paste parts of the diff from web browser to email client.

  (Of course, if the diff is huge, such as when a large body of new code has been added to the repository, then it makes sense to omit the diff and offer only the URL. Most commit mailers can do this kind of limiting automatically. If yours can't, then it's still better to include diffs, and live with the occasional huge email, than to leave the diffs off entirely. Convenient reviewing and commenting is a cornerstone of cooperative development, much too important to do without.)

- The commit emails should set their Reply-to header to the regular development list, not the commit email list. That is, when someone reviews a commit and writes a response, their response should be automatically directed toward the human development list, where technical issues are normally discussed. There are a few reasons for this. First, you want to keep all technical discussion on one list, because that's where people expect it to happen, and because that way there's only one archive to search. Second, there might be interested parties not subscribed to the commit email list. Third, the commit email list advertises itself as a service for watching commits, not for watching commits *and* occasional technical discussions. Those who subscribed to the commit email list did not sign up for anything but commit emails; sending them other material via that list would violate an implicit contract. Fourth, people often write programs that read the commit email list and process the results (for display on a web page, for example). Those programs are prepared to handle consistently-formatted commit emails, but not inconsistent human-written mails.

  Note that this advice to set Reply-to does not contradict the recommendations in "The Great Reply-to Debate" earlier in this chapter. It's always okay for the *sender* of a message to set Reply-to. In this case, the sender is the version control system itself, and it sets Reply-to in order to indicate that the appropriate place for replies is the development mailing list, not the commit list.

CIA: Another Change Publication Mechanism

Commit emails are not the only way to propagate change news. Recently, another mechanism called CIA (*http://cia.navi.cx/*) has been developed. CIA is a real-time commit statistics aggregator and distributor. The most popular use of CIA is to send commit notifications to IRC channels, so that people logged into those channels see the commits happening in real time. Though of somewhat less technical utility than commit emails, since observers might or might not be around when a commit notice pops up in IRC, this technique is of immense *social* utility. People get the sense of being part of something alive and active, and feel that they can see progress being made right before their eyes.

The way it works is that you invoke the CIA notifier program from your post-commit hook. The notifier formats the commit information into an XML message, and sends to a central server (typically `cia.navi.cx`). That server then distributes the commit information to other forums.

CIA can also be configured to send out RSS (*http://www.xml.com/pub/a/2002/12/18/dive-into-xml.html*) feeds. See the documentation at *http://cia.navi.cx/* for details.

To see an example of CIA in action, point your IRC client at `irc.freenode.net`, channel `#commits`.

Use branches to avoid bottlenecks

Non-expert version control users are sometimes a bit afraid of branching and merging. This is probably a side effect of CVS's popularity: Its interface for branching and merging is somewhat counterintuitive, so many people have learned to avoid those operations entirely.

If you are among those people, resolve right now to conquer any fears you may have and take the time to learn how to do branching and merging. They are not difficult operations, once you get used to them, and they become increasingly important as a project acquires more developers.

Branches are valuable because they turn a scarce resource—working room in the project's code—into an abundant one. Normally, all developers work together in the same sandbox, constructing the same castle. When someone wants to add a new drawbridge, but can't convince everyone else that it would be an improvement, branching makes it possible for her to go to an isolated corner and try it out. If the effort succeeds, she can invite the other developers to examine the result. If everyone agrees that the result is good, they can tell the version control system to move ("merge") the drawbridge from the branch castle over to the main castle.

It's easy to see how this ability helps collaborative development. People need the freedom to try new things without feeling like they're interfering with others' work. Equally important, there are times when code needs to be isolated from the usual development churn, in order to get a bug fixed or a release stabilized (see "Stabilizing a Release" and "Maintaining Multiple Release Lines" in Chapter 7) without worrying about tracking a moving target.

Use branches liberally, and encourage others to use them. But also make sure that a given branch is only active for exactly as long as needed. Every active branch is a slight drain on the community's attention. Even those who are not working in a branch still maintain a peripheral awareness of what's going on in it. Such awareness is desirable, of course, and commit emails should be sent out for branch commits just as for any other commit. But branches should not become a mechanism for dividing the development community. With rare exceptions, the eventual goal of most branches should be to merge their changes back into the main line and disappear.

Singularity of information

Merging has an important corollary: never commit the same change twice. That is, a given change should enter the version control system exactly once. The revision (or set of revisions) in which the change entered is its unique identifier from then on. If it needs to be applied to branches other than the one on which it entered, then it should be merged from its original entry point to those other destinations—as opposed to committing a textually identical change, which would have the same effect in the code, but would make accurate bookkeeping and release management impossible.

The practical effects of this advice differ from one version control system to another. In some systems, merges are special events, fundamentally distinct from commits, and carry their own metadata with them. In others, the results of merges are committed the same way other changes are committed, so the primary means of distinguishing a "merge commit" from a "new change commit" is in the log message. In a merge's log message, don't repeat the log message of the original change. Instead, just indicate that this is a merge, and give the identifying revision of the original change, with at most a one-sentence summary of its effect. If someone wants to see the full log message, he should consult the original revision.

The reason it's important to avoid repeating the log message is that log messages are sometimes edited after they've been committed. If a change's log message were repeated at each merge destination, then even if someone edited the original message, he'd still leave all the repeats uncorrected—which would only cause confusion down the road.

The same principle applies to reverting a change. If a change is withdrawn from the code, then the log message for the reversion should merely state that some specific revision(s) is being reverted, *not* describe the actual code change that results from the reversion, since the semantics of the change can be derived by reading the original log message and change. Of course, the reversion's log message should also state the reason why the change is being reverted, but it should not duplicate anything from the original change's log message. If possible, go back and edit the original change's log message to point out that it was reverted.

All of the above implies that you should use a consistent syntax for referring to revisions. This is helpful not only in log messages, but in emails, the bug tracker, and elsewhere. If you're using CVS, I suggest `path/to/file/in/project/tree:REV`, where REV is a CVS revision number such as `1.76`. If you're using Subversion, the standard syntax for revision 1729 is `r1729` (file paths are not needed because Subversion uses global revision numbers). In other systems, there is usually a standard syntax for expressing the changeset name. Whatever the appropriate syntax is for your system, encourage people to use it when referring to changes. Consistent expression of change names makes project bookkeeping much easier (as we will see in Chapter 6 and Chapter 7), and since a lot of the bookkeeping will be done by volunteers, it needs to be as easy as possible.

See also "Releases and Daily Development" in Chapter 7.

Authorization

Most version control systems offer a feature whereby certain people can be allowed or disallowed from committing in specific sub-areas of the repository. Following the principle that when handed a hammer, people start looking around for nails, many projects use this feature with abandon, carefully granting people access to just those areas where they have been approved to commit, and making sure they can't commit anywhere else. (See "Committers" in Chapter 8 for how projects decide who can commit where.)

There is probably little harm done by exercising such tight control, but a more relaxed policy is fine too. Some projects simply use an honor system: when a person is granted commit access, even for a sub-area of the repository, what he actually receives is a password that allows him to commit anywhere in the project. He's just asked to keep his commits in his area. Remember that there is no real risk here: in an active project, all commits are reviewed anyway. If someone commits where he's not supposed to, others will notice it and say something. If a change needs to be undone, that's simple enough—everything's under version control anyway, so just revert.

There are several advantages to the relaxed approach. First, as developers expand into other areas (which they usually will if they stay with the project), there is no administrative overhead to granting them wider privileges. Once the decision is made, the person can just start committing in the new area right away.

Second, expansion can be done in a more fine-grained manner. Generally, a committer in area X who wants to expand to area Y will start posting patches against Y and asking for review. If someone who already has commit access to area Y sees such a patch and approves of it, he can just tell the submitter to commit the change directly (mentioning the reviewer/approver's name in the log message, of course). That way, the commit will come from the person who actually wrote the change, which is preferable from both an information management standpoint and from a crediting standpoint.

Last, and perhaps most important, using the honor system encourages an atmosphere of trust and mutual respect. Giving someone commit access to a subdomain is a statement about his technical preparedness—it says: "We see you have expertise to make commits in a certain domain, so go for it." But imposing strict authorization controls says: "Not only are we asserting a limit on your expertise, we're also a bit suspicious about your *intentions*." That's not the sort of statement you want to make if you can avoid it. Bringing someone into the project as a committer is an opportunity to initiate him into a circle of mutual trust. A good way to do that is to give him more power than he's supposed to use, then inform him that it's up to him to stay within the stated limits.

The Subversion project has operated on the honor system way for more than four years, with 33 full and 43 partial committers as of this writing. The only distinction the system actually enforces is between committers and non-committers; further subdivisions are maintained solely by humans. Yet we've never had a problem with someone deliberately committing outside their domain. Once or twice there's been an innocent misunderstanding about the extent of someone's commit privileges, but it's always been resolved quickly and amiably.

Obviously, in situations where self-policing is impractical, you must rely on hard authorization controls. But such situations are rare. Even when there are millions of lines of code and hundreds or thousands of developers, a commit to any given code module should still be reviewed by those who work on that module, and they can recognize if someone committed there who wasn't supposed to. If regular commit review *isn't* happening, then the project has bigger problems to deal with than the authorization system anyway.

In summary, don't spend too much time fiddling with the version control authorization system, unless you have a specific reason to. It usually won't bring much tangible benefit, and there are advantages to relying on human controls instead.

None of this should be taken to mean that the restrictions themselves are unimportant, of course. It would be bad for a project to encourage people to commit in areas where they're not qualified. Furthermore, in many projects, full (unrestricted) commit access has a special status: it implies voting rights on project-wide questions. This political aspect of commit access is discussed more in "Who Votes?" in Chapter 4.

Bug Tracker

Bug tracking is a broad topic; various aspects of it are discussed throughout this book. Here I'll try to concentrate mainly on setup and technical considerations, but to get to those, we have to start with a policy question: exactly what kind of information should be kept in a bug tracker?

The term *bug tracker* is misleading. Bug tracking systems are also frequently used to track new feature requests, one-time tasks, unsolicited patches—really anything that has distinct beginning and end states, with optional transition states in between, and that accrues information over its lifetime. For this reason, bug trackers are also called *issue trackers*, *defect trackers*, *artifact trackers*, *request trackers*, *trouble ticket systems*, etc. See Appendix B for a list of software.

In this book, I'll continue to use *bug tracker* for the software that does the tracking, because that's what most people call it, but will use *issue* to refer to a single item in the bug tracker's database. This allows us to distinguish between the behavior or misbehavior that the user encountered (that is, the bug itself), and the tracker's *record* of the bug's discovery, diagnosis, and eventual resolution. Keep in mind that although most issues are about actual bugs, issues can be used to track other kinds of tasks too.

The classic issue life cycle looks like this:

1. Someone files the issue. She provides a summary, an initial description (including a reproduction recipe, if applicable; see "Treat Every User as a Potential Volunteer" in Chapter 8 for how to encourage good bug reports), and whatever other information the tracker asks for. The person who files the issue may be totally unknown to the project—bug reports and feature requests are as likely to come from the user community as from the developers.

   Once filed, the issue is in what's called an *open* state. Because no action has been taken yet, some trackers also label it as *unverified* and/or *unstarted*. It is not assigned to anyone; or, in some systems, it is assigned to a fake user to represent the lack of real assignation. At this point, it is in a holding area: the issue has been recorded, but not yet integrated into the project's consciousness.

2. Others read the issue, add comments to it, and perhaps ask the original filer for clarification on some points.

3. The bug gets *reproduced*. This may be the most important moment in the life cycle. Although the bug is not actually fixed yet, the fact that someone besides the original filer was able to make it happen proves that it is genuine, and, no less importantly, confirms to the original filer that she's contributed to the project by reporting a real bug.

4. The bug gets *diagnosed*: its cause is identified, and if possible, the effort required to fix it is estimated. Make sure these things get recorded in the issue; if the person who diagnosed the bug suddenly has to step away from the project for a while (as can often happen with volunteer developers), someone else should be able to pick up where she left off.

   In this stage, or sometimes the previous one, a developer may "take ownership" of the issue and *assign* it to herself ("Distinguish clearly between inquiry and assignment" in Chapter 8 examines the assignment process in more detail). The issue's *priority* may also be set at this stage. For example, if it is so severe that it should delay the next release, that fact needs to be identified early, and the tracker should have some way of noting it.

5. The issue gets scheduled for resolution. Scheduling doesn't necessarily mean naming a date by which it will be fixed. Sometimes it just means deciding which future release (not necessarily the next one) the bug should be fixed by, or deciding that it need not block any particular release. Scheduling may also be dispensed with, if the bug is quick to fix.

6. The bug gets fixed (or the task completed, or the patch applied, or whatever). The change or set of changes that fixed it should be recorded in a comment in the issue, after which the issue is *closed* and/or marked as *resolved*.

There are some common variations on this life cycle. Sometimes an issue is closed very soon after being filed, because it turns out not to be a bug at all, but rather a misunderstanding on the part of the user. As a project acquires more users, more and more such invalid issues will come in, and developers will close them with increasingly short-tempered responses. Try to guard against the latter tendency. It does no one any good, as the individual user in each case is not responsible for all the previous invalid issues; the statistical trend is visible only from the developers' point of view, not the user's. (In "Prefiltering the Bug Tracker" later in this chapter, we'll look at techniques for reducing the number of invalid issues.) Also, if different users are experiencing the same misunderstanding over and over, it might mean that aspect of the software needs to be redesigned. This sort of pattern is easiest to notice when there is an issue manager monitoring the bug database; see "Issue Manager" in Chapter 8.

Another common life cycle variation is for the issue to be closed as a *duplicate* soon after Step 1. A duplicate is when someone files an issue that's already known to the project. Duplicates are not confined to open issues: it's possible for a bug to come back after having been fixed (this is known as a *regression*), in which case the preferred course is usually to reopen the original issue and close any new reports as duplicates of the original one. The bug tracking system should keep track of this relationship bidirectionally, so that reproduction information in the duplicates is available to the original issue, and vice versa.

A third variation is for the developers to close the issue, thinking they have fixed it, only to have the original reporter reject the fix and reopen it. This is usually because the developers simply don't have access to the environment necessary to reproduce the bug, or because they didn't test the fix using the exact same reproduction recipe as the reporter.

Aside from these variations, there may be other small details of the life cycle that vary depending on the tracking software. But the basic shape is the same, and while the life cycle itself is not specific to open source software, it has implications for how open source projects use their bug trackers.

As Step 1 implies, the tracker is as much a public face of the project as the mailing lists or web pages. Anyone may file an issue, anyone may look at an issue, and anyone may browse the list of currently open issues. It follows that you never know how many people are waiting to see progress on a given issue. While the size and skill of the development community constrains the rate at which issues can be resolved, the project should at least try to acknowledge each issue the moment it appears. Even if the issue lingers for a while, a response encourages the reporter to stay involved, because she feels that a human has registered what she has done (remember that filing an issue usually involves more effort than, say, posting an email). Furthermore, once an issue is seen by a developer, it enters the project's consciousness, in the sense that the developer can be on the lookout for other instances of the issue, can talk about it with other developers, etc.

The need for timely reactions implies two things:

- The tracker must be connected to a mailing list, such that every change to an issue, including its initial filing, causes a mail to go out describing what happened. This mailing list is usually different from the regular development list, since not all developers may want to receive automated bug mails, but (just as with commit mails) the Reply-to header should be set to the development mailing list.

- The form for filing issues should capture the reporter's email address, so she can be contacted for more information. (However, it should not *require* the reporter's email address, as some people prefer to report issues anonymously. See "Anonymity and involvement" later in this chapter for more on the importance of anonymity.)

Interaction with Mailing Lists

Make sure the bug tracker doesn't turn into a discussion forum. Although it is important to maintain a human presence in the bug tracker, it is not fundamentally suited to real-time discussion. Think of it rather as an archiver, a way to organize facts and references to other discussions, primarily those that take place on mailing lists.

There are two reasons to make this distinction. First, the bug tracker is more cumbersome to use than the mailing lists (or than real-time chat forums, for that matter). This is not because bug trackers have bad user interface design; it's just that their interfaces were designed for capturing and presenting discrete states, not free-flowing discussions. Second, not everyone who should be involved in discussing a given issue is necessarily watching the bug tracker. Part of good issue management (see "Share Management Tasks as Well as Technical Tasks" in Chapter 8) is to make sure each issue is brought to the right peoples' attention, rather than requiring every developer to monitor all issues. In "No Conversations in the Bug Tracker" in Chapter 6, we'll look at ways to make sure people don't accidentally siphon discussions out of appropriate forums and into the bug tracker.

Some bug trackers can monitor mailing lists and automatically log all emails that are about a known issue. Typically they do this by recognizing the issue's identifying number in the subject line of the mail, as part of a special string; developers learn to include these strings in their mails to attract the tracker's notice. The bug tracker may either save the entire email, or (even better) just record a link to the mail in the regular mailing list archive. Either way, this is a very useful feature; if your tracker has it, make sure both to turn it on and to remind people to take advantage of it.

Prefiltering the Bug Tracker

Most issue databases eventually suffer from the same problem: a crushing load of duplicate or invalid issues filed by well-meaning but inexperienced or ill-informed users. The first step in combatting this trend is usually to put a prominent notice on the front page of the bug tracker, explaining how to tell if a bug is really a bug, how to search to see if it's already been filed, and finally, how to effectively report it if one still thinks it's a new bug.

This will reduce the noise level for a while, but as the number of users increases, the problem will eventually come back. No individual user can be blamed for it. Each one is just trying to contribute to the project's well-being, and even if their first bug report isn't helpful, you still want to encourage them to stay involved and file better issues in the future. In the meantime, though, the project needs to keep the issue database as free of junk as possible.

The two things that will do the most to prevent this problem are: making sure there are people watching the bug tracker who have enough knowledge to close issues as invalid or duplicates the moment they come in, and requiring (or strongly encouraging) users to confirm their bugs with other people before filing them in the tracker.

The first technique seems to be used universally. Even projects with huge issue databases (say, the Debian bug tracker at *http://bugs.debian.org/*, which contained 315,929 issues as of this writing) still arrange things so that *someone* sees each issue that comes in. It may be a different person depending on the category of the issue. For example, the Debian project is a collection of software packages, so Debian automatically routes each issue to the appropriate package maintainers. Of course, users can sometimes misidentify an issue's category, with the result that the issue is sent to the wrong person initially, who may then have to reroute it. However, the important thing is that the burden is still shared—whether the user guesses right or wrong when filing, issue watching is still distributed more or less evenly among the developers, so each issue is able to receive a timely response.

The second technique is less widespread, probably because it's harder to automate. The essential idea is that every new issue gets "buddied" into the database. When a user thinks he's found a problem, he is asked to describe it on one of the mailing lists, or in an IRC channel, and get confirmation from someone that it is indeed a bug. Bringing in that second pair of eyes early can prevent a lot of spurious reports. Sometimes the second party is able to identify that the behavior is not a bug, or is fixed in recent releases. Or she may be familiar with the symptoms from a previous issue, and can prevent a duplicate filing by pointing the user to the older issue. Often it's enough just to ask the user "Did you search the bug tracker to see if it's already been reported?" Many people simply don't think of that, yet are happy to do the search once they know someone's *expecting* them to.

The buddy system can really keep the issue database clean, but it has some disadvantages too. Many people will file solo anyway, either through not seeing, or through disregarding, the instructions to find a buddy for new issues. Thus it is still necessary for volunteers to watch the issue database. Furthermore, because most new reporters don't understand how difficult the task of maintaining the issue database is, it's not fair to chide them too harshly for ignoring the guidelines. Thus the volunteers must be vigilant, and yet exercise restraint in how they bounce unbuddied issues back to their reporters. The goal is to train each reporter to use the buddying system in the future, so that there is an ever-growing pool of people who understand the issue-filtering system. On seeing an unbuddied issue, here are the ideal steps:

1. Immediately respond to the issue, politely thanking the user for filing, but pointing them to the buddying guidelines (which should, of course, be prominently posted on the web site).

2. If the issue is clearly valid and not a duplicate, approve it anyway, and start it down the normal life cycle. After all, the reporter's now been informed about buddying, so there's no point wasting the work done so far by closing a valid issue.

3. Otherwise, if the issue is not clearly valid, close it, but ask the reporter to reopen it if they get confirmation from a buddy. When they do, they should put a reference to the confirmation thread (e.g., a URL into the mailing list archives).

Remember that although this system will improve the signal/noise ratio in the issue database over time, it will never completely stop the misfilings. The only way to prevent misfilings entirely is to close off the bug tracker to everyone but developers—a cure that is almost always worse than the disease. It's better to accept that cleaning out invalid issues will always be part of the project's routine maintenance, and to try to get as many people as possible to help.

See also "Issue Manager" in Chapter 8.

IRC/Real-Time Chat Systems

Many projects offer real-time chat rooms using Internet Relay Chat (IRC), forums where users and developers can ask each other questions and get instant responses. While you *can* run an IRC server from your own website, it is generally not worth the hassle. Instead, do what everyone else does: run your IRC channels at Freenode (*http://freenode.net/*). Freenode gives you the control you need to administer your project's IRC channels,[2] while sparing you the not-insignificant trouble of maintaining an IRC server yourself.

The first thing to do is choose a channel name. The most obvious choice is the name of your project—if that's available at Freenode, then use it. If not, try to choose something as close to your project's name, and as easy to remember, as possible. Advertise the channel's availability from your project's web site, so a visitor with a quick question will see it right away. For example, this appears in a prominently placed box at the top of Subversion's home page:

> If you're using Subversion, we recommend that you join the *users@subversion. tigris.org* mailing list, and read the Subversion Book (*http://svnbook.red-bean.com/*) and FAQ (*http://subversion.tigris.org/faq.html*). You can also ask questions on IRC at *irc.freenode.net* channel #svn.

Some projects have multiple channels, one per subtopic. For example, one channel for installation problems, another for usage questions, another for development chat, etc. ("Handling Growth" in Chapter 6 discusses how to divide into multiple channels). When your project is young, there should only be one channel, with everyone talking together. Later, as the user-to-developer ratio increases, separate channels may become necessary.

How will people know all the available channels, let alone which channel to talk in? And when they talk, how will they know what the local conventions are?

---

2   There is no requirement or expectation that you donate to Freenode, but if you or your project can afford it, please consider a contribution. They are a tax-exempt charity in the Unitd States, and they perform a valuable service.

The answer is to tell them by setting the *channel topic.*[3] The channel topic is a brief message each user sees when they first enter the channel. It gives quick guidance to newcomers, and pointers to further information. For example:

```
You are now talking on #svn

Topic for #svn is Forum for Subversion user questions, see also
http://subversion.tigris.org/. || Development discussion happens in
#svn-dev. || Please don't paste long transcripts here, instead use
a pastebin site like http://pastebin.ca/. || NEWS: Subversion 1.1.0
is released, see http://svn110.notlong.com/ for details.
```

That's terse, but it tells newcomers what they need to know. It says exactly what the channel is for, gives the project home page (in case someone wanders into the channel without having first been to the project web site), mentions a related channel, and gives some guidance about pasting.

Bots

Many technically oriented IRC channels have a non-human member, a so-called *bot* that is capable of storing and regurgitating information in response to specific commands. Typically, the bot is addressed just like any other member of the channel, that is, the commands are delivered by "speaking to" the bot. For example:

```
<kfogel> ayita: learn diff-cmd = http://subversion.tigris.org/faq.html#diff-cmd
<ayita>  Thanks!
```

That told the bot (who is logged into the channel as ayita) to remember a certain URL as the answer to the query `diff-cmd`. Now we can address ayita, asking the bot to tell another user about `diff-cmd`:

```
<kfogel> ayita: tell jrandom about diff-cmd
<ayita>  jrandom: http://subversion.tigris.org/faq.html#diff-cmd
```

The same thing can be accomplished via a convenient shorthand:

```
<kfogel> !a jrandom diff-cmd
<ayita>  jrandom: http://subversion.tigris.org/faq.html#diff-cmd
```

The exact command set and behaviors differ from bot to bot. The above example is with ayita (*http://hix.nu/svn-public/alexis/trunk/*), of which there is usually an instance running in #svn at freenode. Other bots include Dancer (*http://dancer.sf.net*) and

---

3   To set a channel topic, use the **/topic** command. All commands in IRC start with a slash (**/**). See *http://www.irchelp.org/* if you're not familiar with IRC usage and administration; in particular, *http://www.irchelp.org/irchelp/irctutorial.html* is an excellent tutorial.

Paste Sites

An IRC channel is a shared space: everyone can see what everyone else is saying. Normally, this is a good thing, as it allows people to jump into a conversation when they think they have something to contribute, and allows spectators to learn by watching. But it becomes problematic when someone has to provide a large quantity of information at once, such as a debugging session transcript, because pasting too many lines of output into the channel will disrupt other conversations.

The solution is to use one of the *pastebin* or *pastebot* sites. When requesting a large amount of data from someone, ask them not to paste it into the channel, but instead to go to (for example) *http://pastebin.ca/*, paste their data into the form there, and tell the resulting new URL to the IRC channel. Anyone can then visit the URL and view the data.

There are a number of free paste sites available now, too many for a comprehensive list, but here are some of the ones I've seen used: *http://www.nomorepasting. com/*, *http://pastebin.ca/*, *http://nopaste.php.cd/*, *http://rafb.net/paste/*, *http:// sourcepost.sytes.net/*, *http://extraball.sunsite.dk/notepad.php*, and *http://www. pastebin.com/*.

Supybot (*http://supybot.sf.net*). Note that no special server privileges are required to run a bot. A bot is a client program; anyone can set one up and direct it to listen to a particular server/channel.

If your channel tends to get the same questions over and over, I highly recommend setting up a bot. Only a small percentage of channel users will acquire the expertise needed to manipulate the bot, but those users will answer a disproportionately high percentage of questions because the bot enables them to respond much more efficiently.

Archiving IRC

Although it is possible to archive everything that happens in an IRC channel, it's not necessarily expected. IRC conversations may be nominally public, but many people think of them as informal, semi-private conversations. Users may be careless with grammar, and often express opinions (for example, about other software or other programmers) that they wouldn't want preserved forever in an online archive.

Of course, there will sometimes be *excerpts* that should be preserved, and that's fine. Most IRC clients can log a conversation to a file at the user's request, or failing that, one can always just cut and paste the conversation from IRC into a more permanent forum (most often the bug tracker). But indiscriminate logging may make some users uneasy. If you do archive everything, make sure you state so clearly in the channel topic, and give a URL to the archive.

Wikis

A *wiki* is a web site that allows any visitor to edit or extend its content; the term "wiki" (from a Hawaiian word meaning "quick" or "super-fast") is also used to refer to the software that enables such editing. Wikis were invented in 1995, but their popularity has really started to take off since 2000 or 2001, boosted partly by the success of Wikipiedia (*http://www.wikipedia.org/*), a wiki-based free-content encyclopedia. Think of a wiki as falling somewhere between IRC and web pages: wikis don't happen in real time, so people get a chance to ponder and polish their contributions, but they are also very easy to add to, involving less interface overhead than editing a regular web page.

Wikis are not yet standard equipment for open source projects, but they probably will be soon. As they are relatively new technology, and people are still experimenting with different ways of using them, I will just offer a few words of caution here—at this stage, it's easier to analyze misuses of wikis than to analyze their successes.

If you decide to run a wiki, put a lot of effort into having a clear page organization and pleasing visual layout, so that visitors (i.e., potential editors) will instinctively know how to fit in their contributions. Equally important, post those standards on the wiki itself, so people have somewhere to go for guidance. Too often, wiki administrators fall victim to the fantasy that because hordes of visitors are individually adding high quality content to the site, the sum of all these contributions must therefore also be of high quality. That's not how web sites work. Each individual page or paragraph may be good when considered by itself, but it will not be good if embedded in a disorganized or confusing whole. Too often, wikis suffer from:

Lack of navigational principles
> A well-organized web site makes visitors feel like they know where they are at any time. For example, if the pages are well-designed, people can intuitively tell the difference between a "table of contents" region and a "content" region. Contributors to a wiki will respect such differences too, but only if the differences are present to begin with.

Duplication of information

Wikis frequently end up with different pages saying similar things, because the individual contributors did not notice the duplications. This can be partly a consequence of the lack of navigational principles noted above, in that people may not find the duplicate content if it is not where they expect it to be.

Inconsistent target audience

To some degree this problem is inevitable when there are so many authors, but it can be lessened if there are written guidelines about how to create new content. It also helps to aggressively edit new contributions at the beginning, as an example, so that the standards start to sink in.

The common solution to all these problems is the same: have editorial standards, and demonstrate them not only by posting them, but by editing pages to adhere to them. In general, wikis will amplify any failings in their original material, since contributors imitate whatever patterns they see in front of them. Don't just set up the wiki and hope everything falls into place. You must also prime it with well-written content, so people have a template to follow.

The shining example of a well-run wiki is Wikipedia, though this may be partly because the content (encyclopedia entries) is naturally well suited to the wiki format. But if you examine Wikipedia closely, you'll see that its administrators laid a *very* thorough foundation for cooperation. There is extensive documentation on how to write new entries, how to maintain an appropriate point of view, what sorts of edits to make, what edits to avoid, a dispute resolution process for contested edits (involving several stages, including eventual arbitration), and so forth. They also have authorization controls, so that if a page is the target of repeated inappropriate edits, they can lock it down until the problem is resolved. In other words, they didn't just throw some templates onto a web site and hope for the best. Wikipedia works because its founders thought carefully about how to get thousands of strangers to tailor their writing to a common vision. While you may not need the same level of preparedness to run a wiki for a free software project, the spirit is worth emulating.

For more information about wikis, see *http://en.wikipedia.org/wiki/Wiki*. Also, the first wiki remains alive and well, and contains a lot of discussion about running wikis: see *http://www.c2.com/cgi/wiki?WelcomeVisitors*, *http://www.c2.com/cgi/wiki?WhyWikiWorks*, and *http://www.c2.com/cgi/wiki?WhyWikiDoesntWork* for various points of view.

Web Site

There is not much to say about setting up the project web site from a technical point of view: setting up a web server and writing web pages are fairly simple tasks, and most of the important things to say about layout and arrangement were covered in the previous chapter. The web site's main function is to present a clear and welcoming overview of the project, and to bind together the other tools (the version control system, bug tracker, etc). If you don't have the expertise to set up a web server yourself, it's usually not hard to find someone who does and is willing to help out. Nonetheless, to save time and effort, people often prefer to use one of the canned hosting sites.

Canned Hosting

There are two main advantages to using a canned site. The first is server capacity and bandwidth: their servers are beefy boxes sitting on really fat pipes. No matter how successful your project gets, you're not going to run out of disk space or swamp the network connection. The second advantage is simplicity. They have already chosen a bug tracker, a version control system, a mailing list manager, an archiver, and everything else you need to run a site. They've configured the tools, and are taking care of backups for all the data stored in the tools. You don't need to make many decisions. All you have to do is fill in a form, press a button, and suddenly you've got a project web site.

These are pretty significant benefits. The disadvantage, of course, is that you must accept *their* choices and configurations, even if something different would be better for your project. Usually canned sites are adjustable within certain narrow parameters, but you will never get the fine-grained control you would have if you set up the site yourself and had full administrative access to the server.

A perfect example of this is the handling of generated files. Certain project web pages may be generated files—for example, there are systems for keeping FAQ data in an easy-to-edit master format, from which HTML, PDF, and other presentation formats can be generated. As explained in "Version everything" earlier in this chapter, you wouldn't want to version the generated formats, only the master file. But when your web site is hosted on someone else's server, it may be impossible to set up a custom hook to regenerate the online HTML version of the FAQ whenever the master file is changed. The only workaround is to version the generated formats too, so that they show up on the web site.

There can be larger consequences as well. You may not have as much control over presentation as you would wish. Some of the canned hosting sites allow you to customize your web pages, but the site's default layout usually ends up showing through in various awkward ways. For example, some projects that host themselves at SourceForge have completely customized home pages, but still point developers to their "SourceForge page" for more information. The SourceForge page is what would be the project's home page, had the project not used a custom home page. The SourceForge page has links to the bug tracker, the CVS repository, downloads, etc. Unfortunately, a SourceForge page also contains a great deal of extraneous noise. The top is a banner ad, often an animated image. The left side is a vertical arrangement of links of little relevance to someone interested in the project. The right side is often another advertisement. Only the center of the page is devoted to truly project-specific material, and even that is arranged in a confusing way that often makes visitors unsure of what to click on next.

Behind every individual aspect of SourceForge's design, there is no doubt a good reason—good from SourceForge's point of view, such as the advertisements. But from an individual project's point of view, the result can be a less-than-ideal web page. I don't mean to pick on SourceForge; similar concerns apply to many of the canned hosting sites. The point is that there's a trade off. You get relief from the technical burdens of running a project site, but only at the price of accepting someone else's way of running it.

Only you can decide whether canned hosting is best for your project. If you choose a canned site, leave open the option of switching to your own servers later, by using a custom domain name for the project's "home address." You can forward the URL to the canned site, or have a fully customized home page at the public URL and hand users off to the canned site for sophisticated functionality. Just make sure to arrange things such that if you later decide to use a different hosting solution, the project's address doesn't need to change.

Choosing a canned hosting site

The largest and most well-known hosting site is SourceForge (*http://www.sourceforge. net/*). Two other sites providing the same or similar services are savannah.gnu.org (*http://savannah.gnu.org/*) and BerliOS.de (*http://www.berlios.de/*). A few organizations, such as the Apache Software Foundation (*http://www.apache.org/*) and Tigris.org[4]

---

4   Disclaimer: I am employed by CollabNet (*http://www.collab.net/*), which sponsors Tigris.org, and
    I use Tigris regularly.

(*http://www.tigris.org/*) give free hosting to open source projects that fit well with their missions and their community of existing projects.

Haggen So did a thorough evaluation of various canned hosting sites, as part of the research for his Ph.D. thesis, *Construction of an Evaluation Model for Free/Open Source Project Hosting (FOSPHost) sites*. The results are at *http://www.ibiblio.org/ fosphost/*; see especially the very readable comparison chart at *http://www.ibiblio.org/ fosphost/exhost.htm*.

Anonymity and involvement

A problem that is not strictly limited to the canned sites, but is most often found there, is the abuse of user login functionality. The functionality itself is simple enough: the site allows each visitor to register himself with a username and password. From then on it keeps a profile for that user, and project administrators can assign the user certain permissions, for example, the right to commit to the repository.

This can be extremely useful, and in fact it's one of the prime advantages of canned hosting. The problem is that sometimes user login ends up being required for tasks that ought to be permitted to unregistered visitors, specifically the ability to file issues in the bug tracker, and to comment on existing issues. By requiring a logged-in username for such actions, the project raises the involvement bar for what should be quick, convenient tasks. Of course, one wants to be able to contact someone who's entered data into the issue tracker, but having a field where he can enter his email address (if he wants to) is sufficient. If a new user spots a bug and wants to report it, he'll only be annoyed at having to fill out an account creation form before he can enter the bug into the tracker. He may simply decide not to file the bug at all.

The advantages of user management generally outweigh the disadvantages. But if you can choose which actions can be done anonymously, make sure not only that *all* read-only actions are permitted to non-logged-in visitors, but also some data entry actions, especially in the bug tracker and, if you have them, wiki pages.

## CHAPTER 4

Social and Political Infrastructure

The first questions people usually ask about free software are "How does it work? What keeps a project running? Who makes the decisions?" I'm always dissatisfied with bland responses about meritocracy, the spirit of cooperation, code speaking for itself, etc. The fact is, the question is not easy to answer. Meritocracy, cooperation, and running code are all part of it, but they do little to explain how projects actually run on a day-to-day basis, and say nothing about how conflicts are resolved.

This chapter tries to show the structural underpinnings successful projects have in common. I mean "successful" not just in terms of technical quality, but also operational health and survivability. Operational health is the project's ongoing ability to incorporate new code contributions and new developers, and to be responsive to incoming bug reports. Survivability is the project's ability to exist independently of any individual participant or sponsor—think of it as the likelihood that the project would continue even if all of its founding members were to move on to other things. Technical success is not hard to achieve, but without a robust developer base and social foundation, a project may be unable to handle the growth that initial success brings, or the departure of charismatic individuals.

There are various ways to achieve this kind of success. Some involve a formal governance structure, by which debates are resolved, new developers are invited in (and sometimes out), new features planned, and so on. Others involve less formal structure, but more conscious self-restraint, to produce an atmosphere of fairness that people can rely on as a de facto form of governance. Both ways lead to the same result: a sense of institutional permanence, supported by habits and procedures that are well understood by everyone who participates. These features are even more important in self-organizing systems than in centrally controlled ones, because in self-organizing systems, everyone is conscious that a few bad apples can spoil the whole barrel, at least for a while.

Forkability

The indispensable ingredient that binds developers together on a free software project, and makes them willing to compromise when necessary, is the code's *forkability*: the ability of anyone to take a copy of the source code and use it to start a competing project, known as a *fork*. The paradoxical thing is that the *possibility* of forks is usually a much greater force in free software projects than actual forks, which are very rare. Because a fork is bad for everyone (for reasons examined in detail in "Forks" in Chapter 8), the more serious the threat of a fork becomes, the more willing people are to compromise to avoid it.

Forks, or rather the potential for forks, are the reason there are no true dictators in free software projects. This may seem like a surprising claim, considering how common it is to hear someone called the "dictator" or "tyrant" in a given open source project. But this kind of tyranny is special, quite different from the conventional understanding of the word. Imagine a king whose subjects could copy his entire kingdom at any time and move to the copy to rule as they see fit. Would not such a king govern very differently from one whose subjects were bound to stay under his rule no matter what he did?

This is why even projects that are not formally organized as democracies are, in practice, democracies when it comes to important decisions. Replicability implies forkability; forkability implies consensus. It may well be that everyone is willing to defer to one leader (the most famous example being Linus Torvalds in Linux kernel development), but this is because they *choose* to do so, in an entirely non-cynical and non-sinister way. The dictator has no magical hold over the project. A key property of all open source licenses is that they do not give one party more power than any other in deciding how the code can be changed or used. If the dictator were to suddenly start making bad decisions, there would be restlessness, followed eventually by revolt and a fork. Except, of course, things rarely get that far, because the dictator compromises first.

But just because forkability puts an upper limit on how much power anyone can exert in a project doesn't mean there aren't important differences in how projects are governed. You don't want every decision to come down to the last-resort question of who is considering a fork. That would get tiresome very quickly, and sap energy away from real work. The next two sections examine different ways to organize projects such that most decisions go smoothly. These two examples are somewhat idealized extremes; many projects fall somewhere along a continuum between them.

Benevolent Dictators

The *benevolent dictator* model is exactly what it sounds like: final decision-making authority rests with one person, who by virtue of personality and experience, is expected to use it wisely.

Although "benevolent dictator" (or BD) is the standard term for this role, it would be better to think of it as "community-approved arbitrator" or "judge". Generally, benevolent dictators do not actually make all the decisions, or even most of the decisions. It's unlikely that one person could have enough expertise to make consistently good decisions across all areas of the project, and anyway, quality developers won't stay around unless they have some influence on the project's direction. Therefore, benevolent dictators commonly do not dictate much. Instead, they let things work themselves out through discussion and experimentation whenever possible. They participate in those discussions themselves, but as regular developers, often deferring to an area maintainer who has more expertise. Only when it is clear that no consensus can be reached, and that most of the group *wants* someone to guide the decision so that development can move on, do they put their foot down and say "This is the way it's going to be." Reluctance to make decisions by fiat is a trait shared by virtually all successful benevolent dictators; it is one of the reasons they manage to keep the role.

Who Can Be a Good Benevolent Dictator?

Being a BD requires a combination of traits. It needs, first of all, a well-honed sensitivity to one's own influence in the project, which in turn brings self-restraint. In the early stages of a discussion, one should not express opinions and conclusions with so much certainty that others feel like it's pointless to dissent. People must be free to air ideas, even stupid ideas. It is inevitable that the BD will post a stupid idea from time to time too, of course, and therefore the role also requires an ability to recognize and acknowledge when one has made a bad decision—though this is simply a trait that *any* good developer should have, especially if she stays with the project a long time. But the difference is that the BD can afford to slip from time to time without worrying about long-term damage to her credibility. Developers with less seniority may not feel so secure, so the BD should phrase critiques or contrary decisions with some sensitivity for how much weight her words carry, both technically and psychologically.

The BD does *not* need to have the sharpest technical skills of anyone in the project. She must be skilled enough to work on the code herself, and to understand and comment on any change under consideration, but that's all. The BD position is neither acquired nor held by virtue of intimidating coding skills. What *is* important is experience and overall design sense—not necessarily the ability to produce good design on demand, but the ability to recognize good design, whatever its source.

It is common for the benevolent dictator to be a founder of the project, but this is more a correlation than a cause. The sorts of qualities that make one able to successfully start a project—technical competence, ability to persuade other people to join, etc.—are exactly the qualities any BD would need. And of course, founders start out with a sort of automatic seniority, which can often be enough to make benevolent dictatorship appear the path of least resistance for all concerned.

Remember that the potential to fork goes both ways. A BD can fork a project just as easily as anyone else, and some have occasionally done so, when they felt that the direction they wanted to take the project was different from where the majority of other developers wanted to go. Because of forkability, it does not matter whether the benevolent dictator has root (system administrator privileges) on the project's main servers or not. People sometimes talk of server control as though it were the ultimate source of power in a project, but in fact it is irrelevant. The ability to add or remove people's commit passwords on one particular server affects only the copy of the project that resides on that server. Prolonged abuse of that power, whether by the BD or someone else, would simply lead to development moving to a different server.

Whether your project should have a benevolent dictator, or would run better with some less centralized system, largely depends on who is available to fill the role. As a general rule, if it's simply obvious to everyone who should be the BD, then that's the way to go. But if no candidate for BD is immediately obvious, then the project should probably use a decentralized decision-making process, as described in the next section.

Consensus-Based Democracy

As projects get older, they tend to move away from the benevolent dictatorship model and toward more openly democratic systems. This is not necessarily out of dissatisfaction with a particular BD. It's simply that group-based governance is more "evolutionarily stable," to borrow a biological metaphor. Whenever a benevolent dictator steps down, or attempts to spread decision-making responsibility more evenly, it is an opportunity for the group to settle on a new, non-dictatorial system—establish a constitution, as it were. The group may not take this opportunity the first time, or the second, but eventually they will; once they do, the decision is unlikely ever to be reversed. Common sense explains why: if a group of N people were to vest one person with special power, it would mean that N–1 people were each agreeing to decrease their individual influence. People usually don't want to do that. Even if they did, the resulting dictatorship would still be conditional: the group anointed the BD, clearly the group could depose the BD. Therefore, once a project has moved from leadership by a charismatic individual to a more formal, group-based system, it rarely moves back.

The details of how these systems work vary widely, but there are two common elements: one, the group works by consensus most of the time; two, there is a formal voting mechanism to fall back on when consensus cannot be reached.

Consensus merely means an agreement that everyone is willing to live with. It is not an ambiguous state: a group has reached consensus on a given question when someone proposes that consensus has been reached, and no one contradicts the assertion. The person proposing consensus should, of course, state specifically what the consensus is, and what actions would be taken in consequence of it, if they're not obvious.

Most conversation in a project is on technical topics, such as the right way to fix a certain bug, whether or not to add a feature, how strictly to document interfaces, etc. Consensus-based governance works well because it blends seamlessly with the technical discussion itself. By the end of a discussion, there is often general agreement on what course to take. Someone will usually make a concluding post, which is simultaneously a summary of what has been decided and an implicit proposal of consensus. This provides a last chance for someone else to say, "Wait, I didn't agree to that. We need to hash this out some more."

For small, uncontroversial decisions, the proposal of consensus is implicit. For example, when a developer spontaneously commits a bug fix, the commit itself is a proposal of consensus: "I assume we all agree that this bug needs to be fixed, and that this is the way to fix it." Of course, the developer does not actually say that; she just commits the fix, and the others in the project do not bother to state their agreement, because silence is consent. If someone commits a change that turns out *not* to have consensus, the result is simply for the project to discuss the change as though it had not already been committed. The reason this works is the topic of the next section.

Version Control Means You Can Relax

The fact that the project's source code is kept under version control means that most decisions can be easily unmade. The most common way this happens is that someone commits a change mistakenly thinking everyone would be happy with it, only to be met with objections after the fact. It is typical for such objections to start out with an obligatory apology for having missed out on prior discussion, though this may be omitted if the objector finds no record of such a discussion in the mailing list archives. Either way, there is no reason for the tone of the discussion to be different after the change has been committed than before. Any change can be reverted, at least until dependent changes are introduced (i.e., new code that would break if the original change were suddenly removed). The version control system gives the project a way to undo the effects of bad or hasty judgement. This, in turn, frees people to trust their instincts about how much feedback is necessary before doing something.

This also means that the process of establishing consensus need not be very formal. Most projects handle it by feel. Minor changes can go in with no discussion, or with minimal discussion followed by a few nods of agreement. For more significant changes, especially ones with the potential to destabilize a lot of code, people should wait a day or two before assuming there is consensus, the rationale being that no one should be marginalized in an important conversation simply because he didn't check email frequently enough.

Thus, when someone is confident he knows what needs to be done, he should just go ahead and do it. This applies not only to software fixes, but to web site updates, documentation changes, and anything else unlikely to be controversial. Usually there will be only a few instances where an action needs to be undone, and these can be handled on a case-by-case basis. Of course, one shouldn't encourage people to be headstrong. There is still a psychological difference between a decision under discussion and one that has already taken effect, even if it is technically reversible. People always feel that momentum is allied to action, and will be slightly more reluctant to revert a change than to prevent it in the first place. If a developer abuses this fact by committing potentially controversial changes too quickly, however, people can and should complain, and hold that developer to a stricter standard until things improve.

When Consensus Cannot Be Reached, Vote

Inevitably, some debates just won't reach a consensus. When all other means of breaking a deadlock fail, the solution is to vote. But before a vote can be taken, there must be a clear set of choices on the ballot. Here, again, the normal process of technical discussion blends serendipitously with the project's decision-making procedures. The kinds of questions that come to a vote often involve complex, multifaceted issues. In any such complex discussion, there are usually one or two people playing the role of *honest broker*: posting periodic summaries of the various arguments and keeping track of where the core points of disagreement (and agreement) lie. These summaries help everyone measure how much progress has been made, and remind everyone of what issues remain to be addressed. Those same summaries can serve as prototypes for a ballot sheet, should a vote become necessary. If the honest brokers have been doing their job well, they will be able to credibly call for a vote when the time comes, and the group will be willing to use a ballot sheet based on their summary of the issues. The brokers themselves may be participants in the debate; it is not necessary for them to remain above the fray, as long as they can understand and fairly represent others' views, and not let their partisan sentiments prevent them from summarizing the state of the debate in a neutral fashion.

The actual content of the ballot is usually not controversial. By the time matters reach a vote, the disagreement has usually boiled down to a few key issues, with recognizable labels and brief descriptions. Occasionally a developer will object to the form of the ballot itself. Sometimes his concern is legitimate, for example, that an important choice was left off or not described accurately. But other times a developer may be merely trying to stave off the inevitable, perhaps knowing that the vote probably won't go his way. See "Difficult People" in Chapter 6 for how to deal with this sort of obstructionism.

Remember to specify the voting system, as there are many different kinds, and people might make wrong assumptions about which procedure is being used. A good choice in most cases is *approval voting*, whereby each voter can vote for as many of the choices on the ballot as he likes. Approval voting is simple to explain and to count, and unlike some other methods, it only involves one round of voting. See *http://en.wikipedia.org/wiki/Voting_system#List_of_systems* for more details about approval voting and other voting systems, but try to avoid getting into a long debate about which voting system to use (because, of course, you will then find yourself in a debate about which voting system to use to decide the voting system!). One reason approval voting is a good choice is that it's very hard for anyone to object to—it's about as fair as a voting system can be.

Finally, conduct votes in public. There is no need for secrecy or anonymity in a vote on matters that have been debated publicly anyway. Have each participant post their votes to the project mailing list, so that any observer can tally and check the results for herself, and so that everything is recorded in the archives.

When to Vote

The hardest thing about voting is determining when to do it. In general, taking a vote should be very rare—a last resort for when all other options have failed. Don't think of voting as a great way to resolve debates. It isn't. It ends discussion, and thereby ends creative thinking about the problem. As long as discussion continues, there is the possibility that someone will come up with a new solution everyone likes. This happens surprisingly often: a lively debate can produce a new way of thinking about the problem, and lead to a proposal that eventually satisfies everyone. Even when no new proposal arises, it's still usually better to broker a compromise than to hold a vote. After a compromise, everyone is a little bit unhappy, whereas after a vote, some people are unhappy while others are happy. From a political standpoint, the former situation is preferable: at least each person can feel he extracted a price for his unhappiness. He may be dissatisfied, but so is everyone else.

Voting's main advantage is that it finally settles a question so everyone can move on. But it settles it by a head count, instead of by rational dialogue leading everyone to the same conclusion. The more experienced people are with open source projects, the less eager I find them to be to settle questions by vote. Instead they will try to explore previously unconsidered solutions, or compromise more severely than they'd originally planned. Various techniques are available to prevent a premature vote. The most obvious is simply to say "I don't think we're ready for a vote yet," and explain why not. Another is to ask for an informal (non-binding) show of hands. If the response clearly tends toward one side or another, this will make some people suddenly more willing to compromise, obviating the need for a formal vote. But the most effective way is simply to offer a new solution, or a new viewpoint on an old suggestion, so that people re-engage with the issues instead of merely repeating the same arguments.

In certain rare cases, everyone may agree that all the compromise solutions are worse than any of the non-compromise ones. When that happens, voting is less objectionable, both because it is more likely to lead to a superior solution and because people will not be overly unhappy no matter how it turns out. Even then, the vote should not be rushed. The discussion leading up to a vote is what educates the electorate, so stopping that discussion early can lower the quality of the result.

(Note that this advice to be reluctant to call votes does not apply to the change-inclusion voting described in "Stabilizing a Release" in Chapter 7. There, voting is more of a communications mechanism, a means of registering one's involvement in the change review process so that everyone can tell how much review a given change has received.)

Who Votes?

Having a voting system raises the question of electorate: who gets to vote? This has the potential to be a sensitive issue, because it forces the project to officially recognize some people as being more involved, or as having better judgement, than others.

The best solution is to simply take an existing distinction, commit access, and attach voting privileges to it. In projects that offer both full and partial commit access, the question of whether partial committers can vote largely depends on the process by which partial commit access is granted. If the project hands it out liberally, for example as a way of maintaining many third-party contributed tools in the repository, then it should be made clear that partial commit access is really just about committing, not voting. The reverse implication naturally holds as well: since full committers *will* have voting privileges, they must be chosen not only as programmers, but as members of the electorate. If someone shows disruptive or obstructionist tendencies on the mailing list, the group should be very cautious about making her a committer, even if the person is technically skilled.

The voting system itself should be used to choose new committers, both full and partial. But here is one of the rare instances where secrecy is appropriate. You can't have votes about potential committers posted to a public mailing list, because the candidate's feelings (and reputation) could be hurt. Instead, the usual way is that an existing committer posts to a private mailing list consisting only of the other committers, proposing that someone be granted commit access. The other committers speak their minds freely, knowing the discussion is private. Often there will be no disagreement, and therefore no vote necessary. After waiting a few days to make sure every committer has had a chance to respond, the proposer mails the candidate and offers him commit access. If there is disagreement, discussion ensues as for any other question, possibly resulting in a vote. For this process to be open and frank, the mere fact that the discussion is taking place at all should be secret. If the person under consideration knew it was going on, and then were never offered commit access, he could conclude that he had lost the vote, and would likely feel hurt. Of course, if someone explicitly asks for commit access, then there is no choice but to consider the proposal and explicitly accept or reject him. If the latter, then it should be done as politely as possible, with a clear explanation: "We liked your patches, but haven't seen enough of them yet," or "We appreciate all your patches, but they required considerable adjustments before they could be applied, so we don't feel comfortable giving you commit access yet. We hope that this will change over time, though." Remember, what you're saying could come as a blow, depending on the person's level of confidence. Try to see it from their point of view as you write the mail.

Because adding a new committer is more consequential than most other one-time decisions, some projects have special requirements for the vote. For example, they may require that the proposal receive at least *n* positive votes and no negative votes, or that a super majority vote in favor. The exact parameters are not important; the main idea is to get the group to be careful about adding new committers. Similar, or even stricter, special requirements can apply to votes to *remove* a committer, though hopefully that will never be necessary. See "Committers" in Chapter 8 for more on the non-voting aspects of adding and removing committers.

Polls Versus Votes

For certain kinds of votes, it may be useful to expand the electorate. For example, if the developers simply can't figure out whether a given interface choice matches the way people actually use the software, one solution is to ask to all the subscribers of the project's mailing lists to vote. These are really *polls* rather than votes, but the developers may choose to treat the result as binding. As with any poll, be sure to make it clear to the participants that there's a write-in option: if someone thinks of a better option not offered in the poll questions, her response may turn out to be the most important result of the poll.

Vetoes

Some projects allow a special kind of vote known as a *veto*. A veto is a way for a developer to put a halt to a hasty or ill-considered change, at least long enough for everyone to discuss it more. Think of a veto as somewhere between a very strong objection and a filibuster. Its exact meaning varies from one project to another. Some projects make it very difficult to override a veto; others allow them to be overridden by regular majority vote, perhaps after an enforced delay for more discussion. Any veto should be accompanied by a thorough explanation; a veto without such an explanation should be considered invalid on arrival.

With vetoes comes the problem of veto abuse. Sometimes developers are too eager to raise the stakes by casting a veto, when really all that was called for was more discussion. You can prevent veto abuse by being very reluctant to use vetoes yourself, and by gently calling it out when someone else uses her veto too often. If necessary, you can also remind the group that vetoes are binding for only as long as the group agrees they are—after all, if a clear majority of developers wants X, then X is going to happen one way or another. Either the vetoing developer will back down, or the group will decide to weaken the meaning of a veto.

You may see people write "-1" to express a veto. This usage comes from the Apache Software Foundation, which has a highly structured voting and veto process, described at *http://www.apache.org/foundation/voting.html*. The Apache standards have spread to other projects, and you will see their conventions used to varying degrees in a lot of places in the open source world. Technically, "-1" does not always indicate a formal veto even according to the Apache standards, but informally it is usually taken to mean a veto, or at least a very strong objection.

Like votes, vetoes can apply retroactively. It's not okay to object to a veto on the grounds that the change in question has already been committed, or the action taken (unless it's something irrevocable, like putting out a press release). On the other hand, a veto that arrives weeks or months late isn't likely to be taken very seriously, nor should it be.

Writing It All Down

At some point, the number of conventions and agreements floating around in your project may become so great that you need to record it somewhere. In order to give such a document legitimacy, make it clear that it is based on mailing list discussions and on agreements already in effect. As you compose it, refer to the relevant threads in the mailing list archives, and whenever there's a point you're not sure about, ask again. The document should not contain any surprises: it is not the source of the agreements, it is merely a description of them. Of course, if it is successful, people will start citing it as a source of authority in itself but that just means it reflects the overall will of the group accurately.

This is the document alluded to in "Developer Guidelines" in Chapter 2. Naturally, when the project is very young, you will have to lay down guidelines without the benefit of a long project history to draw on. But as the development community matures, you can adjust the language to reflect the way things actually turn out.

Don't try to be comprehensive. No document can capture everything people need to know about participating in a project. Many of the conventions a project evolves remain forever unspoken, never mentioned explicitly, yet adhered to by all. Other things are simply too obvious to be mentioned, and would only distract from important but non-obvious material. For example, there's no point writing guidelines like "Be polite and respectful to others on the mailing lists, and don't start flame wars," or "Write clean, readable, bug-free code." Of course these things are desirable, but since there's no conceivable universe in which they might *not* be desirable, they are not worth mentioning. If people are being rude on the mailing list, or writing buggy code, they're not going to stop just because the project guidelines said to. Such situations need to be dealt with as they arise, not by blanket admonitions to be good. On the other hand, if the project has specific guidelines about *how* to write good code, such as rules about documenting every API in a certain format, then those guidelines should be written down as completely as possible.

A good way to determine what to include is to base the document on the questions that newcomers ask most often, and on the complaints experienced developers make most often. This doesn't necessarily mean it should turn into a FAQ sheet—it probably needs a more coherent narrative structure than FAQs can offer. But it should follow the same reality-based principle of addressing the issues that actually arise, rather than those you anticipate might arise.

If the project is a benevolent dictatorship, or has officers endowed with special powers (president, chair, whatever), then the document is also a good opportunity to codify succession procedures. Sometimes this can be as simple as naming specific people as replacements in case the BD suddenly leaves the project for any reason. Generally, if there is a BD, only the BD can get away with naming a successor. If there are elected officers, then the nomination and election procedure that was used to choose them in the first place should be described in the document. If there was no procedure originally, then get consensus on a procedure on the mailing lists *before* writing about it. People can sometimes be touchy about hierarchical structures, so the subject needs to be approached with sensitivity.

Perhaps the most important thing is to make it clear that the rules can be reconsidered. If the conventions described in the document start to hamper the project, remind everyone that it is supposed to be a living reflection of the group's intentions, not a source of frustration and blockage. If someone makes a habit of inappropriately asking for rules to be reconsidered every time the rules get in her way, you don't always need to debate it with her—sometimes silence is the best tactic. If other people agree with the complaints, they'll chime in, and it will be obvious that something needs to change. If no one else agrees, then the person won't get much response, and the rules will stay as they are.

Two good examples of project guidelines are the Subversion HACKING file, at *http:// svn.collab.net/repos/svn/trunk/HACKING*, and the Apache Software Foundation governance documents, at *http://www.apache.org/foundation/how-it-works.html* and *http:// www.apache.org/foundation/voting.html*. The ASF is really a collection of software projects, legally organized as a non-profit corporation, so its documents tend to describe governance procedures more than development conventions. They're still worth reading, though, because they represent the accumulated experience of a lot of open source projects.

## CHAPTER 5

Money

This chapter examines how to bring funding into a free software environment. It is aimed not only at developers who are paid to work on free software projects, but also at their managers, who need to understand the social dynamics of the development environment. In the sections that follow, the addressee ("you") is presumed to be either a paid developer, or one who manages such developers. The advice will often be the same for both; when it's not, the intended audience will be made clear from context.

Corporate funding of free software development is not a new phenomenon. A lot of development has always been informally subsidized. When a system administrator writes a network analysis tool to help him do his job, then posts it online and gets bug fixes and feature contributions from other system administrators, what's happened is that an unofficial consortium has been formed. The consortium's funding comes from the sysadmins' salaries, and its office space and network bandwidth are donated, albeit unknowingly, by the organizations they work for. Those organizations benefit from the investment, of course, although they may not be institutionally aware of it at first.

The difference today is that many of these efforts are being formalized. Corporations have become conscious of the benefits of open source software, and started involving themselves more directly in its development. Developers, too, have come to expect that really important projects will attract at least donations, and possibly even long-term sponsors. While the presence of money has not changed the basic dynamics of free software development, it has greatly changed the scale at which things happen, both in terms of the number of developers and time-per-developer. It has also had effects on how projects are organized, and on how the parties involved in them interact. The issues are not merely about how the money is spent, or how return on investment is measured. They are also about management and process: how can the hierarchical command structures of corporations and the semi-decentralized volunteer communities of free software projects work productively with each other? Will they even agree on what "productively" means?

Financial backing is, in general, welcomed by open source development communities. It can reduce a project's vulnerability to the Forces of Chaos, which sweep away so many projects before they really get off the ground, and therefore it can make people more willing to give the software a chance—they feel they're investing their time into something that will still be around six months from now. After all, credibility is contagious, to a point. When, say, IBM backs an open source project, people pretty much assume the project won't be allowed to fail, and their resultant willingness to devote effort to it can make that a self-fulfilling prophecy.

However, funding also brings a perception of control. If not handled carefully, money can divide a project into in-group and out-group developers. If the unpaid volunteers get the feeling that design decisions or feature additions are simply available to the highest bidder, they'll head off to a project that seems more like a meritocracy and less like unpaid labor for someone else's benefit. They may never complain overtly on the mailing lists. Instead, there will simply be less and less noise from external sources, as the volunteers gradually stop trying to be taken seriously. The buzz of small-scale activity will continue, in the form of bug reports and occasional small fixes. But there won't be any large code contributions or outside participation in design discussions. People sense what's expected of them, and live up (or down) to those expectations.

Although money needs to be used carefully, that doesn't mean it can't buy influence. It most certainly can. The trick is that it can't buy influence directly. In a straightforward commercial transaction, you trade money for what you want. If you need a feature added, you sign a contract, pay for it, and it gets done. In an open source project, it's not so simple. You may sign a contract with some developers, but they'd be fooling themselves—and you—if they guaranteed that the work you paid for would be accepted by the development community simply because you paid for it. The work can only be accepted on its own merits and on how it fits into the community's vision for the software. You may have some say in that vision, but you won't be the only voice.

So money can't purchase influence, but it can purchase things that *lead to* influence. The most obvious example are programmers. If good programmers are hired, and they stick around long enough to get experience with the software and credibility in the community, then they can influence the project by the same means as any other member. They will have a vote, or if there are many of them, they will have a voting bloc. If they are respected in the project, they will have influence beyond just their votes. There is no need for paid developers to disguise their motives, either. After all, everyone who wants a change made to the software wants it for a reason. Your company's reasons are no less legitimate than anyone else's. It's just that the weight given to your company's goals will be determined by its representatives' status in the project, not by the company's size, budget, or business plan.

Types of Involvement

There are many different reasons open source projects get funded. The items in this list aren't mutually exclusive; often a project's financial backing will result from several, or even all, of these motivations:

Sharing the burden

> Separate organizations with related software needs often find themselves duplicating effort, either by redundantly writing similar code in-house, or by purchasing similar products from proprietary vendors. When they realize what's going on, the organizations may pool their resources and create (or join) an open source project tailored to their needs. The advantages are obvious: the costs of development are divided, but the benefits accrue to all. Although this scenario seems most intuitive for non-profits, it can make strategic sense for even for-profit competitors.

> Examples: *http://www.openadapter.org/, http://www.koha.org/*

Augmenting services

> When a company sells services that depend on, or are made more attractive by, particular open source programs, it is naturally in that company's interests to ensure those programs are actively maintained.

> Example: CollabNet's (*http://www.collab.net/*) support of *http://subversion.tigris.org/* (disclaimer: that's my day job, but it's also a perfect example of this model).

Supporting hardware sales

> The value of computers and computer components is directly related to the amount of software available for them. Hardware vendors—not just whole-machine vendors, but also makers of peripheral devices and microchips—have

found that having high-quality free software to run on their hardware is important to customers.

Undermining a competitor

Sometimes companies support a particular open source project as a means of undermining a competitor's product, which may or may not be open source itself. Eating away at a competitor's market share is usually not the sole reason for getting involved with an open source project, but it can be a factor.

Example: *http://www.openoffice.org/* (no, this isn't the only reason OpenOffice exists, but the software is at least partly a response to Microsoft Office).

Marketing

Having your company associated with a popular open source application can be simply good brand management.

Dual licensing

Dual licensing is the practice of offering software under a traditional proprietary license for customers who want to resell it as part of a proprietary application of their own, and simultaneously under a free license for those willing to use it under open source terms (see "Dual Licensing Schemes" in Chapter 9). If the open source developer community is active, the software gets the benefits of wide-area debugging and development, yet the company still gets a royalty stream to support some full-time programmers.

Two well-known examples are MySQL (*http://www.mysql.com/*), makers of the database software of the same name, and Sleepycat (*http://www.sleepycat.com/*), which offers distributions and support for the Berkeley Database. It's no coincidence that they're both database companies. Database software tends to be integrated into applications rather than marketed directly to users, so it's very well suited to the dual-licensing model.

Donations

A widely used project can sometimes get significant contributions, from both individuals and organizations, just by having an online donation button, or sometimes by selling branded merchandise such as coffee mugs, T-shirts, mousepads, etc. A word of caution: if your project accepts donations, plan out how the money will be used *before* it comes in, and state the plans on the project's web site. Discussions about how to allocate money tend to go a lot more smoothly when held before there's actual money to spend; and anyway, if there are significant disagreements, it's better to find that out while it's still academic.

A funder's business model is not the only factor in how it relates to an open source community. The historical relationship between the two also matters: did the company start the project, or is it joining an existing development effort? In both cases, the funder will have to earn credibility, but, not surprisingly, there's a bit more earning to be done in the latter case. The organization needs to have clear goals with respect to the project. Is the company trying to keep a position of leadership, or simply trying to be one voice in the community, to guide but not necessarily govern the project's direction? Or does it just want to have a couple of committers around, able to fix customers' bugs and get the changes into the public distribution without any fuss?

Keep these questions in mind as you read the guidelines that follow. They are meant to apply to any sort of organizational involvement in a free software project, but every project is a human environment, and therefore no two are exactly alike. To some degree, you will always have to play by ear, but following these principles will increase the likelihood of things turning out the way you want.

Hire for the Long Term

If you're managing programmers on an open source project, keep them there long enough that they acquire both technical and political expertise—a couple of years, at a minimum. Of course, no project, whether open or closed-source, benefits from swapping programmers in and out too often. The need for a newcomer to learn the ropes each time would be a deterrent in any environment. But the penalty is even stronger in open source projects, because outgoing developers take with them not only their knowledge of the code, but also their status in the community and the human relationships they have made there.

The credibility a developer has accumulated cannot be transferred. To pick the most obvious example, an incoming developer can't inherit commit access from an outgoing one (see "Money Can't Buy You Love" later in this chapter), so if the new developer doesn't already have commit access, he will have to submit patches until he does. But commit access is only the most measurable manifestation of lost influence. A long-time developer also knows all the old arguments that have been hashed and rehashed on the discussion lists. A new developer, having no memory of those conversations, may try to raise the topics again, leading to a loss of credibility for your organization; the others might wonder "Can't they remember anything?" A new developer will also have no political feel for the project's personalities, and will not be able to influence development directions as quickly or as smoothly as one who's been around a long time.

Train newcomers through a program of supervised engagement. The new developer should be in direct contact with the public development community from the very first day, starting off with bug fixes and cleanup tasks, so he can learn the code base and acquire a reputation in the community, yet not spark any long and involved design discussions. All the while, one or more experienced developers should be available for questioning, and should be reading every post the newcomer makes to the development lists, even if they're in threads that the experienced developers normally wouldn't pay attention to. This will help the group spot potential rocks before the newcomer runs aground. Private, behind-the-scenes encouragement and pointers can also help a lot, especially if the newcomer is not accustomed to massively parallel peer review of his code.

When CollabNet hires a new developer to work on Subversion, we sit down together and pick some open bugs for the new person to cut his teeth on. We'll discuss the technical outlines of the solutions, and then assign at least one experienced developer to (publicly) review the patch that the new developer will (also publicly) post. We typically don't even look at the patch before the main development list sees it, although we could if there were some reason to. The important thing is that the new developer go through the process of public review, learning the code base while simultaneously becoming accustomed to receiving critiques from complete strangers. But we try to coordinate the timing so that our own review comes immediately after the posting of the patch. That way the first review the list sees is ours, which can help set the tone for the others' reviews. It also contributes to the idea that this new person is to be taken seriously: if others see that we're putting in the time to give detailed reviews, with thorough explanations and references into the archives where appropriate, they'll appreciate that a form of training is going on, and that it probably signifies a long-term investment. This can make them more positively disposed toward that developer, at least to the degree of spending a little extra time answering questions and reviewing patches.

Appear as Many, Not as One

Your developers should strive to appear in the project's public forums as individual participants, rather than as a monolithic corporate presence. This is not because there is some negative connotation inherent in monolithic corporate presences (well, perhaps there is, but that's not what this book is about). Rather, it's because individuals are the only sort of entity open source projects are structurally equipped to deal with. An individual contributor can have discussions, submit patches, acquire credibility, vote, and so forth. A company cannot.

Furthermore, by behaving in a decentralized manner, you avoid stimulating centralization of opposition. Let your developers disagree with each other on the mailing lists. Encourage them to review each other's code as often, and as publicly, as they would anyone else's. Discourage them from always voting as a bloc, because if they do, others may start to feel that, just on general principles, there should be an organized effort to keep them in check.

There's a difference between actually being decentralized and simply striving to appear that way. Under certain circumstances, having your developers behave in concert can be quite useful, and they should be prepared to coordinate behind the scenes when necessary. For example, when making a proposal, having several people chime in with agreement early on can help it along, by giving the impression of a growing consensus. Others will feel that the proposal has momentum, and that if they were to object, they'd be stopping that momentum. Thus, people will object only if they have a good reason to do so. There's nothing wrong with orchestrating agreement like this, as long as objections are still taken seriously. The public manifestations of a private agreement are no less sincere for having been coordinated beforehand, and are not harmful as long as they are not used to prejudicially snuff out opposing arguments. Their purpose is merely to inhibit the sort of people who like to object just to stay in shape; see "The Softer the Topic, the Longer the Debate" in Chapter 6 for more about them.

Be Open About Your Motivations

Be as open about your organization's goals as you can without compromising business secrets. If you want the project to acquire a certain feature because, say, your customers have been clamoring for it, just say so outright on the mailing lists. If the customers wish to remain anonymous, as is sometimes the case, then at least ask them if they can be used as unnamed examples. The more the public development community knows about *why* you want what you want, the more comfortable they'll be with whatever you're proposing.

This runs counter to the instinct—so easy to acquire, so hard to shake off—that knowledge is power, and that the more others know about your goals, the more control they have over you. But that instinct would be wrong here. By publicly advocating the feature (or bug fix, or whatever it is), you have *already* laid your cards on the table. The only question now is whether you will succeed in guiding the community to share your goal. If you merely state that you want it, but can't provide concrete examples of why, your argument is weak, and people will start to suspect a hidden agenda. But if you give just a few real-world scenarios showing why the proposed feature is important, that can have a dramatic effect on the debate.

To see why this is so, consider the alternative. Too frequently, debates about new features or new directions are long and tiresome. The arguments people advance often reduce to "I personally want X," or the ever-popular "In my years of experience as a software designer, X is extremely important to users/a useless frill that will please no one." Predictably, the absence of real-world usage data neither shortens nor tempers such debates, but instead allows them to drift farther and farther from any mooring in actual user experience. Without some countervailing force, the end result is as likely as not to be determined by whoever was the most articulate, or the most persistent, or the most senior.

As an organization with plentiful customer data available, you have the opportunity to provide just such a countervailing force. You can be a conduit for information that might otherwise have no means of reaching the development community. The fact that the information supports your desires is nothing to be embarrassed about. Most developers don't individually have very broad experience with how the software they write is used. Each developer uses the software in her own idiosyncratic way; as far as other usage patterns go, she's relying on intuition and guesswork, and deep down, she knows this. By providing credible data about a significant number of users, you are giving the public development community something akin to oxygen. As long as you present it right, they will welcome it enthusiastically, and it will propel things in the direction you want to go.

The key, of course, is presenting it right. It will never do to insist that simply because you deal with a large number of users, and because they need (or think they need) a given feature, therefore your solution ought to be implemented. Instead, you should focus your initial posts on the problem, rather than on one particular solution. Describe in great detail the experiences your customers are encountering, offer as much analysis as you have available, and as many reasonable solutions as you can think of. When people start speculating about the effectiveness of various solutions, you can continue to draw on your data to support or refute what they say. You may have one particular solution in mind all along, but don't single it out for special consideration at first. This is not deception, it is simply standard "honest broker" behavior. After all, your true goal is to solve the problem; a solution is merely a means to that end. If the solution you prefer really is superior, other developers will recognize that on their own eventually—and then they will get behind it of their own free will, which is much better than you browbeating them into implementing it. (There is also the possibility that they will think of a better solution.)

This is not to say that you can't ever come out in favor of a specific solution. But you must have the patience to see the analysis you've already done internally repeated on the public development lists. Don't post saying "Yes, we've been over all that here, but it doesn't work for reasons A, B, and C. When you get right down to it, the only way to solve this is...." The problem is not so much that it sounds arrogant as that it gives the impression that you have *already* devoted some unknown (but, people will presume, large) amount of analytical resources to the problem, behind closed doors. It makes it seem as though efforts have been going on, and perhaps decisions made, that the public is not privy to, and that is a recipe for resentment.

Naturally, *you* know how much effort you've devoted to the problem internally, and that knowledge is, in a way, a disadvantage. It puts your developers in a slightly different mental space than everyone else on the mailing lists, reducing their ability to see things from the point of view of those who haven't yet thought about the problem as much. The earlier you can get everyone else thinking about things in the same terms as you do, the smaller this distancing effect will be. This logic applies not only to individual technical situations, but to the broader mandate of making your goals as clear as you can. The unknown is always more destabilizing than the known. If people understand why you want what you want, they'll feel comfortable talking to you even when they disagree. If they can't figure out what makes you tick, they'll assume the worst, at least some of the time.

You won't be able to publicize everything, of course, and people won't expect you to. All organizations have secrets; perhaps for-profits have more of them, but non-profits have them too. If you must advocate a certain course, but can't reveal anything about why, then simply offer the best arguments you can under that handicap, and accept the fact that you may not have as much influence as you want in the discussion. This is one of the compromises you make in order to have a development community not on your payroll.

Money Can't Buy You Love

If you're a paid developer on a project, then set guidelines early on about what the money can and cannot buy. This does not mean you need to post twice a day to the mailing lists reiterating your noble and incorruptible nature. It merely means that you should be on the lookout for opportunities to defuse the tensions that *could* be created by money. You don't need to start out assuming that the tensions are there; you do need to demonstrate an awareness that they have the potential to arise.

A perfect example of this came up in the Subversion project. Subversion was started in 2000 by CollabNet (*http://www.collab.net/*), which has been the project's primary funder since its inception, paying the salaries of several developers (disclaimer: I'm one of them). Soon after the project began, we hired another developer, Mike Pilato, to join the effort. By then, coding had already started. Although Subversion was still very much in the early stages, it already had a development community with a set of basic ground rules.

Mike's arrival raised an interesting question. Subversion already had a policy about how a new developer gets commit access. First, he submits some patches to the development mailing list. After enough patches have gone by for the other committers to see that the new contributor knows what he's doing, someone proposes that he just commit directly (that proposal is private, as described in "Committers" in Chapter 8). Assuming the committers agree, one of them mails the new developer and offers him direct commit access to the project's repository.

CollabNet had hired Mike specifically to work on Subversion. Among those who already knew him, there was no doubt about his coding skills or his readiness to work on the project. Furthermore, the volunteer developers had a very good relationship with the CollabNet employees, and most likely would not have objected if we'd just given Mike commit access the day he was hired. But we knew we'd be setting a precedent. If we granted Mike commit access by fiat, we'd be saying that CollabNet had the right to ignore project guidelines, simply because it was the primary funder. While the damage from this would not necessarily be immediately apparent, it would gradually result in the non-salaried developers feeling disenfranchised. Other people have to earn their commit access—CollabNet just buys it.

So Mike agreed to start out his employment at CollabNet like any other volunteer developer, without commit access. He sent patches to the public mailing list, where they could be, and were, reviewed by everyone. We also said on the list that we were doing things this way deliberately, so there could be no missing the point. After a couple of weeks of solid activity by Mike, someone (I can't remember if it was a CollabNet developer or not) proposed him for commit access, and he was accepted, as we knew he would be.

That kind of consistency gets you a credibility that money could never buy. And credibility is a valuable currency to have in technical discussions: it's immunization against having one's motives questioned later. In the heat of argument, people will sometimes look for non-technical ways to win the battle. The project's primary funder, because of its deep involvement and obvious concern over the directions the project takes, presents a wider target than most. By being scrupulous to observe all project guidelines right from the start, the funder makes itself the same size as everyone else.

Check out Danese Cooper's blog at *http://blogs.sun.com/roller/page/DaneseCooper/ 20040916* for a similar story about commit access. Cooper was then Sun Microsystems' "Open Source Diva"—I believe that was her official title—and in the blog entry, she describes how the Tomcat development community got Sun to hold its own developers to the same commit-access standards as the non-Sun developers.

The need for the funders to play by the same rules as everyone else means that the benevolent dictatorship governance model (see "Benevolent Dictators" in Chapter 4) is slightly harder to pull off in the presence of funding, particularly if the dictator works for the primary funder. Since a dictatorship has few rules, it is hard for the funder to prove that it's abiding by community standards, even when it is. It's certainly not impossible; it just requires a project leader who is able to see things from the point of view of the outside developers, as well as that of the funder, and act accordingly. Even then, it's probably a good idea to have a proposal for non-dictatorial governance sitting in your back pocket, ready to be brought out the moment there are any indications of widespread dissatisfaction in the community.

Contracting

Contracted work needs to be handled carefully in free software projects. Ideally, you want a contractor's work to be accepted by the community and folded into the public distribution. In theory, it wouldn't matter who the contractor is, as long as his work is good and meets the project's guidelines. Theory and practice can sometimes match, too: a complete stranger who shows up with a good patch *will* generally be able to get it into the software. The trouble is, it's very hard to produce a good patch for a non-trivial enhancement or new feature while truly being a complete stranger; one must first discuss it with the rest of the project. The duration of that discussion cannot be precisely predicted. If the contractor is paid by the hour, you may end up paying more than you expected; if he is paid a flat sum, he may end up doing more work than he can afford.

There are two ways around this. The preferred way is to make an educated guess about the length of the discussion process, based on past experience, add in some padding for error, and base the contract on that. It also helps to divide the problem into as many small, independent chunks as possible, to increase the predictability of each chunk. The other way is to contract solely for delivery of a patch, and treat the patch's acceptance into the public project as a separate matter. Then it becomes much easier to write the contract, but you're stuck with the burden of maintaining a private patch for as long as you depend on the software, or at least for as long as it takes you to get that patch or equivalent functionality into the mainline. Of course, even with the preferred way, the contract itself cannot require that the patch be accepted into the code, because that would involve selling something that's not for sale. (What if the rest of the project unexpectedly decides not to support the feature?) However, the contract can require a bona fide effort to get the change accepted by the community, and that it be committed to the repository if the community agrees with it. For example, if the project has written standards regarding code changes, the contract can reference those standards and specify that the work must meet them. In practice, this usually works out the way everyone hopes.

The best tactic for successful contracting is to hire one of the project's developers—preferably a committer—as the contractor. This may seem like a form of purchasing influence, and, well, it is. But it's not as corrupt as it might seem. A developer's influence in the project is due mainly to the quality of his code and to his interactions with other developers. The fact that he has a contract to get certain things done doesn't raise his status in any way, and doesn't lower it either, though it may make people scrutinize him more carefully. Most developers would not risk their long-term position in the project by backing an inappropriate or widely disliked new feature. In fact, part of what you get, or should get, when you hire such a contractor is advice about what sorts of changes are likely to be accepted by the community. You also get a slight shift in the project's priorities. Because prioritization is just a matter of who has time to work on what, when you pay for someone's time, you cause their work to move up in the priority queue a bit. This is a well-understood fact of life among experienced open source developers, and at least some of them will devote attention to the contractor's work simply because it looks like it's going to *get done*, so they want to help it get done right. Perhaps they won't write any of the code, but they'll still discuss the design and review the code, both of which can be very useful. For all these reasons, the contractor is best drawn from the ranks of those already involved with the project.

This immediately raises two questions: Should contracts ever be private? And when they're not, should you worry about creating tensions in the community by the fact that you've contracted with some developers and not others?

It's best to be open about contracts, when you can. Otherwise, the contractor's behavior may seem strange to others in the community—perhaps he's suddenly giving inexplicably high priority to features that previously he'd never been interested in. When people ask him why he wants them now, how can he answer convincingly if he can't talk about the fact that he's been contracted to write them?

At the same time, neither you nor the contractor should act as though others should treat your arrangement as a big deal. Too often I've seen contractors waltz onto a development list with the attitude that their posts should be taken more seriously simply because they're being paid. That kind of attitude signals to the rest of the project that the contractor regards the fact of the contract—as opposed to the code *resulting* from the contract—to be the important thing. But from the other developers' point of view, only the code matters. At all times, the focus of attention should be kept on technical issues, not on the details of who is paying whom. For example, one of the developers in the Subversion community handles contracting in a particularly graceful way. While discussing his code changes in IRC, he'll mention as an aside (often in a private remark, an IRC *privmsg*, to one of the other committers) that he's being paid for his work on this particular bug or feature. But he also consistently gives the impression that he'd want to be working on that change anyway, and that he's happy the money is making it possible for him to do that. He may or may not reveal his customer's identity, but in any case, he doesn't dwell on the contract. His remarks about it are just an ornament to an otherwise technical discussion about how to get something done.

That example shows another reason why it's good to be open about contracts. There may be multiple organizations sponsoring contracts on a given open source project, and if each knows what the others are trying to do, they may be able to pool their resources. In the above case, the project's largest funder (CollabNet) is not involved in any way with these piecework contracts, but knowing that someone else is sponsoring certain bug fixes allows CollabNet to redirect its resources to other bugs, resulting in greater efficiency for the project as a whole.

Will other developers resent that some are paid for working on the project? In general, no, particularly when those who are paid are established, well-respected members of the community anyway. No one expects contract work to be distributed equally among all the committers. People understand the importance of long-term relationships: the uncertainties involved in contracting are such that once you find someone you can work reliably with, you would be reluctant to switch to a different person just for the sake of evenhandedness. Think of it this way: the first time you hire, there will be no complaints, because clearly you had to pick *someone*—it's not your fault you can't hire everyone. Later, when you hire the same person a second time, that's just common sense: you already know him, the last time was successful, so why take unnecessary risks? Thus, it's perfectly natural to have one or two go-to people in the community, instead of spreading the work around evenly.

Review and Acceptance of Changes

The community is still important to the success of contract work. Their involvement in the design and review process for sizeable changes cannot be an afterthought. It must be considered part of the work, and fully embraced by the contractor. Don't think of community scrutiny as an obstacle to be overcome—think of it as a free design board and QA department. It is a benefit to be aggressively pursued, not merely endured.

Case study: the CVS password-authentication protocol

In 1995, I was one half of a partnership that provided support and enhancements for CVS (the Concurrent Versions System; see *http://www.cvshome.org/*). My partner Jim and I were, informally, the maintainers of CVS by that point. But we'd never thought carefully about how we ought to relate to the existing, mostly volunteer CVS development community. We just assumed that they'd send in patches, and we'd apply them, and that was pretty much how it worked.

Back then, networked CVS could be done only over a remote login program such as rsh. Using the same password for CVS access as for login access was an obvious security risk, and many organizations were put off by it. A major investment bank hired us to add a new authentication mechanism, so they could safely use networked CVS with their remote offices.

Jim and I took the contract and sat down to design the new authentication system. What we came up with was pretty simple (the United States had export controls on cryptographic code at the time, so the customer understood that we couldn't implement strong authentication), but as we were not experienced in designing such protocols, we still made a few gaffes that would have been obvious to an expert. These mistakes would easily have been caught had we taken the time to write up a proposal and run it by the other developers for review. But we never did so, because it didn't occur to us to think of the development list as a resource to be used. We knew that people were probably going to accept whatever we committed, and—because we didn't know what we didn't know—we didn't bother to do the work in a visible way, e.g., posting patches frequently, making small, easily digestible commits to a special branch, etc. The resulting authentication protocol was not very good, and of course, once it became established, it was difficult to improve, because of compatibility concerns.

The root of the problem was not lack of experience; we could easily have learned what we needed to know. The problem was our attitude toward the volunteer development community. We regarded acceptance of the changes as a hurdle to leap, rather than as a process by which the quality of the changes could be improved. Since we were confident that almost anything we did would be accepted (as it was), we made little effort to get others involved.

Obviously, when you're choosing a contractor, you want someone with the right technical skills and experience for the job. But it's also important to choose someone with a track record of constructive interaction with the other developers in the community. That way you're getting more than just a single person; you're getting an agent who will be able to draw on a network of expertise to make sure the work is done in a robust and maintainable way.

Funding Non-Programming Activities

Programming is only part of the work that goes on in an open source project. From the point of view of the project's volunteers, it's the most visible and glamorous part. This unfortunately means that other activities, such as documentation, formal testing, etc., can sometimes be neglected, at least compared to the amount of attention they often receive in proprietary software. Corporate organizations are sometimes able to make up for this, by devoting some of their internal software development infrastructure to open source projects.

The key to doing this successfully is to translate between the company's internal processes and those of the public development community. Such translation is not effortless: often the two are not a close match, and the differences can be bridged only via human intervention. For example, the company may use a different bug tracker from the public project. Even if they use the same tracking software, the data stored in it will be very different, because the bug-tracking needs of a company are very different from those of a free software community. A piece of information that starts in one tracker may need to be reflected in the other, with confidential portions removed or, in the other direction, added.

The sections that follow are about how to build and maintain such bridges. The end result should be that the open source project runs more smoothly, the community recognizes the company's investment of resources, and yet does not feel that the company is inappropriately steering things toward its own goals.

Quality Assurance (i.e., Professional Testing)

In proprietary software development, it is normal to have teams of people dedicated solely to quality assurance: bug hunting, performance and scalability testing, interface and documentation checking, etc. As a rule, these activities are not pursued as vigorously by the volunteer community on a free software project. This is partly because it's hard to get volunteer labor for unglamorous work like testing, partly because people tend to assume that having a large user community gives the project good testing coverage, and, in the case of performance and scalability testing, partly because volunteers often don't have access to the necessary hardware resources anyway.

The assumption that having many users is equivalent to having many testers is not entirely baseless. Certainly there's little point assigning testers for basic functionality in common environments: bugs there will quickly be found by users in the natural course of things. But because users are just trying to get work done, they do not consciously set out to explore uncharted edge cases in the program's functionality, and are likely to leave certain classes of bugs not found. Furthermore, when they discover a bug with an easy workaround, they often silently implement the workaround without bothering to report the bug. Most insidiously, the usage patterns of your customers (the people who drive *your* interest, the software) may differ in statistically significant ways from the usage patterns of the Average User in the Street.

A professional testing team can uncover these sorts of bugs, and can do so as easily with free software as with proprietary software. The challenge is to convey the testing team's results back to the public in a useful form. In-house testing departments usually have their own way of reporting test results, involving company-specific jargon, or specialized knowledge about particular customers and their data sets. Such reports would be inappropriate for the public bug tracker, both because of their form and because of confidentiality concerns. Even if your company's internal bug tracking software were the same as that used by the public project, management might need to make company-specific comments and metadata changes to the issues (for example, to raise an issue's internal priority, or schedule its resolution for a particular customer). Usually such notes are confidential—sometimes they're not even shown to the customer. But even when they're not confidential, they're of no concern to the public project, and therefore the public should not be distracted with them.

Yet the core bug report itself *is* important to the public. In fact, a bug report from your testing department is in some ways more valuable than one received from users at large, since the testing department probes for things that other users won't. Given that you're unlikely to get that particular bug report from any other source, you definitely want to preserve it and make it available to the public project.

To do this, either the QA department can file issues directly in the public issue tracker, if they're comfortable with that, or an intermediary (usually one of the developers) can "translate" the testing department's internal reports into new issues in the public tracker. Translation simply means describing the bug in a way that makes no reference to customer-specific information. The reproduction recipe may use customer data, assuming the customer approves it, of course.

It is somewhat preferable to have the QA department filing issues in the public tracker directly. That gives the public a more direct appreciation of your company's involvement with the project: useful bug reports add to your organization's credibility just as any technical contribution would. It also gives developers a direct line of communication to the testing team. For example, if the internal QA team is monitoring the public issue tracker, a developer can commit a fix for a scalability bug (which the developer may not have the resources to test herself), and then add a note to the issue asking the QA team to see if the fix had the desired effect. Expect a bit of resistance from some of the developers; programmers have a tendency to regard QA as, at best, a necessary evil. The QA team can easily overcome this by finding significant bugs and filing comprehensible reports; on the other hand, if their reports are not at least as good as those coming from the regular user community, then there's no point having them interact directly with the development team.

Either way, once a public issue exists, the original internal issue should simply reference the public issue for technical content. Management and paid developers may continue to annotate the internal issue with company-specific comments as necessary, but use the public issue for information that should be available to everyone.

You should go into this process expecting extra overhead. Maintaining two issues for one bug is, naturally, more work than maintaining one issue. The benefit is that many more coders will see the report and be able to contribute to a solution.

Legal Advice and Protection

Corporations, for-profit or non-profit, are almost the only entities that ever pay attention to complex legal issues in free software. Individual developers often understand the nuances of various open source licenses, but they generally do not have the time or resources to follow copyright, trademark, and patent law in detail. If your company has a legal department, it can help a project by vetting the copyright status of the code, and helping developers understand possible patent and trademark issues.

The exact forms this help could take are discussed in Chapter 9. The main thing is to make sure that communications between the legal department and the development community, if they happen at all, happen with a mutual appreciation of the very different universes the parties are coming from. On occasion, these two groups talk past each other, each side assuming domain-specific knowledge that the other does not have. A good strategy is to have a liaison (usually a developer, or else a lawyer with technical expertise) stand in the middle and translate for as long as needed.

Documentation and Usability

Documentation and usability are both famous weak spots in open source projects, although I think, at least in the case of documentation, that the difference between free and proprietary software is frequently exaggerated. Nevertheless, it is empirically true that much open source software lacks first-class documentation and usability research.

If your organization wants to help fill these gaps for a project, probably the best thing it can do is hire people who are *not* regular developers on the project, but who will be able to interact productively with the developers. Not hiring regular developers is good for two reasons: one, that way you don't take development time away from the project; two, those closest to the software are usually the wrong people to write documentation or investigate usability anyway, because they have trouble seeing the software from an outsider's point of view.

However, it will still be necessary for whoever works on these problems to communicate with the developers. Find people who are technical enough to talk to the coding team, but not so expert in the software that they can't empathize with regular users anymore.

Providing Hosting/Bandwidth

For a project that's not using one of the free canned hosting sites (see "Canned Hosting" in Chapter 3), providing a server and network connection—and most importantly, system administration help—can be of significant assistance. Even if this is all your organization does for the project, it can be a moderately effective way to obtain good public relations karma, though it will not bring any influence over the direction of the project.

You can probably expect a banner ad or an acknowledgment on the project's home page, thanking your company for providing hosting. If you set up the hosting so that the project's web address is under your company's domain name, then you will get some additional association just through the URL. This will cause most users to think of the software as having *something* to do with your company, even if you don't contribute to development at all. The problem is, the developers are aware of this associative tendency too, and may not be very comfortable with having the project in your domain unless you're contributing more resources than just bandwidth. After all, there are a lot of places to host these days. The community may eventually feel that the implied misallocation of credit is not worth the convenience brought by hosting, and take the project elsewhere. So if you want to provide hosting, do so—but either plan to get even more involved soon, or be circumspect about how much involvement you claim.

Marketing

Although most open source developers would probably hate to admit it, marketing works. A good marketing campaign *can* create buzz around an open source product, even to the point where hardheaded coders find themselves having vaguely positive thoughts about the software for reasons they can't quite put their finger on. It is not my place here to dissect the arms-race dynamics of marketing in general. Any corporation involved in free software will eventually find itself considering how to market either themselves, the software, or their relationship to the software. The advice below is about how to avoid common pitfalls in such an effort; see also "Publicity" in Chapter 6.

Remember That You Are Being Watched

For the sake of keeping the volunteer developer community on your side, it is *very* important not to say anything that isn't demonstrably true. Audit all claims carefully before making them, and give the public the means to check your claims on their own. Independent fact checking is a major part of open source, and it applies to more than just the code.

Naturally no one would advise companies to make unverifiable claims anyway. But with open source activities, there is an unusually high quantity of people with the expertise to verify claims—people who are also likely to have high-bandwidth Internet access and the right social contacts to publicize their findings in a damaging way, should they choose to. When Global Megacorp Chemical Industries pollutes a stream, that's verifiable, but only by trained scientists, who can then be refuted by Global Megacorp's scientists, leaving the public scratching their heads and wondering what to think. On the other hand, your behavior in the open source world is not only visible and recorded; it is also easy for many people to check it independently, come to their own conclusions, and spread those conclusions by word of mouth. These communications networks are already in place; they are the essence of how open source operates, and they can be used to transmit any sort of information. Refutation is usually difficult, if not impossible, especially when what people are saying is true.

For example, it's okay to refer to your organization as having "founded project X" if you really did. But don't refer to yourself as the "makers of X" if most of the code was written by outsiders. Conversely, don't claim to have a deeply involved volunteer developer community if anyone can look at your repository and see that there are few or no code changes coming from outside your organization.

Not too long ago, I saw an announcement by a very well-known computer company, stating that they were releasing an important software package under an open source license. When the initial announcement came out, I took a look at their now-public version control repository and saw that it contained only three revisions. In other words, they had done an initial import of the source code, but hardly anything had happened since then. That in itself was not worrying—they'd just made the announcement, after all. There was no reason to expect a lot of development activity right away.

Some time later, they made another announcement. Here is what it said, with the name and release number replaced by pseudonyms:

> We are pleased to announce that following rigorous testing by the Singer Community, Singer 5 for Linux and Windows are now ready for production use.

Curious to know what the community had uncovered in "rigorous testing," I went back to the repository to look at its recent change history. The project was still on revision 3. Apparently, they hadn't found a *single* bug worth fixing before the release! Thinking that the results of the community testing must have been recorded elsewhere, I next examined the bug tracker. There were exactly six open issues, four of which had been open for several months already.

This beggars belief, of course. When testers pound on a large and complex piece of software for any length of time, they will find bugs. Even if the fixes for those bugs don't make it into the upcoming release, one would still expect some version control activity as a result of the testing process, or at least some new issues. Yet to all appearances, nothing had happened between the announcement of the open source license and the first open source release.

The point is not that the company was lying about the community testing. I have no idea if they were or not. But they were oblivious to how much it *looked* like they were lying. Since neither the version control repository nor the issue tracker gave any indication that the alleged rigorous testing had occurred, the company should either not have made the claim in the first place, or provided a clear link to some tangible result of that testing ("We found 278 bugs; click here for details"). The latter would have allowed anyone to get a handle on the level of community activity very quickly. As it was, it only took me a few minutes to determine that whatever this community testing was, it had not left traces in any of the usual places. That's not a lot of effort, and I'm sure I'm not the only one who took the trouble.

Transparency and verifiability are also an important part of accurate crediting, of course. See "Credit" in Chapter 8 for more on this.

Don't Bash Competing Open Source Products

Refrain from giving negative opinions about competing open source software. It's perfectly okay to give negative *facts*—that is, easily confirmable assertions of the sort often seen in good comparison charts. But negative characterizations of a less rigorous nature are best avoided, for two reasons. First, they are liable to start flame wars that detract from productive discussion. Second, and more importantly, some of the volunteer developers in *your* project may turn out to work on the competing project as well. This is more likely than it at first might seem: the projects are already in the same domain (that's why they're in competition), and developers with expertise in that domain may make contributions wherever their expertise is applicable. Even when there is no direct developer overlap, it is likely that developers on your project are at least acquainted with developers on related projects. Their ability to maintain constructive personal ties could be hampered by overly negative marketing messages.

Bashing competing closed-source products seems to be more widely accepted in the open source world, especially when those products are made by Microsoft. Personally, I deplore this tendency (though again, there's nothing wrong with straightforward factual comparisons), not merely because it's rude, but also because it's dangerous for a project to start believing its own hype and thereby ignore the ways in which the competition may actually be superior. In general, watch out for the effect that marketing statements can have on your own development community. People may be so excited at being backed by marketing dollars that they lose objectivity about their software's true strengths and weaknesses. It is normal, and even expected, for a company's developers to exhibit a certain detachment toward marketing statements, even in public forums. Clearly, they should not come out and contradict the marketing message directly (unless it's actually wrong, though one hopes that sort of thing would have been caught earlier). But they may poke fun at it from time to time, as a way of bringing the rest of the development community back down to earth.

## CHAPTER 6

Communications

The ability to write clearly is perhaps the most important skill one can have in an open source environment. In the long run it matters more than programming talent. A great programmer with lousy communications skills can get only one thing done at a time, and even then may have trouble convincing others to pay attention. But a lousy programmer with good communications skills can coordinate and persuade many people to do many different things, and thereby have a significant effect on a project's direction and momentum.

There does not seem to be much correlation, in either direction, between the ability to write good code and the ability to communicate with one's fellow human beings. There is some correlation between programming well and describing technical issues well, but describing technical issues is only a tiny part of the communications in a project. Much more important is the ability to empathize with one's audience, to see one's own posts and comments as others see them, and to cause others to see their own posts with similar objectivity. Equally important is noticing when a given medium or communications method is no longer working well, perhaps because it doesn't scale as the number of users increases, and taking the time to do something about it.

All of which is obvious in theory—what makes it hard in practice is that free software development environments are bewilderingly diverse both in audiences and in communications mechanisms. Should a given thought be expressed in a post to the mailing list, as an annotation in the bug tracker, or as a comment in the code? When answering a question in a public forum, how much knowledge can you assume on the part of the reader, given that "the reader" is not only the one who asked the question in the first place, but all those who might see your response? How can the developers stay in constructive contact with the users, without getting swamped by feature requests, spurious bug reports, and general chatter? How do you tell when a medium has reached the limits of its capacity, and what do you do about it?

Solutions to these problems are usually partial, because any particular solution is eventually made obsolete by project growth or changes in project structure. They are also often ad hoc, because they're improvised responses to dynamic situations. All participants need is to be aware of when and how communications can become bogged down, and be involved in solutions. Helping people do this is a big part of managing an open source project. The sections that follow discuss both how to conduct your own communications, and how to make maintenance of communications mechanisms a priority for everyone in the project.[1]

You Are What You Write

Consider this: the only thing anyone knows about you on the Internet comes from what you write, or what others write about you. You may be brilliant, perceptive, and charismatic in person—but if your emails are rambling and unstructured, people will assume that's the real you. Or perhaps you really are rambling and unstructured in person, but no one need ever know it, if your posts are lucid and informative.

Devoting some care to your writing will pay off hugely. Long-time free software hacker Jim Blandy tells the following story:

> Back in 1993, I was working for the Free Software Foundation, and we were beta-testing version 19 of GNU Emacs. We'd make a beta release every week or so, and people would try it out and send us bug reports. There was this one guy whom none of us had met in person but who did great work: his bug reports were always clear and led us straight to the problem, and when he provided a fix himself, it was almost always right. He was top-notch.
>
> Now, before the FSF can use code written by someone else, we have them do some legal paperwork to assign their copyright interest to that code to the FSF. Just taking code from complete strangers and dropping it in is a recipe for legal disaster.

---

1   There has been some interesting academic research on this topic; for example, see *Group Awareness in Distributed Software Development* by Gutwin, Penner, and Schneider, at *http://hci.usask.ca/publications/2004/awareness-cscw04/*.

So I emailed the guy the forms, saying, "Here's some paperwork we need, here's what it means, you sign this one, have your employer sign that one, and then we can start putting in your fixes. Thanks very much."

He sent me back a message saying, "I don't have an employer."

So I said, "Okay, that's fine, just have your university sign it and send it back."

After a bit, he wrote me back again, and said, "Well, actually…I'm 13 years old, and I live with my parents."

Because that kid didn't write like a 13-year-old, no one knew that's what he was. Following are some ways to make your writing give a good impression too.

Structure and Formatting

Don't fall into the trap of writing everything as though it were a cell phone text message. Write in complete sentences, capitalizing the first word of each sentence, and use paragraph breaks where needed. This is most important in emails and other composed writings. In IRC or similarly ephemeral forums, it's generally okay to leave out capitalization, use compressed forms of common expressions, etc. Just don't carry those habits over into more formal, persistent forums. Emails, documentation, bug reports, and other pieces of writing that are intended to have a permanent life should be written using standard grammar and spelling, and have a coherent narrative structure. This is not because there's anything inherently good about following arbitrary rules, but rather that these rules are *not* arbitrary: they evolved into their present forms because they make text more readable, and you should adhere to them for that reason. Readability is desirable not only because it means more people will understand what you write, but because it makes you look like the sort of person who takes the time to communicate clearly: that is, someone worth paying attention to.

For email in particular, experienced open source developers have settled on certain conventions.

Send plain text mails only, not HTML, RichText, or other formats that might be opaque to text-only mail readers. Format your lines to be around 72 columns long. Don't exceed 80 columns, which has become the de facto standard terminal width (that is, some people may use wider terminals, but no one uses a narrower one). By making your lines a little *less* than 80 columns, you leave room for a few levels of quoting characters to be added in others' replies without forcing a rewrapping of your text.

Use real line breaks. Some mailers do a kind of fake line wrapping, whereby when you're composing an email, the display shows line breaks that aren't actually there.

When the mail goes out, it may not have the line breaks you thought it had, and it will wrap awkwardly on some people's screens. If your mailer might use fake line breaks, look for a setting you can tweak to make it show the true line breaks as you compose.

When including screen output, snippets of code, or other preformatted text, offset it clearly, so that even a lazy eye can easily see the boundaries between your prose and the material you're quoting. (I never expected to write that advice when I started this book, but on a number of open source mailing lists lately, I've seen people mix texts from different sources without making it clear which is which. The effect is very frustrating. It makes their posts significantly harder to understand, and frankly makes those people look a little bit disorganized.)

When quoting someone else's mail, insert your responses where they're most appropriate, at several different places if necessary, and trim off the parts of their mail you didn't use. If you're writing a quick comment that applies to their entire post, it's okay to *top-post* (that is, to put your response above the quoted text of their mail); otherwise, you should quote the relevant portion of the original text first, followed by your response.

Construct the subject lines of new mails carefully. It's the most important line in your mail, because it allows each other person in the project to decide whether or not to read more. Modern mail-reading software organizes groups of related messages into threads, which can be defined not only by a common subject, but by various other headers (which are sometimes not displayed). It follows that if a thread starts to drift to a new topic, you can—and should—adjust the subject line accordingly when replying. The thread's integrity will be preserved, due to those other headers, but the new subject will help people looking at an overview of the thread know that the topic has drifted. Likewise, if you really want to start a new topic, do it by posting a fresh mail, not by replying to an existing mail and changing the subject. Otherwise, your mail would still be grouped into the same thread as what you're replying to, and thus fool people into thinking it's about something it's not. Again, the penalty would not only be the waste of their time, but the slight dent in your credibility as someone fluent in using communications tools.

Content

Well-formatted mails attract readers, but content keeps them. No set of fixed rules can guarantee good content, of course, but there are some principles that make it more likely.

Make things easy for your readers. There's a ton of information floating around in any active open source project, and readers cannot be expected to be familiar with most of it—indeed, they cannot always be expected to know how to become familiar. Wherever possible, your posts should provide information in the form most convenient for readers. If you have to spend an extra two minutes to dig up the URL to a particular thread in the mailing list archives, in order to save your readers the trouble of doing so, it's worth it. If you have to spend an extra 5 or 10 minutes summarizing the conclusions so far of a complex thread, in order to give people context in which to understand your post, then do so. Think of it this way: the more successful a project, the higher the reader-to-writer ratio in any given forum. If every post you make is seen by *n* people, then as *n* rises, the worthwhileness of expending extra effort to save those people time rises with it. And as people see you imposing this standard on yourself, they will work to match it in their own communications. The result is, ideally, an increase in the global efficiency of the project: when there is a choice between *n* people making an effort and one person doing so, the project prefers the latter.

Don't engage in hyperbole. Exaggerating in online posts is a classic arms race. For example, a person reporting a bug may worry that the developers will not pay sufficient attention, so he'll describe it as a severe, showstopper problem that is preventing him (and all his friends/coworkers/cousins) from using the software productively, when it's actually only a mild annoyance. But exaggeration is not limited to users—programmers often do the same thing during technical debates, particularly when the disagreement is over a matter of taste rather than correctness:

> Doing it that way would make the code totally unreadable. It'd be a maintenance nightmare, compared to J. Random's proposal...

The same sentiment actually becomes *stronger* when phrased less sharply:

> That works, but it's less than ideal in terms of readability and maintainability, I think. J. Random's proposal avoids those problems because it...

You will not be able to get rid of hyperbole completely, and in general, it's not necessary to do so. Compared to other forms of miscommunication, hyperbole is not globally damaging—it hurts mainly the perpetrator. The recipients can compensate; it's just that the sender loses a little more credibility each time. Therefore, for the sake of your own influence in the project, try to err on the side of moderation. That way, when you *do* need to make a strong point, people will take you seriously.

Edit twice. For any message longer than a medium-sized paragraph, reread it from top to bottom before sending it but after you think it's done the first time. This is familiar advice to anyone who's taken a composition class, but it's especially important in online discussion. Because the process of online composition tends to be highly discontinuous (in the course of writing a message, you may need to go back and check other mails, visit certain web pages, run a command to capture its debugging output, etc.), it's especially easy to lose your sense of narrative place. Messages that were composed discontinuously and not checked before being sent are often recognizable as such, much to the chagrin (or so one would hope) of their authors. Take the time to review what you send. The more your posts hold together structurally, the more they will be read.

Tone

After writing thousands of messages, you will probably find your style tending toward the terse. This seems to be the norm in most technical forums, and there's nothing wrong with it, per se. A degree of terseness that would be unacceptable in normal social interactions is simply the default for free software hackers. Here's a response I once drew on a mailing list about some free content management software, quoted in full:

```
Can you possibly elaborate a bit more on exactly what problems
you ran into, etc?

Also:

What version of Slash are you using? I couldn't tell from your
original message.

Exactly how did you build the apache/mod_perl source?

Did you try the Apache 2.0 patch that was posted about on
slashcode.com?

    Shane
```

Now *that's* terse! No greeting, no sign-off other than his name, and the message itself is just a series of questions phrased as compactly as possible. His one declarative sentence was an implicit criticism of my original message. And yet, I was happy to see Shane's mail, and didn't take his terseness as a sign of anything other than him being a busy person. The mere fact that he was asking questions, instead of ignoring my post, meant that he was willing to spend some time on my problem.

Will all readers react positively to this style? Not necessarily; it depends on the person and the context. For example, if someone has just posted acknowledging that she made a mistake (perhaps she wrote a bug), and you know from past experience that this person tends to be a bit insecure, then while you may still write a compact response, you should make sure to leaven it with some sort of acknowledgment of her feelings. The bulk of your response might be a brief, engineer's-eye analysis of the situation, as terse as you want. But at the end, sign off with something indicating that your terseness is not to be taken as coldness. For example, if you've just given reams of advice about exactly how the person should fix the bug, then sign off with "Good luck, <your name here>" to indicate that you wish them well and are not mad. A strategically placed smiley face or other emoticlue can often be enough to reassure an interlocutor, too.

It may seem odd to focus as much on the participant's feelings as on the surface of what they say, but to put it baldly, feelings affect productivity. Feelings are important for other reasons too, but even confining ourselves to purely utilitarian grounds, we may note that unhappy people write worse software, and less of it. Given the restricted nature of most electronic media, though, there will often be no overt clue as to how a person is feeling. You will have to make an educated guess based on a) how most people would feel in that situation, and b) what you know of this particular person from past interactions. Some people prefer a more hands-off attitude, and simply deal with everyone at face value, the idea being that if a participant doesn't say outright that she feels a particular way, then one has no business treating her as though she does. I don't buy this approach, for a couple of reasons. One, people don't behave that way in real life, so why would they online? Two, since most interactions take place in public forums, people tend to be even more restrained in expressing emotions than they might be in private. To be more precise, they are often willing to express emotions directed at others, such as gratitude or outrage, but not emotions directed inwardly, such as insecurity or pride. Yet most humans work better when they know that others are aware of their state of mind. By paying attention to small clues, you can usually guess right most of the time, and motivate people to stay involved to a greater degree than they otherwise might.

I don't mean, of course, that your role is to be a group therapist, constantly helping everyone to get in touch with their feelings. But by paying careful attention to long-term patterns in people's behavior, you will begin to get a sense of them as individuals even if you never meet them face-to-face. And by being sensitive to the tone of your own writing, you can have a surprising amount of influence over how others feel, to the ultimate benefit of the project.

Recognizing Rudeness

One of the defining characteristics of open source culture is its distinctive notions of what does and does not constitute rudeness. While the conventions described below are not unique to free software development, nor even to software in general—they would be familiar to anyone working in mathematics, the hard sciences, or engineering disciplines—free software, with its porous boundaries and constant influx of newcomers, is an environment where these conventions are especially likely to be encountered by people unfamiliar with them.

Let's start with the things that are *not* rude.

Technical criticism, even when direct and unpadded, is not rude. Indeed, it can be a form of flattery: the critic is saying, by implication, that the target is worth taking seriously, and is worth spending some time on. That is, the more viable it would have been to simply ignore someone's post, the more of a compliment it becomes to take the time to criticize it (unless the critique descends into an *ad hominem* attack or some other form of obvious rudeness, of course).

Blunt, unadorned questions, such as Shane's questions to me in the previously quoted email, are not rude either. Questions that in other contexts might seem cold, rhetorical, or even mocking, are often intended seriously, and have no hidden agenda other than eliciting information as quickly as possible. The famous technical support question "Is your computer plugged in?" is a classic example of this. The support person really does need to know if your computer is plugged in, and after the first few days on the job, has gotten tired of prefixing her question with polite blandishments ("I beg your pardon, I just want to ask a few simple questions to rule out some possibilities. Some of these might seem pretty basic, but bear with me..."). At this point, she doesn't bother with the padding anymore, she just asks straight out; is it plugged in or not? Equivalent questions are asked all the time on free software mailing lists. The intent is not to insult the recipient, but to quickly rule out the most obvious (and perhaps most common) explanations. Recipients who understand this and react accordingly win points for taking a broad-minded point of view without prompting. But recipients who react badly should not be reprimanded, either. It's just a collision of cultures, not anyone's fault. Explain amiably that your question (or criticism) had no hidden meanings; it was just meant to get (or transmit) information as efficiently as possible, nothing more.

So what is rude?

By the same principle under which detailed technical criticism is a form of flattery, failure to provide quality criticism can be a kind of insult. I don't mean simply ignoring someone's work, be it proposal, code change, new issue filing, or whatever.

Unless you explicitly promised a detailed reaction in advance, it's usually okay to simply not react at all. People will assume you just didn't have time to say anything. But if you *do* react, don't skimp: take the time to really analyze things, provide concrete examples where appropriate, dig around in the archives to find related posts from the past, etc. Or if you don't have time to put in that kind of effort, but still need to write some sort of brief response, then state the shortcoming openly in your message ("I think there's an issue filed for this, but unfortunately didn't have time to search for it, sorry"). The main thing is to recognize the existence of the cultural norm, either by fulfilling it or by openly acknowledging that one has fallen short this time. Either way, the norm is strengthened. But failing to meet that norm, while at the same time not explaining *why* you failed to meet it, is like saying the topic (and those participating in it) was not worth much of your time. Better to show that your time is valuable by being terse than by being lazy.

There are many other forms of rudeness, of course, but most of them are not specific to free software development, and common sense is a good enough guide to avoid them. See also "Nip Rudeness in the Bud" in Chapter 2, if you haven't already.

Face

There is a region in the human brain devoted specifically to recognizing faces. It is known informally as the "fusiform face area," and its capabilities are mostly inborn, not learned. It turns out that recognizing individual people is such a crucial survival skill that we have evolved specialized hardware to do it.

Internet-based collaboration is therefore psychologically odd, because it involves tight cooperation between human beings who almost never get to identify each other by the most natural, intuitive methods: facial recognition first of all, but also sound of voice, posture, etc. To compensate for this, try to use a consistent *screen name* everywhere. It should be the front part of your email address (the part before the @ sign), your IRC username, your repository committer name, your issue tracker username, and so on. This name is your online "face": a short identifying string that serves some of the same purpose as your real face, although it does not, unfortunately, stimulate the same built-in hardware in the brain.

The screen name should be some intuitive permutation of your real name (mine, for example, is "kfogel"). In some situations it will be accompanied by your full name anyway, for example in mail headers:

```
From: "Karl Fogel" <kfogel@whateverdomain.com>
```

Actually, there are two things going on in that example. As mentioned earlier, the screen name matches the real name in an intuitive way. But also, the real name is *real*. That is, it's not some made-up appellation like:

```
From: "Wonder Hacker" <wonderhacker@whateverdomain.com>
```

There's a famous cartoon by Paul Steiner, from the July 5, 1993 issue of *The New Yorker*, that shows one dog logged into a computer terminal, looking down and telling another conspiratorially: "On the Internet, nobody knows you're a dog." This kind of thought probably lies behind a lot of the self-aggrandizing, meant-to-be-hip online identities people give themselves—as if calling oneself "Wonder Hacker" will actually cause people to believe one is a wonderful hacker. But the fact remains: even if no one knows you're a dog, you're still a dog. A fantastical online identity never impresses readers. Instead, it makes them think you're more into image than substance, or that you're simply insecure. Use your real name for all interactions, or if for some reason you require anonymity, then make up a name that sounds like a perfectly normal real name, and use it consistently.

In addition to keeping your online face consistent, there are some things you can do to make it more attractive. If you have an official title (e.g., "doctor," "professor," or "director"), don't flaunt it, nor even mention it except when it's directly relevant to the conversation. Hackerdom in general, and free software culture in particular, tends to view title displays as exclusionary and a sign of insecurity. It's okay if your title appears as part of a standard signature block at the end of every mail you send, just don't ever use it as a tool to bolster your position in a discussion—the attempt is guaranteed to backfire. You want folks to respect the person, not the title.

Speaking of signature blocks: keep them small and tasteful, or better yet, nonexistent. Avoid large legal disclaimers tacked on to the end of every mail, especially when they express sentiments incompatible with participation in a free software project. For example, the following classic of the genre appears at the end of every post a particular user makes to a public mailing list I'm on:

```
IMPORTANT NOTICE

If you have received this e-mail in error or wish to read our e-mail
disclaimer statement and monitoring policy, please refer to the
statement below or contact the sender.

This communication is from Deloitte & Touche LLP.  Deloitte &
Touche LLP is a limited liability partnership registered in England
and Wales with registered number OC303675.  A list of members' names
is available for inspection at Stonecutter Court, 1 Stonecutter
```

For someone who's just showing up to ask a question now and then, that huge disclaimer looks a bit silly but probably doesn't do any lasting harm. However, if this person wanted to participate actively in the project, that legal boilerplate would start to have a more insidious effect. It would send at least two potentially destructive signals: first, that this person doesn't have full control over his tools—he's trapped inside some corporate mailer that tacks an annoying message to the end of every email, and he hasn't got any way to route around it—and second, that he has little or no organizational support for his free software activities. True, the organization has clearly not banned him outright from posting to public lists, but it has made his posts look distinctly unwelcoming, as though the risk of letting out confidential information must trump all other priorities.

If you work for an organization that insists on adding such signature blocks to all outgoing mail, consider getting a free email account from, for example, *gmail.google.com*, *www.hotmail.com*, or *www.yahoo.com*, and using that as your address for the project.

Avoiding Common Pitfalls

Email lists can be highly efficient, but their use can also drag people into activities that waste a lot of time. This is sometimes because postings are spread over time, and nobody really pays attention to whether the postings contribute to the purpose of the list. In any case, certain subtle patterns of disfunctioning have been observed over and over.

Don't Post Without a Purpose

A common pitfall in online project participation is to think that you have to respond to everything. You don't. First of all, there will usually be more threads going on than you can keep track of, at least after the project is past its first few months. Second, even in the threads that you have decided to engage in, much of what people say will not require a response. Development forums in particular tend to be dominated by three kinds of messages:

- Messages proposing something non-trivial
- Messages expressing support or opposition to something someone else has said
- Summing-up messages

None of these *inherently* requires a response, particularly if you can be fairly sure, based on watching the thread so far, that someone else is likely to say what you would have said anyway. (If you're worried that you'll be caught in a wait-wait loop because all the others are using this tactic too, don't be; there's almost always *someone* out there who'll feel like jumping into the fray.) A response should be motivated by a definite purpose. Ask yourself first: do you know what you want to accomplish? And second: will it not get accomplished unless you say something?

Two good reasons to add your voice to a thread are a) when you see a flaw in a proposal and suspect that you're the only one who sees it, and b) when you see that miscommunication is happening between others, and know that you can fix it with a clarifying post. It's also generally fine to post just to thank someone for doing something, or to say "Me too!", because a reader can tell right away that such posts do not require any response or further action, and therefore the mental effort demanded by the post ends cleanly when the reader reaches the last line of the mail. But even then, think twice before saying something; it's always better to leave people wishing you'd post more than wishing you'd post less. (See the second half of Appendix C for more thoughts about how to behave on a busy mailing list.)

Productive Versus Unproductive Threads

On a busy mailing list, you have two imperatives. One, obviously, is to figure out what you need to pay attention to and what you can ignore. The other is to behave in a way that avoids *causing* noise: not only do you want your own posts to have a high signal/noise ratio, you also want them to be the sorts of messages that stimulate *other* people to either post with a similarly high signal/noise ratio, or not post at all.

To see how to do that, let's consider the context in which it is done. What are some of the hallmarks of an unproductive thread?

- Arguments that have been made already start being repeated, as though the poster thinks no one heard them the first time.

- Levels of hyperbole and involvement increase as the stakes get smaller and smaller.

- A majority of comments are coming from people who do little or nothing, while the people who tend to get things done are silent.

- Many ideas are discussed without clear proposals ever being made. (Of course, any interesting idea starts out as an imprecise vision; the important question is what direction it goes from there. Does the thread seem to be turning the vision into something more concrete, or is it spinning off into sub-visions, side-visions, and ontological disputes?)

Just because a thread is not productive at first doesn't mean it's a waste of time. It might be about an important topic, in which case the fact that it's not making any headway is all the more troublesome.

Guiding a thread toward usefulness without being pushy is an art. It won't work to simply admonish people to stop wasting their time, or to ask them not to post unless they have something constructive to say. You may, of course, think these things privately, but if you say them out loud then you will be offensive. Instead, you have to suggest conditions for further progress—give people a route, a path to follow that leads to the results you want, yet without sounding like you're dictating conduct. The distinction is largely one of tone. For example, this is bad:

> This discussion is going nowhere. Can we please drop this topic until someone has a patch to implement one of these proposals? There's no reason to keep going around and around saying the same things. Code speaks louder than words, folks.

Whereas this is good:

> Several proposals have been floated in this thread, but none have had all the
> details fleshed out, at least not enough for an up-or-down vote. Yet we're also
> not saying anything new now; we're just reiterating what has been said before.
> So the best thing at this point would probably be for further posts to contain
> either a complete specification for the proposed behavior, or a patch. Then at
> least we'd have a definite action to take (i.e., get consensus on the specification,
> or apply and test the patch).

Contrast the second approach with the first. The second way does not draw a line
between you and the others, or accuse them of taking the discussion into a spiral. It
talks about "we," which is important whether or not you actually participated in the
thread before now, because it reminds everyone that even those who have been silent
thus far still have a stake in the thread's outcome. It describes why the thread is
going nowhere, but does so without pejoratives or judgements—it just dispassionately states some facts. Most importantly, it offers a positive course of action, so that
instead of people feeling like discussion is being closed off (a restriction against
which they can only be tempted to rebel), they will feel as if they're being offered a
way to take the conversation to a more constructive level. This is a standard people
will naturally want to meet.

You won't always want a thread to make it to the next level of constructiveness—
sometimes you'll want it to just go away. The purpose of your post, then, is to make
it do one or the other. If you can tell from the way the thread has gone so far that no
one is actually *going* to take the steps you suggested, then your post effectively shuts
down the thread without seeming to do so. Of course, there isn't any foolproof way
to shut down a thread, and even if there were, you wouldn't want to use it. But asking participants to either make visible progress or stop posting is perfectly defensi-
ble, if done diplomatically. Be wary of quashing threads prematurely, however. Some
amount of speculative chatter can be productive, depending on the topic, and asking
for it to be resolved too quickly will stifle the creative process, as well as make you
look impatient.

Don't expect any thread to stop on a dime. There will probably still be a few posts
after yours, either because mails got crossed in the pipe, or because people want to
have the last word. This is nothing to worry about, and you don't need to post again.
Just let the thread peter out, or not peter out, as the case may be. You can't have
complete control; on the other hand, you can expect to have a statistically significant
effect across many threads.

The Softer the Topic, the Longer the Debate

Although discussion can meander in any topic, the probability of meandering goes up as the technical difficulty of the topic goes down. After all, the greater the technical difficulty, the fewer participants can really follow what's going on. Those who can are likely to be the most experienced developers, who have already taken part in such discussions thousands of times before and know what sort of behavior is likely to lead to a consensus everyone can live with.

Thus, consensus is hardest to achieve in technical questions that are simple to understand and easy to have an opinion about, and in "soft" topics such as organization, publicity, funding, etc. People can participate in those arguments forever, because there are no qualifications necessary for doing so and no clear ways to decide (even afterward) if a decision was right or wrong. In addition, simply outwaiting other discussants is sometimes a successful tactic.

The principle that the amount of discussion is inversely proportional to the complexity of the topic has been around for a long time, and is known informally as the *Bikeshed Effect*. Here is Poul-Henning Kamp's explanation of it, from a now-famous post made to BSD developers:

> It's a long story, or rather it's an old story, but it is quite short actually. C. Northcote Parkinson wrote a book in the early 1960s, called "Parkinson's Law," which contains a lot of insight into the dynamics of management.
>
> [...]
>
> In the specific example involving the bikeshed, the other vital component is an atomic power-plant, I guess that illustrates the age of the book.
>
> Parkinson shows how you can go in to the board of directors and get approval for building a multi-million or even billion dollar atomic power plant, but if you want to build a bikeshed you will be tangled up in endless discussions.
>
> Parkinson explains that this is because an atomic plant is so vast, so expensive and so complicated that people cannot grasp it, and rather than try, they fall back on the assumption that somebody else checked all the details before it got this far. Richard P. Feynmann gives a couple of interesting, and very much to the point, examples relating to Los Alamos in his books.
>
> A bikeshed on the other hand. Anyone can build one of those over a weekend, and still have time to watch the game on TV. So no matter how well prepared, no matter how reasonable you are with your proposal, somebody will seize the chance to show that he is doing his job, that he is paying attention, that he is *here*.

In Denmark we call it "setting your fingerprint". It is about personal pride and prestige, it is about being able to point somewhere and say "There! *I* did that." It is a strong trait in politicians, but present in most people given the chance. Just think about footsteps in wet cement.

His complete post is very much worth reading, too. See Appendix C.

Anyone who's ever taken regular part in group decision-making will recognize what Kamp is talking about. However, it is usually impossible to persuade *everyone* to avoid painting bikesheds. The best you can do is point out that the phenomenon exists, when you see it happening, and persuade the senior developers—the people whose posts carry the most weight—to drop their paintbrushes early, so at least they're not contributing to the noise. Bikeshed painting parties will never go away entirely, but you can make them shorter and less frequent by spreading an awareness of the phenomenon in the project's culture.

Avoid Holy Wars

A *holy war* is a dispute, often but not always over a relatively minor issue, which is not resolvable on the merits of the arguments, but where people feel passionate enough to continue arguing anyway in the hope that their side will prevail. Holy wars are not quite the same as bikeshed paintings. People painting bikesheds are usually quick to jump in with an opinion (because they can), but they won't necessarily feel strongly about it, and indeed will sometimes express other, incompatible opinions, to show that they understand all sides of the issue. In a holy war, on the other hand, understanding the other sides is a sign of weakness. In a holy war, everyone knows there is One Right Answer; they just don't agree on what it is.

Once a holy war has started, it generally cannot be resolved to everyone's satisfaction. It does no good to point out, in the midst of a holy war, that a holy war is going on. Everyone knows that already. Unfortunately, a common feature of holy wars is disagreement on the very question of *whether* the dispute is resolvable by continued discussion. Viewed from outside, it is clear that neither side is changing the other's mind. Viewed from inside, the other side is being obtuse and not thinking clearly, but they might come around if browbeaten enough. Now, I am *not* saying there's never a right side in a holy war. Sometimes there is—in the holy wars I've participated in, it's always been my side, of course. But it doesn't matter, because there's no algorithm for convincingly demonstrating that one side or the other is right.

A common, but unsatisfactory, way people try to resolve holy wars is to say "We've already spent far more time and energy discussing this than it's worth! Can we please just drop it?" There are two problems with this. First, that time and energy has already been spent and can never be recovered—the only question now is, how much *more* effort remains? If some people feel that just a little more discussion will bring the issue to a close, then it still makes sense (from their point of view) to continue.

The other problem with asking for the matter to be dropped is that this is often equivalent to allowing one side, the status quo, to declare victory by inaction. And in some cases, the status quo is known to be unacceptable anyway: everyone agrees that some decision must be made, some action taken. Dropping the subject would be worse for everyone than simply giving up the argument would be for anyone. But since that dilemma applies to all equally, it's still possible to end up arguing forever about what to do.

So how should you handle holy wars?

The first answer is, try to set things up so they don't happen. This is not as hopeless as it sounds.

You can anticipate certain standard holy wars: they tend to come up over programming languages, licenses (see "The GPL and License Compatibility" in Chapter 9), reply-to munging (see "The Great Reply-to Debate" in Chapter 3), and a few other topics. Each project usually has a holy war or two all its own, as well, which long-time developers will quickly become familiar with. The techniques for stopping holy wars, or at least limiting their damage, are pretty much the same everywhere. Even if you are positive your side is right, try to find *some* way to express sympathy and understanding for the points the other side is making. Often the problem in a holy war is that because each side has built its walls as high as possible, and made it clear that any other opinion is sheer foolishness, the act of surrendering or changing one's mind becomes psychologically unbearable: it would be an admission not just of being wrong, but of having been *certain* and still being wrong. The way you can make this admission palatable for the other side is to express some uncertainty yourself—precisely by showing that you understand the arguments they are making and find them at least sensible, if not finally persuasive. Make a gesture that provides space for a reciprocal gesture, and usually the situation will improve. You are no more or less likely to get the technical result you wanted, but at least you can avoid unnecessary collateral damage to the project's morale.

When a holy war can't be avoided, decide early how much you care, and then be willing to publicly give up. When you do so, you can say that you're backing out because the holy war isn't worth it, but don't express any bitterness and *don't* take the opportunity for a last parting shot at the opposing side's arguments. Giving up is effective only when done gracefully.

Programming language holy wars are a bit of a special case, because they are often highly technical, yet many people feel qualified to take part in them, and the stakes are very high, since the result may determine what language a good portion of the project's code is written in. The best solution is to choose the language early, with buy-in from influential initial developers, and then defend it on the grounds that it's what you are all comfortable writing in, *not* on the grounds that it's better than some other language that could have been used instead. Never let the conversation degenerate into an academic comparison of programming languages (this seems to happen especially often when someone brings up Perl, for some reason); that's a death topic that you must simply refuse to be drawn into.

For more historical background on holy wars, see *http://catb.org/~esr/jargon/html/H/holy-wars.html*, and the paper by Danny Cohen that popularized the term, *http://www.ietf.org/rfc/ien/ien137.txt*.

The "Noisy Minority" Effect

In any mailing list discussion, it's easy for a small minority to give the impression that there is a great deal of dissent, by flooding the list with numerous lengthy emails. It's a bit like a filibuster, except that the illusion of widespread dissent is even more powerful, because it's divided across an arbitrary number of discrete posts and most people won't bother to keep track of who said what, when. They'll just have an instinctive impression that the topic is very controversial, and wait for the fuss to die down.

The best way to counteract this effect is to point it out very clearly and provide supporting evidence showing how small the actual number of dissenters is, compared to those in agreement. In order to increase the disparity, you may want to privately poll people who have been mostly silent, but who you suspect would agree with the majority. Don't say anything that suggests the dissenters were deliberately trying to inflate the impression they were making. Chances are they weren't, and even if they were, there would be no strategic advantage to pointing it out. All you need do is show the actual numbers in a side-by-side comparison, and people will realize that their intuition of the situation does not match reality.

This advice doesn't just apply to issues with clear for-and-against positions. It applies to any discussion where a fuss is being made, but it's not clear that most people consider the issue under discussion to be a real problem. After a while, if you agree that the issue is not worthy of action, and can see that it has failed to get much traction (even if it has generated a lot of mails), you can just observe publicly that it's not getting traction. If the "Noisy Minority" effect has been at work, your post will seem like a breath of fresh air. Most people's impression of the discussion up to that point will have been somewhat murky: "Huh, it sure feels like there's some big deal here, because there sure are a lot of posts, but I can't see any clear progress happening." By explaining how the form of the discussion made it appear more turbulent than it really was, you retrospectively give it a new shape, through which people can recast their understanding of what transpired.

Difficult People

Difficult people are no easier to deal with in electronic forums than they are in person. By "difficult" I don't mean "rude." Rude people are annoying, but they're not necessarily difficult. This book has already discussed how to handle them: comment on the rudeness the first time, and from then on, either ignore them or treat them the same as anyone else. If they continue being rude, they will usually make themselves so unpopular as to have no influence on others in the project, so they are a self-containing problem.

The really difficult cases are people who are not overtly rude, but who manipulate or abuse the project's processes in a way that ends up costing other people time and energy, yet do not bring any benefit to the project. Such people often look for wedge-points in the project's procedures, to give themselves more influence than they might otherwise have. This is much more insidious than mere rudeness, because neither the behavior nor the damage it causes is apparent to casual observers. A classic example is the filibuster, in which someone (always sounding as reasonable as possible, of course) keeps claiming that the matter under discussion is not ready for resolution, and offers more and more possible solutions, or new viewpoints on old solutions, when what is really going on is that he senses that a consensus or a ballot is about to form, and doesn't like where it is probably headed. Another example is when there's a debate that won't converge on consensus, but the group tries to at least clarify the points of disagreement and produce a summary for everyone to refer to from then on. The obstructionist, who knows the summary may lead to a result he doesn't like, will often try to delay even the summary, by relentlessly complicating the question of what should be in it, either by objecting to reasonable suggestions or by introducing unexpected new items.

Handling Difficult People

To counteract such behavior, it helps to understand the mentality of those who engage in it. People generally do not do it consciously. No one wakes up in the morning and says to himself, "Today I'm going to cynically manipulate procedural forms in order to be an irritating obstructionist." Instead, such actions are often preceded by a semi-paranoid feeling of being shut out of group interactions and decisions. The person feels he is not being taken seriously, or (in the more severe cases) that there is almost a conspiracy against him—that the other project members have decided to form an exclusive club, of which he is not a member. This then justifies, in his mind, taking rules literally and engaging in a formal manipulation of the project's procedures, in order to *make* everyone else take him seriously. In extreme cases, the person can even believe that he is fighting a lonely battle to save the project from itself.

It is the nature of such an attack from within that not everyone will notice it at the same time, and some people may not see it at all unless presented with very strong evidence. This means that neutralizing it can be quite a bit of work. It's not enough to persuade yourself that it's happening; you have to marshal enough evidence to persuade others too, and then you have to distribute that evidence in a thoughtful way.

Given that it's so much work to fight, it's often better just to tolerate it for a while. Think of it like a parasitic but mild disease: if it's not too debilitating, the project can afford to remain infected, and medicine might have harmful side effects. However, if it gets too damaging to tolerate, then it's time for action. Start gathering notes on the patterns you see. Make sure to include references to public archives—this is one of the reasons the project keeps records, so you might as well use them. Once you've got a good case built, start having private conversations with other project participants. Don't tell them what you've observed; instead, first ask them what they've observed. This may be your last chance to get unfiltered feedback about how others see the troublemaker's behavior; once you start openly talking about it, opinion will become polarized and no one will be able to remember what she formerly thought about the matter.

If private discussions indicate that at least some others see the problem too, then it's time to do something. That's when you have to get *really* cautious, because it's very easy for this sort of person to try to make it appear as though you're picking on him unfairly. Whatever you do, never accuse him of maliciously abusing the project's procedures, of being paranoid, or, in general, of any of the other things that you suspect are probably true. Your strategy should be to look both more reasonable and more concerned with the overall welfare of the project, with the goal of either reforming the person's behavior, or getting him to go away permanently. Depending on the other developers, and your relationship with them, it may be advantageous to gather allies privately first. Or it may not; that might just create ill will behind the scenes, if people think you're engaging in an improper whispering campaign.

Remember that although the other person may be the one behaving destructively, *you* will be the one who appears destructive if you make a public charge that you can't back up. Be sure to have plenty of examples to demonstrate what you're saying, and say it as gently as possible while still being direct. You may not persuade the person in question, but that's okay as long as you persuade everyone else.

Case Study

I remember only one situation, in more than 10 years of working in free software, where things got so bad that we actually had to ask someone to stop posting altogether. As is so often the case, he was not rude, and sincerely wanted only to be helpful. He just didn't know when to post and when not to post. Our lists were open to the public, and he was posting so often, and asking questions on so many different topics, that it was getting to be a noise problem for the community. We'd already tried asking him nicely to do a little more research for answers before posting, but that had no effect.

The strategy that finally worked is a perfect example of how to build a strong case on neutral, quantitative data. One of our developers did some digging in the archives, and then sent the following message privately to a few developers. The offender (the third name on the list below, shown here as "J. Random") had very little history with the project, and had contributed no code or documentation. Yet he was the third most active poster on the mailing lists:

```
From: "Brian W. Fitzpatrick" <fitz@collab.net>
To: [... recipient list omitted for anonymity ...]
Subject: The Subversion Energy Sink
Date: Wed, 12 Nov 2003 23:37:47 -0600

In the last 25 days, the top 6 posters to the svn [dev|users] list have
been:

    294  kfogel@collab.net
    236  "C. Michael Pilato" <cmpilato@collab.net>
    220  "J. Random" <jrandom@problematic-poster.com>
    176  Branko Čibej <brane@xbc.nu>
    130  Philip Martin <philip@codematters.co.uk>
    126  Ben Collins-Sussman <sussman@collab.net>

I would say that five of these people are contributing to Subversion
hitting 1.0 in the near future.

I would also say that one of these people is consistently drawing time
and energy from the other 5, not to mention the list as a whole, thus
```

```
(albeit unintentionally) slowing the development of Subversion.  I did
not do a threaded analysis, but vgrepping my Subversion mail spool tells
me that every mail from this person is responded to at least once by at
least 2 of the other 5 people on the above list.

I think some sort of radical intervention is necessary here, even if we
do scare the aforementioned person away.  Niceties and kindness have
already proven to have no effect.

dev@subversion is a mailing list to facilitate development of a version
control system, not a group therapy session.

-Fitz, attempting to wade through three days of svn mail that he let
 pile up
```

Though it might not seem so at first, J. Random's behavior was a classic case of abusing project procedures. He wasn't doing something obvious like trying to filibuster a vote, but he was taking advantage of the mailing list's policy of relying on self-moderation by its members. We left it to each individual's judgement when to post and on what topics. Thus, we had no procedural recourse for dealing with someone who either did not have, or would not exercise, such judgement. There was no rule one could point to and say the fellow was violating it, yet everyone knew that his frequent posting was getting to be a serious problem.

Fitz's strategy was, in retrospect, masterful. He gathered damning quantitative evidence, but then distributed it discreetly, sending it first to a few people whose support would be key in any drastic action. They agreed that some sort of action was necessary, and in the end we called J. Random on the phone, described the problem to him directly, and asked him to simply stop posting. He never really did understand the reasons why; if he had been capable of understanding, he probably would have exercised appropriate judgement in the first place. But he agreed to stop posting, and the mailing lists became usable again. Part of the reason this strategy worked was, perhaps, the implicit threat that we could start restricting his posts via the moderation software normally used for preventing spam (see "Spam Prevention" in Chapter 3). But the reason we were able to have that option in reserve was that Fitz had gathered the necessary support from key people first.

Handling Growth

The price of success is heavy in the open source world. As your software gets more popular, the number of people who show up looking for information increases dramatically, while the number of people able to provide information increases much more slowly. Furthermore, even if the ratio were evenly balanced, there is still a fundamental scalability problem with the way most open source projects handle communications. Consider mailing lists, for example. Most projects have a mailing list for general user questions—sometimes the list's name is "users," "discuss," "help," or something else. Whatever its name, the purpose of the list is always the same: to provide a place where people can get their questions answered, while others watch and (presumably) absorb knowledge from observing these exchanges.

These mailing lists work very well up to a few thousand users and/or a couple of hundred posts a day. But somewhere after that, the system starts to break down, because every subscriber sees every post; if the number of posts to the list begins to exceed what any individual reader can process in a day, the list becomes a burden to its members. Imagine, for instance, if Microsoft had such a mailing list for Windows XP. Windows XP has hundreds of millions of users; if even one-tenth of one percent of them had questions in a given 24-hour period, then this hypothetical list would get hundreds of thousands of posts per day! Such a list could never exist, of course, because no one would stay subscribed to it. This problem is not limited to mailing lists; the same logic applies to IRC channels, online discussion forums, indeed to any system in which a group hears questions from individuals. The implications are ominous: the usual open source model of massively parallelized support simply does not scale to the levels needed for world domination.

There will be no explosion when forums reach the breaking point. There is just a quiet negative feedback effect: people unsubscribe from the lists, leave the IRC channel, or at any rate stop bothering to ask questions because they can see they won't be heard in all the noise. As more and more people make this highly rational choice, the forum's activity will seem to stay at a manageable level. But it is staying manageable precisely because the rational (or at least experienced) people have started looking elsewhere for information—while the inexperienced people stay behind and continue posting. In other words, one side effect of continuing to use unscalable communications models as the project grows is that the average quality of both questions and answers tends to go down, which makes it look like new users are dumber than they used to be, when in fact they're probably not. It's just that the benefit/cost ratio of using those high-population forums goes down, so naturally those with the experience to do so start to look elsewhere for answers first. Adjusting communications mechanisms to cope with project growth therefore involves two related strategies.

- Strategy 1: Recognizing when particular parts of a forum are *not* suffering unbounded growth, even if the forum as a whole is, and separating those parts off into new, more specialized forums (i.e., don't let the good be dragged down by the bad).

- Strategy 2: Making sure there are many automated sources of information available, and that they are kept organized, up-to-date, and easy to find.

Strategy 1 is usually not too hard. Most projects start out with one main forum: a general discussion mailing list, on which feature ideas, design questions, and coding problems can all be hashed out. Everyone involved with the project is on the list. After a while, it usually becomes clear that the list has evolved into several distinct topic-based sublists. For example, some threads are clearly about development and design; others are user questions of the "How do I do X?" variety; maybe there's a third topic family centered around processing bug reports and enhancement requests; and so on. A given individual, of course, might participate in many different thread types, but the important thing is that there is not a lot of overlap between the types themselves. They could be divided into separate lists without causing any harmful balkanization, because the threads rarely cross topic boundaries.

Actually doing this division is a two-step process. You create the new list (or IRC channel, or whatever it is to be), and then you spend whatever time is necessary gently nagging and reminding people to *use* the new forums appropriately. That latter step can last for weeks, but eventually people will get the idea. You simply have to make a point of always telling the sender when a post is sent to the wrong destination, and do so visibly, so that other people are encouraged to help out with routing. It's also useful to have a web page providing a guide to all the lists available; your responses can simply reference that web page and, as a bonus, the recipient may learn something about looking for guidelines before posting.

Strategy 2 is an ongoing process, lasting the lifetime of the project and involving many participants. Of course it is partly a matter of having up-to-date documentation (see "Documentation" in Chapter 2) and making sure to point people there. But it is also much more than that; the sections that follow discuss this strategy in detail.

Conspicuous Use of Archives

Typically, all communications in an open source project (except sometimes IRC conversations) are archived. The archives are public and searchable, and have referential stability: that is, once a given piece of information is recorded at a particular address, it stays at that address forever.

Use those archives as much as possible, and as conspicuously as possible. Even when you know the answer to some question off the top of your head, if you think there's a reference in the archives that contains the answer, spend the time to dig it up and present it. Every time you do that in a publicly visible way, some people learn for the first time that the archives are there, and that searching in them can produce answers. Also, by referring to the archives instead of rewriting the advice, you reinforce the social norm against duplicating information. Why have the same answer in two different places? When the number of places it can be found is kept to a minimum, people who have found it before are more likely to remember what to search for to find it again. Well-placed references also contribute to the quality of search results in general, because they strengthen the targeted resource's ranking in Internet search engines.

There are times when duplicating information makes sense, however. For example, suppose there's a response already in the archives, not from you, saying:

```
It appears that your Scanley indexes have become frobnicated.  To
unfrobnicate them, run these steps:

1. Shut down the Scanley server.
2. Run the 'defrobnicate' program that ships with Scanley.
3. Start up the server.
```

Then, months later, you see another post indicating that someone's indexes have become frobnicated. You search the archives and come up with the old response above, but you realize it's missing some steps (perhaps by mistake, or perhaps because the software has changed since that post was written). The classiest way to handle this is to post a new, more complete set of instructions, and explicitly obsolete the old post by mentioning it:

```
It appears that your Scanley indexes have become frobnicated.  We
saw this problem back in July, and J. Random posted a solution at
http://blahblahblah/blah.  Below is a more complete description of
how to unfrobnicate your indexes, based on J. Random's instructions
but extending them a bit:

1. Shut down the Scanley server.
2. Become the user the Scanley server normally runs as.
3. As that user, run the 'defrobnicate' program on the indexes.
4. Run Scanley by hand to see if the indexes work now.
5. Restart the server.
```

(In an ideal world, it would be possible to attach a note to the old post, saying that there is newer information available and pointing to the new post. However, I don't know of any archiving software that offers an "obsoleted by" feature, perhaps because it would be mildly tricky to implement in a way that doesn't violate the archives' integrity as a verbatim record. This is another reason why creating dedicated web pages with answers to common questions is a good idea.)

Archives are probably most often searched for answers to technical questions, but their importance to the project goes well beyond that. If a project's formal guidelines are its statutory law, the archives are its common law: a record of all decisions made and how they were arrived at. In any recurring discussion, it's pretty much obligatory nowadays to start with an archive search. This allows you to begin the discussion with a summary of the current state of things, anticipate objections, prepare rebuttals, and possibly discover angles you hadn't thought of. Also, the other participants will *expect* you to have done an archive search. Even if the previous discussions went nowhere, you should include pointers to them when you re-raise the topic, so people can see for themselves a) that they went nowhere, and b) that you did your homework, and therefore are probably saying something now that has not been said before.

Treat all resources like archives

All of the preceding advice applies to more than just mailing list archives. Having particular pieces of information at stable, conveniently findable addresses should be an organizing principle for all of the project's information. Let's take the project FAQ as a case study.

How do people use a FAQ?

1. They want to search in it for specific words and phrases.
2. They want to browse it, soaking up information without necessarily looking for answers to specific questions.
3. They expect search engines such as Google to know about the FAQ's content, so that searches can result in FAQ entries.
4. They want to be able to refer other people directly to specific items in the FAQ.
5. They want to be able to add new material to the FAQ. But note that this happens much less often than answers are looked up—FAQs are far more often read from than written to.

Point 1 implies that the FAQ should be available in some sort of textual format. Points 2 and 3 imply that the FAQ should be available as an HTML page, with point 2 additionally indicating that the HTML should be designed for readability (i.e., you'll want some control over its look and feel), and should have a table of contents. Point 4 means that each individual entry in the FAQ should be assigned an HTML *named anchor*, a tag that allows people to reach a particular location on the page. Point 5 means the source files for the FAQ should be available in a convenient way (see "Version everything" in Chapter 3), in a format that's easy to edit.

Formatting the FAQ like this is just one example of how to make a resource presentable. The same properties—direct searchability, availability to major Internet search engines, browseability, referential stability, and (where applicable) editability—apply to other web pages, the source code tree, the bug tracker, etc. It just happens that most mailing list archiving software long ago recognized the importance of these properties, which is why mailing lists tend to have this functionality natively, while other formats may require some extra effort on the maintainer's part (Chapter 8 discusses how to spread that maintenance burden across many volunteers).

Codifying Tradition

As a project acquires history and complexity, the amount of data each incoming participant must absorb increases. Those who have been with the project a long time were able to learn, and invent, the project's conventions as they went along. They will often not be consciously aware of what a huge body of tradition has accumulated, and may be surprised at how many missteps recent newcomers seem to make. Of course, the issue is not that the newcomers are of any lower quality than before; it's that they face a bigger acculturation burden than newcomers did in the past.

The traditions a project accumulates are as much about how to communicate and preserve information as they are about coding standards and other technical minutae. We've already looked at both sorts of standards, in "Developer documentation" in Chapter 2 and "Writing It All Down" in Chapter 4 respectively, and examples are given there. What this section is about is how to keep such guidelines up-to-date as the project evolves, especially guidelines about how communications are managed, because those are the ones that change the most as the project grows in size and complexity.

First, watch for patterns in how people get confused. If you see the same situations coming up over and over, especially with new participants, chances are there is a guideline that needs to be documented but isn't. Second, don't get tired of saying the same things over and over again, and don't *sound* like you're tired of saying them. You and other project veterans will have to repeat yourselves often; this is an inevitable side effect of the arrival of newcomers.

Named Anchors and ID Attributes

There are two ways to get a browser to jump to a specific location within a web page: named anchors and ID attributes.

A *named anchor* is just a normal HTML anchor element (<a>...</a>), but with a "name" attribute:

```
<a name="mylabel">...</a>
```

More recent versions of HTML support a generic *ID attribute*, which can be attached to any HTML element, not just to <a>. For example:

```
<p id="mylabel">...</p>
```

Both named anchors and ID attributes are used in the same way. One appends a hash mark and the label to a URL, to cause the browser to jump straight to that spot in the page:

```
http://myproject.example.com/faq.html#mylabel
```

Virtually all browsers support named anchors; most modern browsers support the ID attribute. To play it safe, I would recommend using either named anchors alone, or named anchors *and* ID attributes together (with the same label for both in a given pair, of course). For reasons mysterious to me, doing named anchors as self-closing tags does not seem to work. So even if there's no text inside the element, you should still write it in two-sided form:

```
<a name="mylabel"></a>
```

...though normally there would be some text, such as the title of a section.

Whether you use a named anchor, an ID attribute, or both, remember that the label will not be visible to someone who browses to that location without using the label. But such a person might want to discover the label for a particular location, so she can mail the URL for a FAQ answer to a friend, for example. To help her do this, add a *title attribute* to the same element(s) where you added the "name" and/or "ID" attribute, for example:

```
<a name="mylabel" title="#mylabel">...</a>
```

When the mouse pointer is held over the text inside the title-attributed element, most browsers will pop up a tiny box showing the title. I usually include the hash sign, to remind the user that this is what she would put at the end of the URL to jump straight to this location next time.

Every web page, every mailing list message, and every IRC channel should be considered advertising space—not for commercial advertisements, but for ads about your project's own resources. What you put in that space depends on the demographics of those likely to read it. An IRC channel for user questions, for example, is likely to get people who have never interacted with the project before—often someone who has just installed the software, and has a question he'd like answered immediately (after all, if it could wait, he'd have sent it to a mailing list instead, which would probably use less of his total time, although it would take longer for an answer to come back). People usually don't make a permanent investment in the IRC channel; they'll show up, ask their question, and leave.

Therefore, the channel topic should be aimed at people looking for technical answers about the software *right now*, rather than at, say, people who might get involved with the project in a long term way and for whom community interaction guidelines might be more appropriate. Here's how a really busy channel handles it (compare this with the earlier example in "IRC/Real-Time Chat Systems" in Chapter 3):

```
You are now talking on #linuxhelp

Topic for #linuxhelp is Please READ
http://www.catb.org/~esr/faqs/smart-questions.html &&
http://www.tldp.org/docs.html#howto BEFORE asking questions | Channel
rules are at http://www.nerdfest.org/lh_rules.html | Please consult
http://kerneltrap.org/node/view/799 before asking about upgrading to a
2.6.x kernel | memory read possible: http://tinyurl.com/4s6mc ->
update to 2.6.8.1 or 2.4.27 | hash algo disaster: http://tinyurl.com/6w8rf
| reiser4 out
```

With mailing lists, the "ad space" is a tiny footer appended to every message. Most projects put subscription/unsubscription instructions there, and perhaps a pointer to the project's home page or FAQ page as well. You might think that anyone subscribed to the list would know where to find those things, and they probably do—but many more people than just subscribers see those mailing list messages. An archived post may be linked to from many places; indeed, some posts become so widely known that they eventually have more readers off the list than on it.

Formatting can make a big difference. For example, in the Subversion project, we were having limited success using the bug-filtering technique described in "Prefiltering the Bug Tracker" in Chapter 3. Many bogus bug reports were still being filed by inexperienced people, and each time it happened, the filer had to be educated in exactly the same way as the 500 people before him. One day, after one of our developers had finally gotten to the end of his rope and flamed some poor user who didn't read the issue tracker guidelines carefully enough, another developer decided this pattern had gone on long enough. He suggested that we reformat the issue tracker front page so that the most important part, the injunction to discuss the bug on the mailing lists or IRC channels before filing, would stand out in huge, bold red letters, on a bright yellow background, centered prominently above everything else on the page. We did so (you can see the results at *http://subversion.tigris.org/project_issues.html*), and the result was a noticeable drop in the rate of bogus issue filings. We still get them, of course—we always will—but the rate has slowed considerably, even as the number of users increases. The outcome is not only that the bug database contains less junk, but that those who respond to issue filings stay in a better mood, and are more likely to remain friendly when responding to one of the now-rare bogus filings. This improves both the project's image and the mental health of its volunteers.

The lesson for us was that merely writing up the guidelines was not enough. We also had to put them where they'd be seen by those who need them most, and format them in such a way that their status as introductory material would be immediately clear to people unfamiliar with the project.

Static web pages are not the only venue for advertising the project's customs. A certain amount of interactive policing (in the friendly-reminder sense, not the handcuffs-and-jail sense) is also required. All peer review, even the commit reviews described in "Practice Conspicuous Code Review" in Chapter 2, should include review of people's conformance or non-conformance with project norms, especially with regard to communications conventions.

Another example from the Subversion project: we settled on a convention of "r12908" to mean "revision 12908 in the version control repository." The lowercase "r" prefix is easy to type, and because it's half the height of the digits, it makes an easily-recognizable block of text when combined with the digits. Of course, settling on the convention doesn't mean that everyone will begin using it consistently right away. Thus, when a commit mail comes in with a log message like this:

```
------------------------------------------------------------------------
r12908 | qsimon | 2005-02-02 14:15:06 -0600 (Wed, 02 Feb 2005) | 4 lines

Patch from J. Random Contributor <jrcontrib@gmail.com>

* trunk/contrib/client-side/psvn/psvn.el:
  Fixed some typos from revision 12828.
------------------------------------------------------------------------
```

...part of reviewing that commit is to say "By the way, please use 'r12828', not 'revision 12828' when referring to past changes." This isn't just pedantry; it's important as much for automatic parsability as for human readership.

By following the general principle that there should be canonical referral methods for common entities, and that these referral methods should be used consistently everywhere, the project in effect exports certain standards. Those standards enable people to write tools that present the project's communications in more usable ways—for example, a revision formatted as "r12828" could be transformed into a live link into the repository browsing system. This would be harder to do if the revision were written as "revision 12828", both because that form could be divided across a line break, and because it's less distinct (the word "revision" will often appear alone, and groups of numbers will often appear alone, whereas the combination "r12828" can only mean a revision number). Similar concerns apply to issue numbers, FAQ items (hint: use a URL with a named anchor, as described in the earlier sidebar), etc.

Even for entities where there is not an obvious short, canonical form, people should still be encouraged to provide key pieces of information consistently. For example, when referring to a mailing list message, don't just give the sender and subject; also give the archive URL *and* the Message-ID header. The last allows people who have their own copy of the mailing list (people sometimes keep offline copies, for example to use on a laptop while traveling) to unambiguously identify the right message even if they don't have access to the archives. The sender and subject wouldn't be enough, because the same person might make several posts in the same thread, even on the same day.

The more a project grows, the more important this sort of consistency becomes. Consistency means that everywhere people look, they see the same patterns being followed, so they know to follow those patterns themselves. This, in turn, reduces the number of questions they need to ask. The burden of having a million readers is no greater than that of having one; scalability problems start to arise only when a certain percentage of those readers ask questions. As a project grows, therefore, it must reduce that percentage by increasing the density and accessibility of information, so that any given person is more likely to find what she needs without having to ask.

No Conversations in the Bug Tracker

In any project that's making active use of its bug tracker, there is always a danger of the tracker turning into a discussion forum itself, even though the mailing lists would really be better. Usually it starts off innocently enough: someone annotates an issue with, say, a proposed solution, or a partial patch. Someone else sees this, realizes there are problems with the solution, and attaches another annotation pointing out the problems. The first person responds, again by appending to the issue...and so it goes.

The problem with this is, first, that the bug tracker is a pretty cumbersome place to have a discussion, and second, that other people may not be paying attention—after all, they expect development discussion to happen on the development mailing list, so that's where they look for it. They may not be subscribed to the issue changes list at all, and even if they are, they may not follow it very closely.

But exactly where in the process did something go wrong? Was it when the original person attached her solution to the issue—should she have posted it to the list instead? Or was it when the second person responded in the issue, instead of on the list?

There isn't one right answer, but there is a general principle: if you're just adding data to an issue, do it in the tracker, but if you're starting a *conversation*, do it on the mailing list. You may not always be able to tell which is the case, but just use your best judgement. For example, when attaching a patch that contains a potentially controversial solution, you might be able to anticipate that people are going to have questions about it. So even though you would normally attach the patch to the issue (assuming you don't want to or can't commit the change directly), in this case you might choose to post it to a mailing list instead. At any rate, there eventually will come a point in the exchange where one party or the other can tell that it is about to go from mere appending of data to an actual conversation—in the example that started this section, that would be the second respondent, who on realizing that there were problems with the patch, could predict that a real conversation is about to ensue, and therefore that it should be held in the appropriate medium.

To use a mathematical analogy, if the information looks like it will be quickly convergent, then put it directly in the bug tracker; if it looks like it will be divergent, then a mailing list or IRC channel would be a better place.

This doesn't mean there should never be any exchanges in the bug tracker. Asking for more details of the reproduction recipe from the original reporter tends to be a highly convergent process, for instance. The person's response is unlikely to raise new issues; it's simply going to flesh out information already filed. There's no need to distract the mailing list with that process; by all means, take care of it with a series of comments in the tracker. Likewise, if you're fairly sure that the bug has been misreported (i.e., is not a bug), then you can simply say so right in the issue. Even pointing out a minor problem with a proposed solution is fine, assuming the problem is not a showstopper for the entire solution.

On the other hand, if you're raising philosophical issues about the bug's scope or the software's proper behavior, you can be pretty sure other developers will want to be involved. The discussion is likely to diverge for a while before it converges, so do it on the mailing list.

Always link to the mailing list thread from the issue, when you choose to post to the mailing list. It's still important for someone following the issue to be able to reach the discussion, even if the issue itself isn't the forum of discussion. The person who starts the thread may find this laborious, but open source is fundamentally a writer-responsible culture: it's much more important to make things easy for the tens or hundreds of people who may read the bug than for the three or five people writing about it.

It's fine to take important conclusions or summaries from the list discussion and paste them into the issue, if that will make things convenient for readers. A common idiom is to start a list discussion, put a link to the thread in the issue, and then when the discussion finishes, paste the final summary into the issue (along with a link to the message containing that summary), so someone browsing the issue can easily see what conclusion was reached without having to click to somewhere else. Note that the usual "two masters" data duplication problem does not exist here, because both archives and issue comments are usually static, unchangeable data anyway.

Publicity

In free software, there is a fairly smooth continuum between purely internal discussions and public relations statements. This is partly because the target audience is always ill-defined: given that most or all posts are publicly accessible, the project doesn't have full control over the impression the world gets. Someone—say, a *slashdot.org* editor—may draw millions of readers' attention to a post that no one ever expected to be seen outside the project. This is a fact of life that all open source projects live with, but in practice, the risk is usually small. In general, the announcements that the project most wants publicized are the ones that will be most publicized, assuming you use the right mechanisms to indicate relative newsworthiness to the outside world.

For major announcements, there tend to be four or five main channels of distribution, on which announcements should be made as nearly simultaneously as possible:

- Your project's front page is probably seen by more people than any other part of the project. If you have a really major announcement, put a blurb there. The blurb should be a very brief synopsis that links to the press release (see below) for more information.

- At the same time, you should also have a "News" or "Press Releases" area of the web site, where the announcement can be written up in detail. Part of the purpose of a press release is to provide a single, canonical "announcement object" that other sites can link to, so make sure it is structured accordingly: either as one web page per release, as a discrete blog entry, or as some other kind of entity that can be linked to while still being kept distinct from other press releases in the same area.

- If your project has an RSS feed, make sure the announcement goes out there too. This may happen automatically when you create the press release, depending on how things are set up at your site. (RSS is a mechanism for distributing metadata-rich news summaries to "subscribers," that is, people who have indicated an interest in receiving those summaries. See *http://www.xml.com/pub/a/2002/12/18/dive-into-xml.html* for more information about RSS.)

- If the announcement is about a new release of the software, then update your project's entry on *http://freshmeat.net/* (see "Announcing" in Chapter 2 about creating the entry in the first place). Every time you update a Freshmeat entry, that entry goes onto the Freshmeat change list for the day. The change list is updated not only on Freshmeat itself, but on various portal sites (including *slashdot.org*) that are watched eagerly by hordes of people. Freshmeat also offers the same data via RSS feed, so people who are not subscribed to your project's own RSS feed might still see the announcement via Freshmeat's.

- Send a mail to your project's announcement mailing list. This list's name should actually be "announce", that is, *announce@yourprojectdomain.org*, because that's a fairly standard convention now, and the list's charter should make it clear that it is very low traffic, reserved for major project announcements. Most of those announcements will be about new releases of the software, but occasionally other events, such as a fundraising drive, the discovery of a security vulnerability (see "Announcing Security Vulnerabilities" later in this chapter), or a major shift in project direction may be posted there as well. Because it is low traffic and used only for important things, the *announce* list typically has the highest subscribership of any mailing list in the project (of course, this means you shouldn't abuse it—consider carefully before posting). To avoid random people making announcements, or worse, spam getting through, the *announce* list must always be moderated.

Try to make the announcements in all these places at the same time, as nearly as possible. People might get confused if they see an announcement on the mailing list but then don't see it reflected on the project's home page or in its press releases area. If you get the various changes (emails, web page edits, etc.) queued up, and then send them all in a row, you can keep the window of inconsistency very small.

For a less important event, you can eliminate some or all of the above outlets. The event will still be noticed by the outside world in direct proportion to its importance. For example, while a new release of the software is a major event, merely setting the date of the next release, while still somewhat newsworthy, is not nearly as important as the release itself. Setting a date is worth an email to the daily mailing lists (not the announce list), and an update of the project's timeline or status web page, but no more.

However, you might still see that date appearing in discussions elsewhere on the Internet, wherever there are people interested in the project. People who are lurkers on your mailing lists, just listening and never saying anything, are not necessarily silent elsewhere. Word of mouth gives very broad distribution; you should count on it, and construct even minor announcements in such a way as to encourage accurate informal transmission. Specifically, posts that you expect to be quoted should have a clearly meant-to-be-quoted portion, just as though you were writing a formal press release. For example:

> Just a progress update: we're planning to release version 2.0 of Scanley in mid-August 2005. You can always check *http://www.scanley.org/status.html* for updates. The major new feature will be regular-expression searches.
>
> Other new features include: ... There will also be various bug fixes, including: ...

The first paragraph is short, gives the two most important pieces of information (the release date and the major new feature), and a URL to visit for further news. If that paragraph is the only thing that crosses someone's screen, you're still doing pretty well. The rest of the mail could be lost without affecting the gist of the content. Of course, sometimes people will link to the entire mail anyway, but just as often, they'll quote only a small part. Given that the latter is a possibility, you might as well make it easy for them, and in the bargain get some influence over what gets quoted.

Announcing Security Vulnerabilities

Handling a security vulnerability is different from handling any other kind of bug report. In free software, doing things openly and transparently is normally almost a religious credo. Every step of the standard bug-handling process is visible to all who care to watch: the arrival of the initial report, the ensuing discussion, and the eventual fix.

Security bugs are different. They can compromise users' data, and possibly users' entire computers. To discuss such a problem openly would be to advertise its existence to the entire world—including to all the parties who might make malicious use of the bug. Even merely committing a fix effectively announces the bug's existence (there are potential attackers who watch the commit logs of public projects, systematically looking for changes that indicate security problems in the pre-change code). Most open source projects have settled on approximately the same set of steps to handle this conflict between openness and secrecy, based on the these basic guidelines:

- Don't talk about the bug publicly until a fix is available; then supply the fix at exactly the same moment you announce the bug.

- Come up with that fix as fast as you can—especially if someone outside the project reported the bug, because then you know there's at least one person outside the project who is able to exploit the vulnerability.

In practice, those principles lead to a fairly standardized series of steps, which are described in the sections below.

Receive the report

Obviously, a project needs the ability to receive security bug reports from anyone. But the regular bug reporting address won't do, because it can be watched by anyone too. Therefore, have a separate mailing list for receiving security bug reports. That mailing list must not have publicly readable archives, and its subscribership must be strictly controlled—only longtime, trusted developers can be on the list. If you need a formal definition of "trusted," you can use "anyone who has had commit access for two years or more" or something like that, to avoid favoritism. This is the group that will handle security bugs.

Ideally, the security list should not be spam-protected or moderated, since you don't want an important report to get filtered out or delayed just because no moderators happened to be online that weekend. If you do use automated spam-protection software, try to configure it with high-tolerance settings; it's better to let a few spams through than to miss a report. For the list to be effective, you must advertise its address, of course; but given that it will be unmoderated and, at most, lightly spam-protected, try to never to post its address without some sort of address-hiding transformation, as described in "Address hiding in archives" in Chapter 3. Fortunately, address hiding need not make the address illegible; see *http://subversion.tigris.org/security.html*, and view that page's HTML source, for an example.

Develop the fix quietly

So what does the security list do when it receives a report? The first task is to evaluate the problem's severity and urgency:

1. How serious is the vulnerability? Does it allow a malicious attacker to take over the computer of someone who uses your software? Or does it, say, merely leak information about the sizes of some of their files?

2. How easy is it to exploit the vulnerability? Can an attack be scripted, or does it require circumstantial knowledge, educated guessing, and luck?

3. *Who* reported the problem to you? The answer to this question doesn't change the nature of the vulnerability, of course, but it does give you an idea of how many other people might know about it. If the report comes from one of the project's own developers, you can breathe a little easier (but only a little), because you can trust them not to have told anyone else about it. On the other hand, if it came in an email from *anonymous14@globalhackerz.net*, then you'd better act as fast as you can. The person did you a favor by informing you of the problem at all, but you have no idea how many other people he's told, or how long he'll wait before exploiting the vulnerability on live installations.

Note that the difference we're talking about here is often just a narrow range between *urgent* and *extremely urgent*. Even when the report comes from a known, friendly source, there could be other people on the Net who discovered the bug long ago and just haven't reported it. The only time things aren't urgent is when the bug inherently does not compromise security very severely.

The *anonymous14@globalhackerz.net* example is not facetious, by the way. You really may get bug reports from identity-cloaked people who, by their words and behavior, never quite clarify whether they're on your side or not. It doesn't matter: if they've reported the security hole to you, they'll feel they've done you a good turn, and you should respond in kind. Thank them for the report, give them a date on or before which you plan to release a public fix, and keep them in the loop. Sometimes they may give *you* a date—that is, an implicit threat to publicize the bug on a certain date, whether you're ready or not. This may feel like a bullying power play, but it's more likely a preemptive action resulting from past disappointment with unresponsive software producers who didn't take security reports seriously enough. Either way, you can't afford to tick this person off. After all, if the bug is severe, he has knowledge that could cause your users big problems. Treat such reporters well, and hope that they treat you well.

Another frequent reporter of security bugs is the security professional, someone who audits code for a living and keeps up on the latest news of software vulnerabilities. These people usually have experience on both sides of the fence—they've both received and sent reports, probably more than most developers in your project have. They too will usually give a deadline for fixing a vulnerability before going public. The deadline may be somewhat negotiable, but that's up to the reporter; deadlines have become recognized among security professionals as pretty much the only reliable way to get organizations to address security problems promptly. So don't treat the deadline as rude; it's a time-honored tradition, and there are good reasons for it.

Once you know the severity and urgency, you can start working on a fix. There is sometimes a trade-off between doing a fix elegantly and doing it speedily; this is why you must agree on the urgency before you start. Keep discussion of the fix restricted to the security list members, of course, plus the original reporter (if he wants to be involved) and any developers who need to be brought in for technical reasons.

Do not commit the fix to the repository. Keep it in patch form until the go-public date. If you were to commit it, even with an innocent-looking log message, someone might notice and understand the change. You never know who is watching your repository and why they might be interested. Turning off commit emails wouldn't help; first of all, the gap in the commit mail sequence would itself look suspicious, and anyway, the data would still be in the repository. Just do all development in a patch and keep the patch in some private place, perhaps a separate, private repository known only to the people already aware of the bug. (If you use a decentralized version control system like Arch or SVK, you can do the work under full version control, and just keep that repository inaccessible to outsiders.)

CAN/CVE numbers

You may have seen a *CAN number* or a *CVE number* associated with security problems. These numbers usually look like "CAN-2004-0397" or "CVE-2002-0092," for example.

Both kinds of numbers represent the same type of entity: an entry in the list of "Common Vulnerabilities and Exposures" list maintained at *http://cve.mitre.org/*. The purpose of the list is to provide standardized names for all known security problems, so that everyone has a unique, canonical name to use when discussing one, and a central place to go to find out more information. The only difference between a CAN number and a CVE number is that the former represents a candidate entry, not yet approved for inclusion in the official list by the CVE Editorial Board, and the latter represents an approved entry. However, both types of entries are visible to the public, and an entry's number does not change when it is approved—the CAN prefix is simply replaced with CVE.

A CAN/CVE entry does not itself contain a full description of the bug and how to protect against it. Instead, it contains a brief summary, and a list of references to external resources (such as mailing list archives) where people can go to get more detailed information. The real purpose of *http://cve.mitre.org/* is to provide a well-organized space in which every vulnerability can have a name and a clear route to more data. See *http://cve.mitre.org/cgi-bin/cvename.cgi?name=2002-0092* for an example of an entry. Note that the references can be very terse, with sources appearing as cryptic abbreviations. A key to those abbreviations is at *http://cve.mitre.org/cve/refs/refkey.html*.

If your vulnerability meets the CVE criteria, you may wish to acquire it a CAN number. The process for doing so is deliberately gated: basically, you have to know someone, or know someone who knows someone. This is not as crazy as it might sound. In order for the CVE Editorial Board to avoid being overwhelmed with spurious or poorly written submissions, they take submissions only from sources they already know and trust. In order to get your vulnerability listed, therefore, you need to find a path of acquaintance from your project to the CVE Editorial Board. Ask around among your developers; one of them will probably know someone else who has either done the CAN process before, or knows someone who has, etc. The advantage of doing it this way is also that somewhere along the chain, someone may know enough to tell you that a) it wouldn't count as a vulnerability or exposure according to MITRE's criteria, so there is no point submitting it, or b) the vulnerability already *has* a CAN or CVE number. The latter can happen if the bug has already been published on another security advisory list, for example at *http://www.cert.org/* or on the BugTraq mailing list at *http://www.securityfocus.com/*. (If that happened without your project hearing about it, then you should worry about what else might be going on that you don't know about.)

If you get a CAN/CVE number at all, you usually want to get it in the early stages of your bug investigation, so that all further communications can refer to that number. CAN entries are embargoed until the go-public date; the entry will exist as an empty placeholder (so you don't lose the name), but it won't reveal any information about the vulnerability until the date on which you will be announcing the bug and the fix.

More information about the CAN/CVE process may be found at *http://cve.mitre.org/about/candidates.html*, and a particularly clear exposition of one open source project's use of CAN/CVE numbers is at *http://www.debian.org/security/cve-compatibility*.

Pre-notification

Once your security response team (that is, those developers who are on the security mailing list, or who have been brought in to deal with a particular report) has a fix ready, you need to decide how to distribute it.

If you simply commit the fix to your repository, or otherwise announce it to the world, you effectively force everyone using your software to upgrade immediately or risk being hacked. It is sometimes appropriate, therefore, to provide *pre-notification* for certain important users. This is particularly true with client/server software, where there may be well-known servers that are tempting targets for attackers. Those servers' administrators would appreciate having an extra day or two to do the upgrade, so that they are already protected by the time the exploit becomes public knowledge.

Pre-notification simply means sending mails to those administrators before the go-public date, telling them of the vulnerability and how to fix it. You should send pre-notification only to people you trust to be discreet with the information. That is, the qualification for receiving pre-notification is twofold: the recipient must run a large, important server where a compromise would be a serious matter, *and* the recipient must be known to be someone who won't blab about the security problem before the go-public date.

Send each pre-notification mail individually (one at a time) to each recipient. Do *not* send it to the entire list of recipients at once, because then they would see each others' names—meaning that you would essentially be alerting each recipient to the fact that each *other* recipient may have a security hole in her server. Sending it to them all via blind CC (BCC) isn't a good solution either, because some admins protect their inboxes with spam filters that either block or reduce the priority of BCC'd mail, since so much spam is sent via BCC these days.

Here's a sample pre-notification mail:

```
From: Your Name Here
To: admin@large-famous-server.com
Reply-to: Your Name Here (not the security list's address)
Subject: Confidential Scanley vulnerability notification.


This email is a confidential pre-notification of a security alert
in the Scanley server.

Please *do not forward* any part of this mail to anyone.  The public
announcement is not until May 19th, and we'd like to keep the
information embargoed until then.
```

You are receiving this mail because (we think) you run a Scanley
server, and would want to have it patched before this security hole is
made public on May 19th.

References:
= == == == == ==

   CAN-2004-1771: Scanley stack overflow in queries

Vulnerability:
= == == == == == == == =

   The server can be made to run arbitrary commands if the server's
   locale is misconfigured and the client sends a malformed query.

Severity:
= == == == ==

   Very severe, can involve arbitrary code execution on the server.

Workarounds:
= == == == == == =

   Setting the 'natural-language-processing' option to 'off' in
   scanley.conf closes this vulnerability.

Patch:
= == == =

   The patch below applies to Scanley 3.0, 3.1, and 3.2.

   A new public release (Scanley 3.2.1) will be made on or just before
   May 19th, so that it is available at the same time as this
   vulnerability is made public. You can patch now, or just wait for
   the public release. The only difference between 3.2 and 3.2.1 will
   be this patch.

   [...patch goes here...]

If you have a CAN number, include it in the pre-notification (as shown above), even
though the information is still embargoed and therefore the MITRE page will show
nothing. Including the CAN number allows the recipient to know with certainty that
the bug they were pre-notified about is the same one they later hear about through
public channels, so they don't have to worry whether further action is necessary,
which is precisely the point of CAN/CVE numbers.

Distribute the fix publicly

The last step in handling a security bug is to distribute the fix publicly. In a single,
comprehensive announcement, you should describe the problem, give the CAN/CVE

number if any, describe how to work around it, and how to permanently fix it. Usually "fix" means upgrading to a new version of the software, though sometimes it can mean applying a patch, particularly if the software is normally run in source form anyway. If you do make a new release, it should differ from some existing release by exactly the security patch. That way, conservative admins can upgrade without worrying about what else they might be affecting; they also don't have to worry about future upgrades, because the security fix will be in all future releases as a matter of course. (Details of release procedures are discussed in "Security Releases" in Chapter 7.)

Whether or not the public fix involves a new release, do the announcement with roughly the same priority as you would a new release: send a mail to the project's *announce* list, make a new press release, update the Freshmeat entry, etc. While you should never try to play down the existence of a security bug out of concern for the project's reputation, you may certainly set the tone and prominence of a security announcement to match the actual severity of the problem. If the security hole is just a minor information exposure, not an exploit that allows the user's entire computer to be taken over, then it may not warrant a lot of fuss. You may even decide not to distract the announce list with it. After all, if the project cries wolf every time, users might end up thinking the software is less secure than it actually is, and also might not believe you when you have a really big problem to announce. See *http://cve.mitre. org/about/terminology.html* for a good introduction to the problem of judging severity.

In general, if you're unsure how to treat a security problem, find someone with experience and talk to them about it. Assessing and handling vulnerabilities is very much an acquired skill, and it's easy to make missteps the first few times.

## CHAPTER 7

Packaging, Releasing, and Daily Development

This chapter is about how free software projects package and release their software, and how overall development patterns organize around those goals.

A major difference between open source projects and proprietary ones is the lack of centralized control over the development team. When a new release is being prepared, this difference is especially stark: a corporation can ask its entire development team to focus on an upcoming release, putting aside new feature development and non-critical bug fixing until the release is done. Volunteer groups are not so monolithic. People work on the project for all sorts of reasons, and those not interested in helping with a given release still want to continue regular development work while the release is going on. Because development doesn't stop, open source release processes tend to take longer, but be less disruptive, than commercial release processes. It's a bit like highway repair. There are two ways to fix a road: you can shut it down completely, so that a repair crew can swarm all over it at full capacity until the problem is solved, or you can work on a couple of lanes at a time, while leaving the others open to traffic. The first way is very efficient *for the repair crew*, but not for anyone else—the road is entirely shut down until the job is done. The second way involves much more time and trouble for the repair crew (now they have to work with fewer people and less equipment, in cramped conditions, with flaggers to slow and direct traffic, etc.), but at least the road remains usable, albeit not at full capacity.

Open source projects tend to work the second way. In fact, for a mature piece of software with several different release lines being maintained simultaneously, the project is sort of in a permanent state of minor road repair. There are always a couple of lanes closed; a consistent but low level of background inconvenience is always being tolerated by the development group as a whole, so that releases get made on a regular schedule.

The model that makes this possible generalizes to more than just releases. It's the principle of parallelizing tasks that are not mutually interdependent—a principle that is by no means unique to open source development, of course, but one that open source projects implement in their own particular way. They cannot afford to annoy either the roadwork crew or the regular traffic too much, but they also cannot afford to have people dedicated to standing by the orange cones and flagging traffic along. Thus they gravitate toward processes that have flat, constant levels of administrative overhead, rather than peaks and valleys. Volunteers are generally willing to work with small but consistent amounts of inconvenience; the predictability allows them to come and go without worrying about whether their schedule will clash with what's happening in the project. But if the project were subject to a master schedule in which some activities excluded other activities, the result would be a lot of developers sitting idle a lot of the time—which would be not only inefficient but boring, and therefore dangerous, in that a bored developer is likely to soon be an ex-developer.

Release work is usually the most noticeable non-development task that happens in parallel with development, so the methods described in the following sections are geared mostly toward enabling releases. However, note that they also apply to other parallelizable tasks, such as translations and internationalization, broad API changes made gradually across the entire code base, etc.

Release Numbering

Before we talk about how to make a release, let's look at how to name releases, which requires knowing what releases actually mean to users. A release means that:

- Old bugs have been fixed. This is probably the one thing users can count on being true of every release.

- New bugs have been added. This too can usually be counted on, except sometimes in the case of security releases or other one-offs (see "Security Releases" later in this chapter).

- New features may have been added.

- New configuration options may have been added, or the meanings of old options may have changed subtly. The installation procedures may have changed slightly since the last release too, though one always hopes not.

- Incompatible changes may have been introduced, such that the data formats used by older versions of the software are no longer usable without undergoing some sort of (possibly manual) one-way conversion step.

As you can see, not all of these are good things. This is why experienced users approach new releases with some trepidation, especially when the software is mature and was already mostly doing what they wanted (or thought they wanted). Even the arrival of new features is a mixed blessing, in that it may mean the software will now behave in unexpected ways.

The purpose of release numbering, therefore, is twofold: obviously the numbers should unambiguously communicate the ordering of releases (i.e., by looking at any two releases' numbers, one can know which came later), but also they should indicate as compactly as possible the degree and nature of the changes in the release.

All that in a number? Well, more or less, yes. Release numbering strategies are one of the oldest bikeshed discussions around (see "The Softer the Topic, the Longer the Debate" in Chapter 6), and the world is unlikely to settle on a single, complete standard anytime soon. However, a few good strategies have emerged, along with one universally agreed on principle: *be consistent.* Pick a numbering scheme, document it, and stick with it. Your users will thank you.

Release Number Components

This section describes the formal conventions of release numbering in detail, and assumes very little prior knowledge. It is intended mainly as a reference. If you're already familiar with these conventions, you can skip this section.

Release numbers are groups of digits separated by dots:

> Scanley 2.3
> Singer 5.11.4

...and so on. The dots are *not* decimal points, they are merely separators; 5.3.9 would be followed by 5.3.10. A few projects have occasionally hinted otherwise, most famously the Linux kernel with its 0.95, 0.96... 0.99 sequence leading up to Linux 1.0, but the convention that the dots are not decimals is now firmly established and should be considered a standard. There is no limit to the number of components (digit portions containing no dots), but most projects do not go beyond three or four. The reasons why will become clear later.

In addition to the numeric components, projects sometimes tack on a descriptive label such as Alpha or Beta (see Chapter 2), for example:

> Scanley 2.3.0 (Alpha)
> Singer 5.11.4 (Beta)

An Alpha or Beta qualifier means that this release *precedes* a future release that will have the same number without the qualifier. Thus, 2.3.0 (Alpha) leads eventually to 2.3.0. In order to allow several such candidate releases in a row, the qualifiers themselves can have meta-qualifiers. For example, here is a series of releases in the order that they would be made available to the public:

> Scanley 2.3.0 (Alpha 1)
> Scanley 2.3.0 (Alpha 2)
> Scanley 2.3.0 (Beta 1)
> Scanley 2.3.0 (Beta 2)
> Scanley 2.3.0 (Beta 3)
> Scanley 2.3.0

Notice that when it has the Alpha qualifier, Scanley 2.3 is written as 2.3.0. The two numbers are equivalent—trailing all-zero components can always be dropped for brevity—but when a qualifier is present, brevity is out the window anyway, so one might as well go for completeness instead.

Other qualifiers in semi-regular use include Stable, Unstable, Development, and RC (for "Release Candidate"). The most widely used ones are still Alpha and Beta, with RC running a close third place, but note that RC always includes a numeric meta-qualifier. That is, you don't release Scanley 2.3.0 (RC), you release Scanley 2.3.0 (RC 1), followed by RC 2, etc.

Those three labels—Alpha, Beta, and RC—are pretty widely known now, and I don't recommend using any of the others, even though the others might at first glance seem like better choices because they are normal words, not jargon. But people who install software from releases are already familiar with the big three, and there's no reason to do things gratuitously differently from the way everyone else does them.

Although the dots in release numbers are not decimal points, they do indicate place-value significance. All 0.X.Y releases precede 1.0 (which is equivalent to 1.0.0, of course). The number 3.14.158 immediately precedes 3.14.159, and non-immediately precedes 3.14.160 as well as 3.15.anything, and so on.

A consistent release numbering policy enables a user to look at two release numbers for the same piece of software and tell, just from the numbers, the important differences between those two releases. In a typical three-component system, the first component is the *major number*, the second is the *minor number*, and the third is the *micro number*. For example, release "2.10.17" is the seventeenth micro release in the tenth minor release line within the second major release series. The words "line" and "series" are used informally here, but they mean what one would expect. A major series is simply all the releases that share the same major number, and a minor series (or minor line) consists of all the releases that share the same minor *and* major number. That is, 2.4.0 and 3.4.1 are not in the same minor series, even though they both have 4 for their minor number; on the other hand, 2.4.0 and 2.4.2 are in the same minor line, though they are not adjacent if 2.4.1 was released between them.

The meanings of these numbers are exactly what you'd expect: an increment of the major number indicates that major changes happened; an increment of the minor number indicates minor changes; and an increment of the micro number indicates really trivial changes. Some projects add a fourth component, usually called the *patch number*, for especially fine-grained control over the differences between their releases (confusingly, other projects use "patch" as a synonym for "micro" in a three-component system). There are also projects that use the last component as a *build number*, incremented every time the software is built and representing no change other than that build. This helps the project link every bug report with a specific build, and is probably most useful when binary packages are the default method of distribution.

Although there are many different conventions for how many components to use, and what the components mean, the differences tend to be minor—you get a little leeway, but not a lot. The next two sections discuss some of the most widely used conventions.

The Simple Strategy

Most projects have rules about what kinds of changes are allowed into a release if one is only incrementing the micro number, different rules for the minor number, and still different ones for the major number. There is no set standard for these rules yet, but here I will describe a policy that has been used successfully by multiple projects. You may want to just adopt this policy in your own project, but even if you don't, it's still a good example of the kind of information release numbers should convey. This policy is adapted from the numbering system used by the APR project; see *http://apr.apache.org/versioning.html*.

- Changes to the micro number only (that is, changes within the same minor line) must be both forward- and backward-compatible. That is, the changes should be bug fixes only, or very small enhancements to existing features. New features should not be introduced in a micro release.

- Changes to the minor number (that is, within the same major line) must be backward-compatible, but not necessarily forward-compatible. It's normal to introduce new features in a minor release, but usually not too many new features at once.

- Changes to the major number mark compatibility boundaries. A new major release can be forward- and backward-incompatible. A major release is expected to have new features, and may even have entire new feature sets.

What *backward-compatible* and *forward-compatible* mean, exactly, depends on what your software does, but in context they are usually not open to much interpretation. For example, if your project is a client/server application, then backward-compatible means that upgrading the server to 2.6.0 should not cause any existing 2.5.4 clients to lose functionality or behave differently than they did before (except for bugs that were fixed, of course). On the other hand, upgrading one of those clients to 2.6.0, along with the server, might make *new* functionality available for that client, functionality that 2.5.4 clients don't know how to take advantage of. If that happens, then the upgrade is *not* "forward-compatible": clearly you can't now downgrade that client back to 2.5.4 and keep all the functionality it had at 2.6.0, since some of that functionality was new in 2.6.0.

This is why micro releases are essentially for bug fixes only. They must remain compatible in both directions: if you upgrade from 2.5.3 to 2.5.4, then change your mind and downgrade back to 2.5.3, no functionality should be lost. Of course, the bugs fixed in 2.5.4 would reappear after the downgrade, but you wouldn't lose any features, except insofar as the restored bugs prevent the use of some existing features.

Client/server protocols are just one of many possible compatibility domains. Another is data formats: does the software write data to permanent storage? If so, the formats it reads and writes need to follow the compatibility guidelines promised by the release number policy. Version 2.6.0 needs to be able to read the files written by 2.5.4, but may silently upgrade the format to something that 2.5.4 cannot read, because the ability to downgrade is not required across a minor number boundary. If your project distributes code libraries for other programs to use, then APIs are a compatibility domain too: you must make sure that source and binary compatibility rules are spelled out in such a way that the informed user need never wonder whether or not it's safe to upgrade in place. She will be able to look at the numbers and know instantly.

In this system, you don't get a chance for a fresh start until you increment the major number. This can often be a real inconvenience: there may be features you wish to add, or protocols that you wish to redesign, that simply cannot be done while maintaining compatibility. There's no magic solution to this, except to try to design things in an extensible way in the first place (a topic easily worth its own book, and certainly outside the scope of this one). But publishing a release compatibility policy, and adhering to it, is an inescapable part of distributing software. One nasty surprise can alienate a lot of users. The policy just described is good partly because it's already quite widespread, but also because it's easy to explain and to remember, even for those not already familiar with it.

It is generally understood that these rules do not apply to pre-1.0 releases (although your release policy should probably state so explicitly, just to be clear). A project that is still in initial development can release 0.1, 0.2, 0.3, and so on in sequence, until it's ready for 1.0, and the differences between those releases can be arbitrarily large. Micro numbers in pre-1.0 releases are optional. Depending on the nature of your project and the differences between the releases, you might find it useful to have 0.1. 0, 0.1.1, etc., or you might not. Conventions for pre-1.0 release numbers are fairly loose, mainly because people understand that strong compatibility constraints would hamper early development too much, and because early adopters tend to be forgiving anyway.

Remember that all these injunctions only apply to this particular three-component system. Your project could easily come up with a different three-component system, or even decide it doesn't need such fine granularity and use a two-component system instead. The important thing is to decide early, publish exactly what the components mean, and stick to it.

The Even/Odd Strategy

Some projects use the parity of the minor number component to indicate the stability of the software: even means stable, odd means unstable. This applies only to the minor number, not the major and micro numbers. Increments in the micro number still indicate bug fixes (no new features), and increments in the major number still indicate big changes, new feature sets, etc.

The advantage of the even/odd system, which has been used by the Linux kernel project, among others, is that it offers a way to release new functionality for testing without subjecting production users to potentially unstable code. People can see from the numbers that 2.4.21 is okay to install on their live web server, but that 2.5.1 should probably stay confined to home workstation experiments. The development team handles the bug reports that come in from the unstable (odd-minor-numbered) series, and when things start to settle down after some number of micro releases in that series, they increment the minor number (thus making it even), reset the micro number back to 0, and release a presumably stable package.

This system preserves, or at least does not conflict with, the compatibility guidelines given earlier. It simply overloads the minor number with some extra information. This forces the minor number to be incremented about twice as often as would otherwise be necessary, but there's no great harm in that. The even/odd system is probably best for projects that have very long release cycles, and which by their nature have a high proportion of conservative users who value stability above new features. It is not the only way to get new functionality tested in the wild, however. "Stabilizing a Release," later in this chapter, describes another, perhaps more common, method of releasing potentially unstable code to the public, marked so that people have an idea of the risk/benefit trade-offs immediately on seeing the release's name.

Release Branches

From a developer's point of view, a free software project is in a state of continuous release. Developers usually run the latest available code at all times, because they want to spot bugs, and because they follow the project closely enough to be able to stay away from currently unstable areas of the feature space. They often update their copy of the software every day, sometimes more than once a day, and when they check in a change, they can reasonably expect that every other developer will have it within 24 hours.

How, then, should the project make a formal release? Should it simply take a snapshot of the tree at a moment in time, package it up, and hand it to the world as, say, version 3.5.0? Common sense says no. First, there may be no moment in time when the entire development tree is clean and ready for release. Newly started features could be lying around in various states of completion. Someone might have checked in a major change to fix a bug, but the change could be controversial and under debate at the moment the snapshot is taken. If so, it wouldn't work to simply delay the snapshot until the debate ends, because another, unrelated debate could start in the meantime, and then you'd have wait for *that* one to end too. This process is not guaranteed to halt.

In any case, using full-tree snapshots for releases would interfere with ongoing development work, even if the tree could be put into a releasable state. Say this snapshot is going to be 3.5.0; presumably, the next snapshot would be 3.5.1, and would contain mostly fixes for bugs found in the 3.5.0 release. But if both are snapshots from the same tree, what are the developers supposed to do in the time between the two releases? They can't be adding new features; the compatibility guidelines prevent that. But not everyone will be enthusiastic about fixing bugs in the 3.5.0 code. Some people may have new features they're trying to complete, and will become irate if they are forced to choose between sitting idle and working on things they're not interested in, just because the project's release processes demand that the development tree remain unnaturally quiescent.

The solution to these problems is to always use a *release branch*. A release branch is just a branch in the version control system (see "Version Control Vocabulary" in Chapter 3), on which the code destined for this release can be isolated from mainline development. The concept of release branches is certainly not original to free software; many commercial development organizations use them too. However, in commercial environments, release branches are sometimes considered a luxury—a kind of formal "best practice" that can, in the heat of a major deadline, be dispensed with while everyone on the team scrambles to stabilize the main tree.

Release branches are pretty much required in open source projects, however. I have seen projects do releases without them, but it has always resulted in some developers sitting idle while others—usually a minority—work on getting the release out the door. The result is usually bad in several ways. First, overall development momentum is slowed. Second, the release is of poorer quality than it needed to be, because there were only a few people working on it, and they were hurrying to finish so everyone else could get back to work. Third, it divides the development team psychologically, by setting up a situation in which different types of work interfere with each other unnecessarily. The developers sitting idle would probably be happy to contribute *some* of their attention to a release branch, as long as that were a choice they could make according to their own schedules and interests. But without the branch, their choice becomes "Do I participate in the project today or not?" instead of "Do I work on the release today, or work on that new feature I've been developing in the mainline code?"

Mechanics of Release Branches

The exact mechanics of creating a release branch depend on your version control system, of course, but the general concepts are the same in most systems. A branch usually sprouts from another branch or from the trunk. Traditionally, the trunk is where mainline development goes on, unfettered by release constraints. The first release branch, the one leading to the 1.0 release, sprouts off the trunk. In CVS, the branch command would be something like this

```
$ cd trunk-working-copy
$ cvs tag -b RELEASE_1_0_X
```

or in Subversion, like this:

```
$ svn copy http://.../repos/trunk http://.../repos/branches/1.0.x
```

(All these examples assume a three-component release numbering system. While I can't show the exact commands for every version control system, I'll give examples in CVS and Subversion and hope that the corresponding commands in other systems can be deduced from those two.)

Notice that we created branch 1.0.x (with a literal "x") instead of 1.0.0. This is because the same minor line—i.e., the same branch—will be used for all the micro releases in that line. The actual process of stabilizing the branch for release is covered in "Stabilizing a Release" later in this chapter. Here we are concerned just with the interaction between the version control system and the release process. When the release branch is stabilized and ready, it is time to tag a snapshot from the branch:

```
$ cd RELEASE_1_0_X-working-copy
$ cvs tag RELEASE_1_0_0
```

or:

```
$ svn copy http://.../repos/branches/1.0.x http://.../repos/tags/1.0.0
```

That tag now represents the exact state of the project's source tree in the 1.0.0 release (this is useful in case anyone ever needs to get an old version after the packaged distributions and binaries have been taken down). The next micro release in the same line is likewise prepared on the 1.0.x branch, and when it is ready, a tag is made for 1.0.1. Lather, rinse, repeat for 1.0.2, and so on. When it's time to start thinking about a 1.1.x release, make a new branch from trunk:

```
$ cd trunk-working-copy
$ cvs tag -b RELEASE_1_1_X
```

or:

```
$ svn copy http://.../repos/trunk http://.../repos/branches/1.1.x
```

Maintenance can continue in parallel along both 1.0.x and 1.1.x, and releases can be made independently from both lines. In fact, it is not unusual to publish near-simultaneous releases from two different lines. The older series is recommended for more conservative site administrators, who may not want to make the big jump to (say) 1.1

without careful preparation. Meanwhile, more adventurous people usually take the most recent release on the highest line, to make sure they're getting the latest features, even at the risk of greater instability.

This is not the only release branch strategy, of course. In some circumstances it may not even be the best, though it's worked out pretty well for projects I've been involved in. Use any strategy that seems to work, but remember the main points: the purpose of a release branch is to isolate release work from the fluctuations of daily development, and to give the project a physical entity around which to organize its release process. That process is described in detail in the next section.

Stabilizing a Release

Stabilization is the process of getting a release branch into a releasable state; that is, of deciding which changes will be in the release, which will not, and shaping the branch content accordingly.

There's a lot of potential grief contained in that word, "deciding." The last-minute feature rush is a familiar phenomenon in collaborative software projects: as soon as developers see that a release is about to happen, they scramble to finish their current changes, in order not to miss the boat. This, of course, is the exact opposite of what you want at release time. It would be much better for people to work on features at a comfortable pace, and not worry too much about whether their changes make it into this release or the next one. The more changes one tries to cram into a release at the last minute, the more the code is destabilized, and (usually) the more new bugs are created.

Most software engineers agree in theory on rough criteria for what changes should be allowed into a release line during its stabilization period. Obviously, fixes for severe bugs can go in, especially for bugs without workarounds. Documentation updates are fine, as are fixes to error messages (except when they are considered part of the interface and must remain stable). Many projects also allow certain kinds of low-risk or non-core changes to go in during stabilization, and may have formal guidelines for measuring risk. But no amount of formalization can obviate the need for human judgement. There will always be cases where the project simply has to make a decision about whether a given change can go into a release. The danger is that since each person wants to see their own favorite changes admitted into the release, there will be plenty of people motivated to allow changes, and not enough people motivated to bar them.

Thus, the process of stabilizing a release is mostly about creating mechanisms for saying "no." The trick for open source projects, in particular, is to come up with ways of saying "no" that won't result in too many hurt feelings or disappointed developers, and also won't prevent deserving changes from getting into the release. There are many different ways to do this. It's pretty easy to design systems that satisfy these criteria, once the team has focused on them as the important criteria. Here I'll briefly describe two of the most popular systems, at the extreme ends of the spectrum, but don't let that discourage your project from being creative. Plenty of other arrangements are possible; these are just two that I've seen work in practice.

Dictatorship by Release Owner

The group agrees to let one person be the *release owner*. This person has final say over what changes make it into the release. Of course, it is normal and expected for there to be discussions and arguments, but in the end the group must grant the release owner sufficient authority to make final decisions. For this system to work, it is necessary to choose someone with the technical competence to understand all the changes, and the social standing and people skills to navigate the discussions leading up to the release without causing too many hurt feelings.

A common pattern is for the release owner to say, "I don't think there's anything wrong with this change, but we haven't had enough time to test it yet, so it shouldn't go into this release." It helps a lot if the release owner has broad technical knowledge of the project, and can give reasons why the change could be potentially destabilizing (for example, its interactions with other parts of the software, or portability concerns). People will sometimes ask such decisions to be justified, or will argue that a change is not as risky as it looks. These conversations need not be confrontational, as long as the release owner is able to consider all the arguments objectively and not reflexively dig in his heels.

Note that the release owner need not be the same person as the project leader (in cases where there is a project leader at all; see "Benevolent Dictators" in Chapter 4). In fact, sometimes it's good to make sure they're *not* the same person. The skills that make a good development leader are not necessarily the same as those that make a good release owner. In something as important as the release process, it may be wise to have someone provide a counterbalance to the project leader's judgement.

Contrast the release owner role with the less dictatorial role described in "Release manager" later in this chapter.

Change Voting

At the opposite extreme from dictatorship by release owner, developers can simply vote on which changes to include in the release. However, since the most important function of release stabilization is to *exclude* changes, it's important to design the voting system in such a way that getting a change into the release involves positive action by multiple developers. Including a change should need more than just a simple majority (see "Who Votes?" in Chapter 4). Otherwise, one vote for and none against a given change would suffice to get it into the release, and an unfortunate dynamic would be set up whereby each developer would vote for her own changes, yet would be reluctant to vote against others' changes, for fear of possible retaliation. To avoid this, the system should be arranged such that subgroups of developers must act in cooperation to get any change into the release. This not only means that more people review each change, it also makes any individual developer less hesitant to vote against a change, because she knows that no particular one among those who voted for it would take her vote against as a personal affront. The greater the number of people involved, the more the discussion becomes about the change and less about the individuals.

The system we use in the Subversion project seems to have struck a good balance, so I'll recommend it here. In order for a change to be applied to the release branch, at least three developers must vote in favor of it, and none against. A single "no" vote is enough to stop the change from being included; that is, a no vote in a release context is equivalent to a veto (see "Vetoes" in Chapter 4). Naturally, any such vote must be accompanied by a justification, and in theory the veto could be overridden if enough people feel it is unreasonable and force a special vote over it. In practice, this has never happened, and I don't expect that it ever will. People are conservative around releases anyway, and when someone feels strongly enough to veto the inclusion of a change, there's usually a good reason for it.

Because the release procedure is deliberately biased toward conservativism, the justifications offered for vetoes are sometimes procedural rather than technical. For example, a person may feel that a change is well written and unlikely to cause any new bugs, but vote against its inclusion in a micro release simply because it's too big—perhaps it adds a new feature, or in some subtle way fails to fully follow the compatibility guidelines. I've occasionally even seen developers veto something because they simply had a gut feeling that the change needed more testing, even though they couldn't spot any bugs in it by inspection. People grumbled a little bit, but the vetoes stood and the change was not included in the release (I don't remember if any bugs were found in later testing or not, though).

Managing collaborative release stabilization

If your project chooses a change voting system, it is imperative that the physical mechanics of setting up ballots and casting votes be as convenient as possible. Although there is plenty of open source electronic voting software available, in practice the easiest thing to do is just to set up a text file in the release branch, called *STATUS* or *VOTES* or something like that. This file lists each proposed change—any developer can propose a change for inclusion—along with all the votes for and against it, plus any notes or comments. (Proposing a change doesn't necessarily mean voting for it, by the way, although the two often go together.) An entry in such a file might look like this:

```
* r2401 (issue #49)
  Prevent client/server handshake from happening twice.
  Justification:
    Avoids extra network turnaround; small change and easy to review.
  Notes:
    This was discussed in http://.../mailing-lists/message-7777.html
    and other messages in that thread.
  Votes:
    +1: jsmith, kimf
    -1: tmartin (breaks compatibility with some pre-1.0 servers;
                 admittedly, those servers are buggy, but why be
                 incompatible if we don't have to?)
```

In this case, the change acquired two positive votes, but was vetoed by tmartin, who gave the reason for the veto in a parenthetical note. The exact format of the entry doesn't matter; whatever your project settles on is fine—perhaps tmartin's explanation for the veto should go up in the "Notes:" section, or perhaps the change description should get a "Description:" header to match the other sections. The important thing is that all the information needed to evaluate the change be reachable, and that the mechanism for casting votes be as lightweight as possible. The proposed change is referred to by its revision number in the repository (in this case a single revision, r2401, although a proposed change could just as easily consist of multiple revisions). The revision is assumed to refer to a change made on the trunk; if the change were already on the release branch, there would be no need to vote on it. If your version control system doesn't have an obvious syntax for referring to individual changes, then the project should make one up. For voting to be practical, each change under consideration must be unambiguously identifiable.

Those proposing or voting for a change are responsible for making sure it applies cleanly to the release branch, that is, applies without conflicts (see "Version Control Vocabulary" in Chapter 3). If there are conflicts, then the entry should either point to an adjusted patch that does apply cleanly, or to a temporary branch that holds an adjusted version of the change, for example:

```
* r13222, r13223, r13232
  Rewrite libsvn_fs_fs's auto-merge algorithm
  Justification:
    unacceptable performance (>50 minutes for a small commit) in
    a repository with 300,000 revisions
  Branch:
    1.1.x-r13222@13517
  Votes:
    +1: epg, ghudson
```

That example is taken from real life; it comes from the *STATUS* file for the Subversion 1.1.4 release process. Notice how it uses the original revisions as canonical handles on the change, even though there is also a branch with a conflict-adjusted version of the change (the branch also combines the three trunk revisions into one, r13517, to make it easier to merge the change into the release, should it get approval). The original revisions are provided because they're still the easiest entity to review, since they have the original log messages. The temporary branch wouldn't have those log messages; in order to avoid duplication of information (see "Singularity of information" in Chapter 3), the branch's log message for r13517 should simply say "Adjust r13222, r13223, and r13232 for backport to 1.1.x branch." All other information about the changes can be chased down at their original revisions.

Release manager

The actual process of merging (see "Version Control Vocabulary" in Chapter 3) approved changes into the release branch can be performed by any developer. There does not need to be one person whose job it is to merge changes; if there are a lot of changes, it can be better to spread the burden around.

However, although both voting and merging happen in a decentralized fashion, in practice there are usually one or two people driving the release process. This role is sometimes formally blessed as *release manager*, but it is quite different from a release owner (see "Dictatorship by Release Owner" earlier in this chapter) who has final say over the changes. Release managers keep track of how many changes are currently under consideration, how many have been approved, how many seem likely to be approved, etc. If they sense that important changes are not getting enough attention, and might be left out of the release for lack of votes, they will gently nag other developers to review and vote. When a batch of changes are approved, these people will often take it upon themselves to merge them into the release branch; it's fine if others leave that task to them, as long as everyone understands that they are not obligated to do all the work unless they have explicitly committed to it. When the time comes to put the release out the door (see "Testing and Releasing" later in this chapter), the release managers also take care of the logistics of creating the final release packages, collecting digital signatures, uploading the packages, and making the public announcement.

Packaging

The canonical form for distribution of free software is as source code. This is true regardless of whether the software normally runs in source form (i.e., can be interpreted, like Perl, Python, PHP, etc.) or needs to be compiled first (like C, C++, Java, etc.). With compiled software, most users will probably not compile the sources themselves, but will instead install from pre-built binary packages (see "Binary Packages" later in this chapter). However, those binary packages are still derived from a master source distribution. The point of the source package is to unambiguously define the release. When the project distributes "Scanley 2.5.0", what it means, specifically, is "The tree of source code files that, when compiled (if necessary) and installed, produces Scanley 2.5.0."

There is a fairly strict standard for how source releases should look. One will occasionally see deviations from this standard, but they are the exception, not the rule. Unless there is a compelling reason to do otherwise, your project should follow this standard too.

Format

The source code should be shipped in the standard formats for transporting directory trees. For Unix and Unix-like operating systems, the convention is to use TAR format, compressed by *compress*, *gzip*, *bzip*, or *bzip2*. For MS Windows, the standard method for distributing directory trees is *zip* format, which happens to do compression as well, so there is no need to compress the archive after creating it.

Name and Layout

The name of the package should consist of the software's name, the release number, and the format suffixes appropriate for the archive type. For example, Scanley 2.5.0, packaged for Unix using GNU Zip (gzip) compression, would look like this:

> scanley-2.5.0.tar.gz

or for Windows using zip compression:

> scanley-2.5.0.zip

TAR Files

TAR stands for Tape ARchive because TAR format represents a directory tree as a linear data stream, which makes it ideal for saving directory trees to tape. The same property also makes it the standard for distributing directory trees as a single file. Producing compressed TAR files (or *tarballs*) is pretty easy. On some systems, the *tar* command can produce a compressed archive itself; on others, a separate compression program is used.

Either of these archives, when unpacked, should create a single new directory tree named *scanley-2.5.0* in the current directory. Underneath the new directory, the source code should be arranged in a layout ready for compilation (if compilation is needed) and installation. In the top level of new directory tree, there should be a plain text *README* file explaining what the software does and what release this is, and giving pointers to other resources, such as the project's web site, other files of interest, etc. Among those other files should be an *INSTALL* file, sibling to the *README* file, giving instructions on how to build and install the software for all the operating systems it supports. As mentioned in "How to Apply a License to Your Software" in Chapter 2, there should also be a *COPYING* or *LICENSE* file, giving the software's terms of distribution.

There should also be a *CHANGES* file (sometimes called *NEWS*), explaining what's new in this release. The *CHANGES* file accumulates change lists for all releases, in reverse chronological order, so that the list for this release appears at the top of the file. Completing that list is usually the last thing done on a stabilizing release branch; some projects write the list piecemeal as they're developing, others prefer to save it all up for the end and have one person write it, getting information by combing the version control logs. The list looks something like this:

```
Version 2.5.0
(20 December 2004, from /branches/2.5.x)
http://svn.scanley.org/repos/svn/tags/2.5.0/

New features, enhancements:
    * Added regular expression queries (issue #53)
    * Added support for UTF-8 and UTF-16 documents
    * Documentation translated into Polish, Russian, Malagasy
    * ...
```

```
Bugfixes:
    * fixed reindexing bug (issue #945)
    * fixed some query bugs (issues #815, #1007, #1008)
    * ...
```

The list can be as long as necessary, but don't bother to include every little bug fix and feature enhancement. Its purpose is simply to give users an overview of what they would gain by upgrading to the new release. In fact, the change list is customarily included in the announcement email (see "Testing and Releasing" later in this chapter), so write it with that audience in mind.

CHANGES Versus ChangeLog

Traditionally, a file named *ChangeLog* lists every change ever made to a project—that is, every revision committed to the version control system. There are various formats for ChangeLog files; the details of the formats aren't important here, as they all contain the same information: the date of the change, its author, and a brief summary (or just the log message for that change).

A CHANGES file is different. It, too, is a list of changes, but only the ones thought important for a certain audience to see, and often with metadata like the exact date and author stripped off. To avoid confusion, don't use the terms interchangeably. Some projects use "NEWS" instead of "CHANGES"; although this avoids the potential for confusion with "ChangeLog", it is a bit of a misnomer, since the CHANGES file retains change information for all releases, and thus has a lot of old news in addition to the new news at the top.

ChangeLog files may be slowly disappearing anyway. They were helpful in the days when CVS was the only choice of version control system, because change data was not easy to extract from CVS. However, with more recent version control systems, the data that used to be kept in the ChangeLog can be requested from the version control repository at any time, making it pointless for the project to keep a static file containing that data—in fact, worse than pointless, since the ChangeLog would merely duplicate the log messages already stored in the repository.

The actual layout of the source code inside the tree should be the same as, or as similar as possible to, the source code layout one would get by checking out the project directly from its version control repository. Usually there are a few differences, for example because the package contains some generated files needed for configuration and compilation (see "Compilation and Installation" later in this chapter), or because it includes third-party software that is not maintained by the project, but that is required and that users are not likely to already have. But even if the distributed tree corresponds exactly to some development tree in the version control repository, the distribution itself should not be a working copy (see "Version Control Vocabulary" in Chapter 3). The release is supposed to represent a static reference point—a particular, unchangeable configuration of source files. If it were a working copy, the danger would be that the user might update it, and afterward think that he still has the release when, in fact, he has something different.

Remember that the package is the same regardless of the packaging. The release— that is, the precise entity referred to when someone says "Scanley 2.5.0"—is the tree created by unpacking a zip file or tarball. So the project might offer all of these for download:

scanley-2.5.0.tar.bz2
scanley-2.5.0.gz
scanley-2.5.0.zip

...but the source tree created by unpacking them must be the same. That source tree is the distribution; the form in which it is downloaded is merely a matter of convenience. Certain trivial differences between source packages are allowable: for example, in the Windows package, text files should have lines ending with CRLF (Carriage Return and Line Feed), while Unix packages should use just LF. The trees may be arranged slightly differently between source packages destined for different operating systems, too, if those operating systems require different sorts of layouts for compilation. However, these are all basically trivial transformations. The basic source files should be the same across all the packagings of a given release.

To capitalize or not to capitalize

When referring to a project by name, people generally capitalize it as a proper noun, and capitalize acronyms if there are any: MySQL 5.0, Scanley 2.5.0, etc. Whether this capitalization is reproduced in the package name is up to the project. Either *Scanley-2.5.0.tar.gz* or *scanley-2.5.0.tar.gz* would be fine, for example (I personally prefer the latter, because I don't like to make people hit the Shift key, but plenty of projects ship capitalized packages). The important thing is that the directory created by unpacking the tarball use the same capitalization. There should be no surprises: the user must be able to predict with perfect accuracy the name of the directory that will be created when she unpacks a distribution.

Pre-releases

When shipping a pre-release or candidate release, the qualifier is truly a part of the release number, so include it in the name of the package's name. For example, the ordered sequence of alpha and beta releases given earlier in "Release Number Components" would result in package names like this:

```
scanley-2.3.0-alpha1.tar.gz
scanley-2.3.0-alpha2.tar.gz
scanley-2.3.0-beta1.tar.gz
scanley-2.3.0-beta2.tar.gz
scanley-2.3.0-beta3.tar.gz
scanley-2.3.0.tar.gz
```

The first would unpack into a directory named *scanley-2.3.0-alpha1*, the second into *scanley-2.3.0-alpha2*, and so on.

Compilation and Installation

For software requiring compilation or installation from source, there are usually standard procedures that experienced users expect to be able to follow. For example, for programs written in C, C++, or certain other compiled languages, the standard under Unix-like systems is for the user to type:

```
$ ./configure
$ make
# make install
```

The first command autodetects as much about the environment as it can and prepares for the build process, the second command builds the software in place (but does not install it), and the last command installs it on the system. The first two commands are done as a regular user, the third as root. For more details about setting up this system, see the excellent *GNU Autoconf, Automake, and Libtool* book by Vaughan, Elliston, Tromey, and Taylor. It is published as treeware by New Riders, and its content is also freely available online at *http://sources.redhat.com/autobook/*.

This is not the only standard, though it is one of the most widespread. The Ant (*http://ant.apache.org/*) build system is gaining popularity, especially with projects written in Java, and it has its own standard procedures for building and installing. Also, certain programming languages, such as Perl and Python, recommend that the same method be used for most programs written in that language (for example, Perl modules use the command *perl Makefile.pl*). If it's not obvious to you what the applicable standards are for your project, ask an experienced developer; you can safely assume that *some* standard applies, even if you don't know what it is at first.

Whatever the appropriate standards for you project are, don't deviate from them unless you absolutely must. Standard installation procedures are practically spinal reflexes for a lot of system administrators now. If they see familiar invocations documented in your project's *INSTALL* file, that instantly raises their faith that your project is generally aware of conventions, and that it is likely to have gotten other things right as well. Also, as discussed in "Downloads" in Chapter 2, having a standard build procedure pleases potential developers.

On Windows, the standards for building and installing are a bit less settled. For projects requiring compilation, the general convention seems to be to ship a tree that can fit into the workspace/project model of the standard Microsoft development environments (Developer Studio, Visual Studio, VS.NET, MSVC++, etc.). Depending on the nature of your software, it may be possible to offer a Unix-like build option on Windows via the Cygwin (*http://www.cygwin.com/*) environment. And of course, if you're using a language or programming framework that comes with its own build and install conventions—e.g., Perl or Python—you should simply use whatever the standard method is for that framework, whether on Windows, Unix, Mac OS X, or any other operating system.

Be willing to put in a lot of extra effort in order to make your project conform to the relevant build or installation standards. Building and installing is an entry point: it's okay for things to get harder after that, if they absolutely must, but it would be a shame for the user's or developer's very first interaction with the software to require unexpected steps.

Binary Packages

Although the formal release is a source code package, most users will install from binary packages, either provided by their operating system's software distribution mechanism, or obtained manually from the project web site or from some third party. Here "binary" doesn't necessarily mean "compiled"; it just means any pre-configured form of the package that allows a user to install it on his computer without going through the usual source-based build and install procedures. On RedHat GNU/Linux, it is the RPM system; on Debian GNU/Linux, it is the APT (*.deb*) system; on MS Windows, it's usually *.MSI* files or self-installing *.exe* files.

Whether these binary packages are assembled by people closely associated with the project, or by distant third parties, users are going to *treat* them as equivalent to the project's official releases, and will file issues in the project's bug tracker based on the behavior of the binary packages. Therefore, it is in the project's interest to provide packagers with clear guidelines, and work closely with them to see to it that what they produce represents the software fairly and accurately.

The main thing packagers need to know is that they should always base their binary packages on an official source release. Sometimes packagers are tempted to pull a later incarnation of the code from the repository, or include selected changes that were committed after the release was made, in order to provide users with certain bug fixes or other improvements. The packager thinks he is doing his users a favor by giving them the more recent code, but actually this practice can cause a great deal of confusion. Projects are prepared to receive reports of bugs found in released versions, and bugs found in recent trunk and major branch code (that is, found by people who deliberately run bleeding edge code). When a bug report comes in from these sources, the responder will often be able to confirm that the bug is known to be present in that snapshot, and perhaps that it has since been fixed and that the user should upgrade or wait for the next release. If it is a previously unknown bug, having the precise release makes it easier to reproduce and easier to categorize in the tracker.

Projects are not prepared, however, to receive bug reports based on unspecified intermediate or hybrid versions. Such bugs can be hard to reproduce; also, they may be due to unexpected interactions in isolated changes pulled in from later development, and thereby cause misbehaviors that the project's developers should not have to take the blame for. I have even seen dismayingly large amounts of time wasted because a bug was *absent* when it should have been present: someone was running a slightly patched-up version, based on (but not identical to) an official release, and when the predicted bug did not happen, everyone had to dig around a lot to figure out why.

Still, there will sometimes be circumstances when a packager insists that modifications to the source release are necessary. Packagers should be encouraged to bring this up with the project's developers and describe their plans. They may get approval, but failing that, they will at least have notified the project of their intentions, so the project can watch out for unusual bug reports. The developers may respond by putting a disclaimer on the project's web site, and may ask that the packager do the same thing in the appropriate place, so that users of that binary package know what they are getting is not exactly the same as what the project officially released. There need be no animosity in such a situation, though unfortunately there often is. It's just that packagers have a slightly different set of goals from developers. The packagers mainly want the best out-of-the-box experience for their users. The developers want that too, of course, but they also need to ensure that they know what versions of the software are out there, so they can receive coherent bug reports and make compatibility guarantees. Sometimes these goals conflict. When they do, it's good to keep in mind that the project has no control over the packagers, and that the bonds of obligation run both ways. It's true that the project is doing the packagers a favor simply by producing the software. But the packagers are also doing the project a favor, by taking on a mostly unglamorous job in order to make the software more widely available, often by orders of magnitude. It's fine to disagree with packagers, but don't flame them; just try to work things out as best you can.

Testing and Releasing

Once the source tarball is produced from the stabilized release branch, the public part of the release process begins. But before the tarball is made available to the world at large, it should be tested and approved by some minimum number of developers, usually three or more. Approval is not simply a matter of inspecting the release for obvious flaws; ideally, the developers download the tarball, build and install it onto a clean system, run the regression test suite (see "Automated testing" in Chapter 8), and do some manual testing. Assuming it passes these checks, as well as any other release checklist criteria the project may have, the developers then digitally sign the tarball using GnuPG (*http://www.gnupg.org/*), PGP (*http://www.pgpi.org/*), or some other program capable of producing PGP-compatible signatures.

In most projects, the developers just use their personal digital signatures, instead of a shared project key, and as many developers as want to may sign (i.e., there is a minimum number, but not a maximum). The more developers sign, the more testing the release undergoes, and also the greater the likelihood that a security-conscious user can find a digital trust path from herself to the tarball.

Once approved, the release (that is, all tarballs, zip files, and whatever other formats are being distributed) should be placed into the project's download area, accompanied by the digital signatures, and by MD5/SHA1 checksums (see *http://en.wikipedia.org/wiki/Cryptographic_hash_function*). There are various standards for doing this. One way is to accompany each released package with a file giving the corresponding digital signatures, and another file giving the checksum. For example, if one of the released packages is *scanley-2.5.0.tar.gz*, place in the same directory a file *scanley-2.5.0.tar.gz.asc* containing the digital signature for that tarball, another file *scanley-2.5.0.tar.gz.md5* containing its MD5 checksum, and optionally another, *scanley-2.5.0.tar.gz.sha1*, containing the SHA1 checksum. A different way to provide checking is to collect all the signatures for all the released packages into a single file, *scanley-2.5.0.sigs*; the same may be done with the checksums.

It doesn't really matter which way you do it. Just keep to a simple scheme, describe it clearly, and be consistent from release to release. The purpose of all this signing and checksumming is to give users a way to verify that the copy they receive has not been maliciously tampered with. Users are about to run this code on their computers—if the code has been tampered with, an attacker could suddenly have a back door to all their data. See "Security Releases" later in this chapter for more about paranoia.

Candidate Releases

For important releases containing many changes, many projects prefer to put out *release candidates* first, e.g., *scanley-2.5.0-beta1* before *scanley-2.5.0*. The purpose of a candidate is to subject the code to wide testing before blessing it as an official release. If problems are found, they are fixed on the release branch and a new candidate release is rolled out (*scanley-2.5.0-beta2*). The cycle continues until no unacceptable bugs are left, at which point the last candidate release becomes the official release— that is, the only difference between the last candidate release and the real release is the removal of the qualifier from the version number.

In most other respects, a candidate release should be treated the same as a real release. The *alpha*, *beta*, or *rc* qualifier is enough to warn conservative users to wait until the real release, and of course, the announcement emails for the candidate releases should point out that their purpose is to solicit feedback. Other than that, give candidate releases the same amount of care as regular releases. After all, you want people to use the candidates, because exposure is the best way to uncover bugs, and also because you never know which candidate release will end up becoming the official release.

Announcing Releases

Announcing a release is like announcing any other event, and should use the procedures described in "Publicity" in Chapter 6. There are a few specific things to do for releases, though.

Whenever you give the URL to the downloadable release tarball, make sure to also give the MD5/SHA1 checksums and pointers to the digital signatures file. Since the announcement happens in multiple forums (mailing list, news page, etc.), this means users can get the checksums from multiple sources, which gives the most security-conscious among them extra assurance that the checksums themselves have not been tampered with. Giving the link to the digital signature files multiple times doesn't make those signatures more secure, but it does reassure people (especially those who don't follow the project closely) that the project takes security seriously.

In the announcement email, and on news pages that contain more than just a blurb about the release, make sure to include the relevant portion of the CHANGES file, so people can see why it might be in their interests to upgrade. This is as important with candidate releases as with final releases; the presence of bug fixes and new features is important in tempting people to try out a candidate release.

Finally, don't forget to thank the development team, the testers, and all the people who took the time to file good bug reports. Don't single out anyone by name, though, unless there's someone who is individually responsible for a huge piece of work, the value of which is widely recognized by everyone in the project. Just be wary of sliding down the slippery slope of credit inflation (see "Credit" in Chapter 8).

Maintaining Multiple Release Lines

Most mature projects maintain multiple release lines in parallel. For example, after 1.0.0 comes out, that line should continue with micro (bug fix) releases 1.0.1, 1.0.2, etc., until the project explicitly decides to end the line. Note that merely releasing 1.1.0 is not sufficient reason to end the 1.0.x line. For example, some users make it a policy never to upgrade to the first release in a new minor or major series—they let others shake the bugs out of, say 1.1.0, and wait until 1.1.1. This isn't necessarily selfish (remember, they're forgoing the bug fixes and new features too); it's just that, for whatever reason, they've decided to be very careful with upgrades. Accordingly, if the project learns of a major bug in 1.0.3 right before it's about to release 1.1.0, it would be a bit severe to just put the bug fix in 1.1.0 and tell all the old 1.0.x users they should upgrade. Why not release both 1.1.0 and 1.0.4, so everyone can be happy?

After the 1.1.x line is well under way, you can declare 1.0.x to be at *end of life*. This should be announced officially. The announcement could stand alone, or it could be mentioned as part of a 1.1.x release announcement; however you do it, users need to know that the old line is being phased out, so they can make upgrade decisions accordingly.

Some projects set a window of time during which they pledge to support the previous release line. In an open source context, "support" means accepting bug reports against that line, and making maintenance releases when significant bugs are found. Other projects don't give a definite amount of time, but watch incoming bug reports to gauge how many people are still using the older line. When the percentage drops below a certain point, they declare end of life for the line and stop supporting it.

For each release, make sure to have a *target version* or *target milestone* available in the bug tracker, so people filing bugs will be able to do so against the proper release.

Don't forget to also have a target called "development" or "latest" for the most recent development sources, since some people—not only active developers—will often stay ahead of the official releases.

Security Releases

Most of the details of handling security bugs were covered in "Announcing Security Vulnerabilities" in Chapter 6, but there are some special details to discuss for doing security releases.

A *security release* is a release made solely to close a security vulnerability. The code that fixes the bug cannot be made public until the release is available, which means not only that the fixes cannot be committed to the repository until the day of the release, but also that the release cannot be publicly tested before it goes out the door. Obviously, the developers can examine the fix among themselves, and test the release privately, but widespread real-world testing is not possible.

Because of this lack of testing, a security release should always consist of some existing release plus the fixes for the security bug, with *no other changes*. This is because the more changes you ship without testing, the more likely that one of them will cause a new bug, perhaps even a new security bug! This conservativism is also friendly to administrators who may need to deploy the security fix, but whose upgrade policy prefers that they not deploy any other changes at the same time.

Making a security release sometimes involves some minor deception. For example, the project may have been working on a 1.1.3 release, with certain bug fixes to 1.1.2 already publicly declared, when a security report comes in. Naturally, the developers cannot talk about the security problem until they make the fix available; until then, they must continue to talk publicly as though 1.1.3 will be what it's always been planned to be. But when 1.1.3 actually comes out, it will differ from 1.1.2 only in the security fixes, and all those other fixes will have been deferred to 1.1.4 (which, of course, will now *also* contain the security fix, as will all other future releases).

You could add an extra component to an existing release to indicate that it contains security changes only. For example, people would be able to tell just from the numbers that 1.1.2.1 is a security release against 1.1.2, and they would know that any release higher than that (e.g., 1.1.3, 1.2.0, etc.) contains the same security fixes. For those in the know, this system conveys a lot of information. On the other hand, for those not following the project closely, it can be a bit confusing to see a three-component release number most of the time with an occasional four-component one thrown in seemingly at random. Most projects I've looked at choose consistency and simply use the next regularly scheduled number for security releases, even when it means shifting other planned releases by one.

Releases and Daily Development

Maintaining parallel releases simultaneously has implications for how daily development is done. In particular, it makes practically mandatory a discipline that would be recommended anyway: have each commit be a single logical change, and never mix unrelated changes in the same commit. If a change is too big or too disruptive to do in one commit, break it across N commits, where each commit is a well-partitioned subset of the overall change, and includes nothing unrelated to the overall change.

Here's an example of an ill-thought-out commit:

```
------------------------------------------------------------------------
r6228 | jrandom | 2004-06-30 22:13:07 -0500 (Wed, 30 Jun 2004) | 8 lines

Fix Issue #1729: Make indexing gracefully warn the user when a file
is changing as it is being indexed.

* ui/repl.py
  (ChangingFile): New exception class.
  (DoIndex): Handle new exception.

* indexer/index.py
  (FollowStream): Raise new exception if file changes during indexing.
  (BuildDir): Unrelatedly, remove some obsolete comments, reformat
  some code, and fix the error check when creating a directory.

Other unrelated cleanups:

* www/index.html: Fix some typos, set next release date.
------------------------------------------------------------------------
```

The problem with it becomes apparent as soon as someone needs to port the BuildDir error check fix over to a branch for an upcoming maintenance release. The porter doesn't want any of the other changes—for example, perhaps the fix to issue #1729 wasn't approved for the maintenance branch at all, and the *index.html* tweaks would simply be irrelevant there. But he cannot easily grab just the BuildDir change via the version control tool's merge functionality, because the version control system was told that the change is logically grouped with all these other unrelated things. In fact, the problem would become apparent even before the merge. Merely listing the change for voting would become problematic: instead of just giving the revision number, the proposer would have to make a special patch or change branch just to isolate the portion of the commit being proposed. That would be a lot of work for others to suffer through, and all because the original committer couldn't be bothered to break things into logical groups.

In fact, that commit really should have been *four* separate commits: one to fix issue #1729, another to remove obsolete comments and reformat code in `BuildDir`, another to fix the error check in `BuildDir`, and finally, one to tweak *index.html*. The third of those commits would be the one proposed for the maintenance release branch.

Of course, release stabilization is not the only reason why having each commit be one logical change is desirable. Psychologically, a semantically unified commit is easier to review, and easier to revert if necessary (in some version control systems, reversion is really a special kind of merge anyway). A little up-front discipline on everyone's part can save the project a lot of headache later.

Planning Releases

One area where open source projects have historically differed from proprietary projects is in release planning. Proprietary projects usually have firmer deadlines. Sometimes it's because customers were promised that an upgrade would be available by a certain date, because the new release needs to be coordinated with some other effort for marketing purposes, or because the venture capitalists who invested in the whole thing need to see some results before they put in any more funding. Free software projects, on the other hand, were until recently mostly motivated by amateurism in the most literal sense: they were written for the love of it. No one felt the need to ship before all the features were ready, and why should they? It wasn't as if anyone's job was on the line.

Nowadays, many open source projects are funded by corporations, and are correspondingly more and more influenced by deadline-conscious corporate culture. This is in many ways a good thing, but it can cause conflicts between the priorities of those developers who are being paid and those who are volunteering their time. These conflicts often happen around the issue of when and how to schedule releases. The salaried developers who are under pressure will naturally want to just pick a date when the releases will occur, and have everyone's activities fall into line. But the volunteers may have other agendas—perhaps features they want to complete, or some testing they want to have done—that they feel the release should wait on.

There is no general solution to this problem except discussion and compromise, of course. But you can minimize the frequency and degree of friction caused, by decoupling the proposed *existence* of a given release from the date when it would go out the door. That is, try to steer discussion toward the subject of which releases the project will be making in the near- to medium-term future, and what features will be in them, without at first mentioning anything about dates, except for rough guesses with wide margins of error. By nailing down feature sets early, you reduce the complexity of the discussion centered on any individual release, and therefore improve predictability. This also creates a kind of inertial bias against anyone who proposes to expand the definition of a release by adding new features or other complications. If the release's contents are fairly well defined, the onus is on the proposer to justify the expansion, even though the date of the release may not have been set yet.

In his multivolume biography of Thomas Jefferson, *Jefferson and His Time* (University Press of Virginia, 2005), Dumas Malone tells the story of how Jefferson handled the first meeting held to decide the organization of the future University of Virginia. The University had been Jefferson's idea in the first place, but (as is the case everywhere, not just in open source projects) many other parties had climbed on board quickly, each with their own interests and agendas. When they gathered at that first meeting to hash things out, Jefferson made sure to show up with meticulously prepared architectural drawings, detailed budgets for construction and operation, a proposed curriculum, and the names of specific faculty he wanted to import from Europe. No one else in the room was even remotely as prepared; the group essentially had to capitulate to Jefferson's vision, and the University was eventually founded more or less in accordance with his plans. The facts that construction went far over budget, and that many of his ideas did not, for various reasons, work out in the end, were all things Jefferson probably knew perfectly well would happen. His purpose was strategic: to show up at the meeting with something so substantive that everyone else would have to fall into the role of simply proposing modifications to it, so that the overall shape, and therefore schedule, of the project would be roughly as he wanted.

In the case of a free software project, there is no single "meeting," but instead a series of small proposals made mostly by means of the issue tracker. But if you have some credibility in the project to start with, and you start assigning various features, enhancements, and bugs to target releases in the issue tracker, according to some announced overall plan, people will mostly go along with you. Once you've got things laid out more or less as you want them, the conversations about actual release *dates* will go much more smoothly.

It is crucial, of course, to never present any individual decision as written in stone. In the comments associated with each assignment of an issue to a specific future release, invite discussion, dissent, and be genuinely willing to be persuaded whenever possible. Never exercise control merely for the sake of exercising control: the more deeply others participate in the release planning process (see "Share Management Tasks as Well as Technical Tasks" in Chapter 8), the easier it will be to persuade them to share your priorities on the issues that really count for you.

The other way the project can lower tensions around release planning is to make releases fairly often. When there's a long time between releases, the importance of any individual release is magnified in everyone's minds; people are that much more crushed when their code doesn't make it in, because they know how long it might be until the next chance. Depending on the complexity of the release process and the nature of your project, somewhere between every three and six months is usually about the right gap between releases, though maintenance lines may put out micro releases a bit faster, if there is demand for them.

CHAPTER 8

Managing Volunteers

Getting people to agree on what a project needs, and to work together to achieve it, requires more than just a genial atmosphere and a lack of obvious dysfunction. It requires someone, or several someones, consciously managing all the people involved. Managing volunteers may not be a technical craft in the same sense as computer programming, but it is a craft in the sense that it can be improved through study and practice.

This chapter is a grab-bag of specific techniques for managing volunteers. It draws, perhaps more heavily than previous chapters, on the Subversion project as a case study, partly because I was working on that project as I wrote this and had all the primary sources close at hand, and partly because it's more acceptable to cast critical stones into one's own glass house than into others'. But I have also seen in various other projects the benefits of applying—and the consequences of not applying—the recommendations that follow; when it is politically feasible to give examples from some of those other projects, I will do so.

Speaking of politics, this is as good a time as any to drag that much-maligned word out for a closer look. Many engineers like to think of politics as something other people engage in. "*I'm* just advocating the best course for the project, but *she's* raising objections for political reasons." I believe this distaste for politics (or for what is imagined to be politics) is especially strong in engineers because engineers are bought into the idea that some solutions are objectively superior to others. Thus, when someone acts in a way that seems motivated by outside considerations—say, the maintenance of his own position of influence, the lessening of someone else's influence, outright horse-trading, or avoiding hurting someone's feelings—other participants in the project may get annoyed. Of course, this rarely prevents them from behaving in the same way when their own vital interests are at stake.

If you consider "politics" a dirty word, and hope to keep your project free of it, give up right now. Politics are inevitable whenever people have to cooperatively manage a shared resource. It is absolutely rational that one of the considerations going into each person's decision-making process is the question of how a given action might affect his own future influence in the project. After all, if you trust your own judgement and skills, as most programmers do, then the potential loss of future influence has to be considered a technical result, in a sense. Similar reasoning applies to other behaviors that might seem, on their face, like "pure" politics. In fact, there is no such thing as pure politics: it is precisely because actions have real-world consequences that people become politically conscious in the first place. Politics is, in the end, simply an acknowledgment that *all* consequences of decisions must be taken into account. If a particular decision leads to a result that most participants find technically satisfying, but involves a change in power relationships that leaves key people feeling isolated, the latter is just as important a result as the former. To ignore it would not be high-minded, but shortsighted.

So as you read the advice that follows, and as you work with your own project, remember that there is *no one* who is above politics. Appearing to be above politics is merely one particular political strategy, and sometimes a very useful one, but it is never the reality. Politics is simply what happens when people disagree, and successful projects are those that evolve political mechanisms for managing disagreement constructively.

Getting the Most Out of Volunteers

Why do volunteers work on free software projects?[1]

When asked, many claim they do it because they want to produce good software, or want to be personally involved in fixing the bugs that matter to them. But these reasons are usually not the whole story. After all, could you imagine a volunteer staying with a project even if no one ever said a word in appreciation of his work, or listened

---

[1]   This question was studied in detail, with interesting results, in a paper by Karim Lakhani and Robert G. Wolf, entitled "Why Hackers Do What They Do: Understanding Motivation and Effort in Free/Open Source Software Projects." See *http://freesoftware.mit.edu/papers/lakhaniwolf.pdf*.

to him in discussions? Of course not. Clearly, people spend time on free software for reasons beyond just an abstract desire to produce good code. Understanding volunteers' true motivations will help you arrange things so as to attract and keep them. The desire to produce good software may be among those motivations, along with the challenge and educational value of working on hard problems. But humans also have a built-in desire to work with other humans, and to give and earn respect through cooperative activities. Groups engaged in cooperative activities must evolve norms of behavior such that status is acquired and kept through actions that help the group's goals.

Those norms won't always arise by themselves. For example, on some projects—experienced open source developers can probably name several off the tops of their heads—people apparently feel that status is acquired by posting frequently and verbosely. They don't come to this conclusion accidentally; they come to it because they are rewarded with respect for making long, intricate arguments, whether or not that actually help the project. Following are some techniques for creating an atmosphere in which status-acquiring actions are also constructive actions.

Delegation

Delegation is not merely a way to spread the workload around; it is also a political and social tool. Consider all the effects when you ask someone to do something. The most obvious effect is that, if she accepts, she does the task and you don't. But another effect is that she is made aware that you trusted her to handle the task. Furthermore, if you made the request in a public forum, then she knows that others in the group have been made aware of that trust too. She may also feel some pressure to accept, which means you must ask in a way that allows her to decline gracefully if she doesn't really want the job. If the task requires coordination with others in the project, you are effectively proposing that she become more involved, form bonds that might not otherwise have been formed, and perhaps become a source of authority in some subdomain of the project. The added involvement may be daunting, or it may lead her to become engaged in other ways as well, from an increased feeling of overall commitment.

Because of all these effects, it often makes sense to ask someone else to do something even when you know you could do it faster or better yourself. Of course, there is sometimes a strict economic efficiency argument for this anyway: perhaps the opportunity cost of doing it yourself would be too high—there might be something even more important you could do with that time. But even when the opportunity cost argument doesn't apply, you may *still* want to ask someone else to take on the task, because in the long run you want to draw that person deeper into the project, even if it means spending extra time watching over them at first. The converse technique also applies: if you occasionally volunteer for work that someone else doesn't want or have time to do, you will gain his good will and respect. Delegation and substitution are not just about getting individual tasks done; they're also about drawing people into a closer commitment to the project.

Distinguish clearly between inquiry and assignment

Sometimes it is fair to expect that a person will accept a particular task. For example, if someone writes a bug into the code, or commits code that fails to comply with project guidelines in some obvious way, then it is enough to point out the problem and thereafter behave as though you assume the person will take care of it. But there are other situations where it is by no means clear that you have a right to expect action. The person may do as you ask, or may not. Since no one likes to be taken for granted, you need to be sensitive to the difference between these two types of situations, and tailor your requests accordingly.

One thing that almost always causes people instant annoyance is being asked to do something in a way that implies that you think it is clearly their responsibility to do it, when they feel otherwise. For example, assignment of incoming issues is particularly fertile ground for this kind of annoyance. The participants in a project usually know who is expert in what areas, so when a bug report comes in, there will often be one or two people whom everyone knows could probably fix it quickly. However, if you assign the issue over to one of those people without her prior permission, she may feel she has been put into an uncomfortable position. She senses the pressure of expectation, but also may feel that she is, in effect, being punished for her expertise. After all, the way one acquires expertise is by fixing bugs, so perhaps someone else should take this one! (Note that issue trackers that automatically assign issues to particular people based on information in the bug report are less likely to offend, because everyone knows that the assignment was made by an automated process, and is not an indication of human expectations.)

While it would be nice to spread the load as evenly as possible, there are certain times when you just want to encourage the person who can fix a bug the fastest to do so. Given that you can't afford a communications turnaround for every such assignment ("Would you be willing to look at this bug?" "Yes." "Okay, I'm assigning the issue over to you then." "Okay."), you should simply make the assignment in the form of an inquiry, conveying no pressure. Virtually all issue trackers allow a comment to be associated with the assignment of an issue. In that comment, you can say something like this:

Assigning this over to you, jrandom, because you're most familiar with this code. Feel free to bounce this back if you don't have time to look at it, though. (And let me know if you'd prefer not to receive such requests in the future.)

This distinguishes clearly between the *request* for assignment and the recipient's *acceptance* of that assignment. The audience here isn't only the assignee, it's everyone: the entire group sees a public confirmation of the assignee's expertise, but the message also makes it clear that the assignee is free to accept or decline the responsibility.

Follow up after you delegate

When you ask someone to do something, remember that you have done so, and follow up with him no matter what. Most requests are made in public forums, and are roughly of the form "Can you take care of X? Let us know either way; no problem if you can't, just need to know." You may or may not get a response. If you do, and the response is negative, the loop is closed—you'll need to try some other strategy for dealing with X. If there is a positive response, then keep an eye out for progress on the issue, and comment on the progress you do or don't see (everyone works better when they know someone else is appreciating their work). If there is no response after a few days, ask again, or post saying that you got no response and are looking for someone else to do it. Or just do it yourself, but still make sure to say that you got no response to the initial inquiry.

The purpose of publicly noting the lack of response is *not* to humiliate the person, and your remarks should be phrased so as not to have that effect. The purpose is simply to show that you keep track of what you have asked for, and that you notice the reactions you get. This makes people more likely to say yes next time, because they will observe (even if only unconsciously) that you are likely to notice any work they do, given that you noticed the much less visible event of someone failing to respond.

Notice what people are interested in

Another thing that makes people happy is to have their interests noticed—in general, the more aspects of someone's personality you notice and remember, the more comfortable he will be, and the more he will want to work with groups of which you are a part.

For example, there was a sharp distinction in the Subversion project between people who wanted to reach a definitive 1.0 release (which we eventually did), and people who mainly wanted to add new features and work on interesting problems but who didn't much care when 1.0 came out. Neither of these positions is better or worse than the other; they're just two different kinds of developers, and both kinds do lots of work on the project. But we swiftly learned that it was important to *not* assume that the excitement of the 1.0 drive was shared by everyone. Electronic media can be very deceptive: you may sense an atmosphere of shared purpose when, in fact, it's shared only by the people you happen to have been talking to, while others have completely different priorities.

The more aware you are of what people want out of the project, the more effectively you can make requests of them. Even just demonstrating an understanding of what they want, without making any associated request, is useful, in that it confirms to each person that she's not just another particle in an undifferentiated mass.

Praise and Criticism

Praise and criticism are not opposites; in many ways, they are very similar. Both are primarily forms of attention, and are most effective when specific rather than generic. Both should be deployed with concrete goals in mind. Both can be diluted by inflation: praise too much or too often and you will devalue your praise; the same is true for criticism, though in practice, criticism is usually reactive and therefore a bit more resistant to devaluation.

An important feature of technical culture is that detailed, dispassionate criticism is often taken as a kind of praise (as discussed in "Recognizing Rudeness" in Chapter 6), because of the implication that the recipient's work is worth the time required to analyze it. However, both of those conditions—*detailed, and dispassionate*—must be met for this to be true. For example, if someone makes a sloppy change to the code, it is useless (and actually harmful) to follow up saying simply "That was sloppy." Sloppiness is ultimately a characteristic of a *person*, not of their work, and it's important to keep your reactions focused on the work. It's much more effective to describe all the things wrong with the change, tactfully and without malice. If this is the third or fourth careless change in a row by the same person, it's appropriate to say that— again without anger—at the end of your critique, to make it clear that the pattern has been noticed.

If someone does not improve in response to criticism, the solution is not more or stronger criticism. The solution is for the group to remove that person from the position of incompetence, in a way that minimizes hurt feelings as much as possible; see "Transitions" later in this chapter for examples. That is a rare occurrence, however. Most people respond pretty well to criticism that is specific, detailed, and contains a clear (even if unspoken) expectation of improvement.

Praise won't hurt anyone's feelings, of course, but that doesn't mean it should be used any less carefully than criticism. Praise is a tool: before you use it, ask yourself *why* you want to use it. As a rule, it's not a good idea to praise people for doing what they usually do, or for actions that are a normal and expected part of participating in the group. If you were to do that, it would be hard to know when to stop: should you praise *everyone* for doing the usual things? After all, if you leave some people out, they'll wonder why. It's much better to express praise and gratitude sparingly, in response to unusual or unexpected efforts, with the intention of encouraging more of such efforts. When a participant seems to have moved permanently into a state of higher productivity, adjust your praise threshold for that person accordingly. Repeated praise for normal behavior gradually becomes meaningless anyway. Instead, that person should sense that her high level of productivity is now considered normal and natural, and only work that goes beyond that should be specially noticed.

This is not to say that the person's contributions shouldn't be acknowledged, of course. But remember that if the project is set up right, everything that person does is already visible anyway, and so the group will know (and the person will know that the rest of the group knows) everything she does. There are also ways to acknowledge someone's work by means other than direct praise. You could mention in passing, while discussing a related topic, that she has done a lot of work in the given area and is the resident expert there; you could publicly consult her on some question about the code; or perhaps most effectively, you could conspicuously make further use of the work she has done, so she sees that others are now comfortable relying on the results of her work. It's probably not necessary to do these things in any calculated way. Someone who regularly makes large contributions in a project will know it, and will occupy a position of influence by default. There's usually no need to take explicit steps to ensure this, unless you sense that, for whatever reason, a contributor is underappreciated.

Prevent Territoriality

Watch out for participants who try to stake out exclusive ownership of certain areas of the project, and who seem to want to do all the work in those areas, to the extent of aggressively taking over work that others start. Such behavior may even seem healthy at first. After all, on the surface it looks like the person is taking on more responsibility, and showing increased activity within a given area. But in the long run, it is destructive. When people sense a "no trespassing" sign, they stay away. This results in reduced review in that area, and greater fragility, because the lone developer becomes a single point of failure. Worse, it fractures the cooperative, egalitarian spirit of the project. The theory should always be that any developer is welcome to help out on any task at any time. Of course, in practice, things work a bit differently: people do have areas where they are more and less influential, and non-experts frequently defer to experts in certain domains of the project. But the key is that this is all voluntary: informal authority is granted based on competence and proven judgement, but it should never be actively *taken*. Even if the person desiring the authority really is competent, it is still crucial that he hold that authority informally, through the consensus of the group, and that the authority never cause him to exclude others from working in that area.

Rejecting or editing someone's work for technical reasons is an entirely different matter, of course. There, the decisive factor is the content of the work, not who happened to act as gatekeeper. It may be that the same person happens to do most of the reviewing for a given area, but as long as he never tries to prevent someone else from doing that work too, things are probably okay.

In order to combat incipient territorialism, or even the appearance of it, many projects have taken the step of banning the inclusion of author names or designated maintainer names in source files. I wholeheartedly agree with this practice: we follow it in the Subversion project, and it is more or less official policy at the Apache Software Foundation. ASF member Sander Striker puts it this way:

> At the Apache Software foundation we discourage the use of author tags in source code. There are various reasons for this, apart from the legal ramifications. Collaborative development is about working on projects as a group and caring for the project as a group. Giving credit is good, and should be done, but in a way that does not allow for false attribution, even by implication. There is no clear line for when to add or remove an author tag. Do you add your name when you change a comment? When you put in a one-line fix? Do you remove other author tags when you refactor the code and it looks 95% different? What do you do about people who go about touching every file, changing just enough to make the virtual author tag quota, so that their name will be everywhere?
>
> There are better ways to give credit, and our preference is to use those. From a technical standpoint author tags are unnecessary; if you wish to find out who wrote a particular piece of code, the version control system can be consulted to figure that out. Author tags also tend to get out of date. Do you really wish to be contacted in private about a piece of code you wrote five years ago and were glad to have forgotten?

A software project's source code files are the core of its identity. They should reflect the fact that the developer community as a whole is responsible for them, and not be divided up into little fiefdoms.

People sometimes argue in favor of author or maintainer tags in source files on the grounds that this gives visible credit to those who have done the most work there. There are two problems with this argument. First, the tags inevitably raise the awkward question of how much work one must do to get one's own name listed there too. Second, they conflate the issue of credit with that of authority: having done work in the past does not imply ownership of the area where the work was done, but it's difficult if not impossible to avoid such an implication when individual names are listed at the tops of source files. In any case, credit information can already be obtained from the version control logs and other out-of-band mechanisms like mailing list archives, so no information is lost by banning it from the source files themselves.

If your project decides to ban individual names from source files, make sure not to go overboard. For instance, many projects have a *contrib/* area where small tools and helper scripts are kept, often written by people who are otherwise not associated with the project. It's fine for those files to contain author names, because they are not really maintained by the project as a whole. On the other hand, if a contributed tool starts getting hacked on by other people in the project, eventually you may want to move it to a less isolated location and, assuming the original author approves, remove the author's name, so that the code looks like any other community-maintained resource. If the author is sensitive about this, compromise solutions are acceptable, for example:

```
# indexclean.py: Remove old data from a Scanley index.
#
# Original Author: K. Maru <kobayashi@yetanotheremailservice.com>
# Now Maintained By: The Scanley Project <http://www.scanley.org/>
#                    and K. Maru.
#
# ...
```

But it's better to avoid such compromises, if possible, and most authors are willing to be persuaded, because they're happy that their contribution is being made a more integral part of the project.

The important thing is to remember that there is a continuum between the core and the periphery of any project. The main source code files for the software are clearly part of the core, and should be considered as maintained by the community. On the other hand, companion tools or pieces of documentation may be the work of single individuals, who maintain them essentially alone, even though the works may be associated with, and even distributed with, the project. There is no need to apply a one-size-fits-all rule to every file, as long as the principle that community-maintained resources are not allowed to become individual territories is upheld.

The Automation Ratio

Try not to let humans do what machines could do instead. As a rule of thumb, automating a common task is worth at least 10 times the effort a developer would spend doing that task manually one time. For very frequent or very complex tasks, that ratio could easily go up to 20 or even higher.

Thinking of yourself as a "project manager," rather than just another developer, may be a useful attitude here. Sometimes individual developers are too wrapped up in low-level work to see the big picture and realize that everyone is wasting a lot of effort performing automatable tasks manually. Even those who do realize it may not take the time to solve the problem: because each individual performance of the task does not feel like a huge burden, no one ever gets annoyed enough to do anything about it. What makes automation compelling is that the small burden is multiplied by the number of times each developer incurs it, and then *that* number is multiplied by the number of developers.

Here, I am using the term "automation" broadly, to mean not only repeated actions where one or two variables change each time, but any sort of technical infrastructure that assists humans. The minimum standard automation required to run a project these days was described in Chapter 3, but each project may have its own special problems too. For example, a group working on documentation might want to have a web site displaying the most up-to-date versions of the documents at all times. Since documentation is often written in a markup language like XML, there may be a compilation step, often quite intricate, involved in creating displayable or download-able documents. Arranging a web site where such compilation happens automatically on every commit can be complicated and time-consuming—but it is worth it, even if it costs you a day or more to set up. The overall benefits of having up-to-date pages available at all times are huge, even though the cost of *not* having them might seem like only a small annoyance at any single moment, to any single developer.

Taking such steps eliminates not merely wasted time, but the griping and frustration that ensue when humans make missteps (as they inevitably will) in trying to perform complicated procedures manually. Multi-step, deterministic operations are exactly what computers were invented for; save your humans for more interesting things.

Automated testing

Automated test runs are helpful for any software project, but especially so for open source projects, because automated testing (especially regression testing) allows developers to feel comfortable changing code in areas they are unfamiliar with, and thus encourages exploratory development. Since detecting breakage is so hard to do by hand—one essentially has to guess where one might have broken something, and try various experiments to prove that one didn't—having automated ways to detect such breakage saves the project a *lot* of time. It also makes people much more relaxed about refactoring large swaths of code, and therefore contributes to the software's long-term maintainability.

Regression Testing

Regression testing means testing for the reappearance of bugs that were already fixed. The purpose of regression testing is to reduce the chances that code changes will break the software in unexpected ways. As a software project gets bigger and more complicated, the chances of such unexpected side effects increase steadily. Good design can reduce the rate at which the chances increase, but it cannot eliminate the problem entirely.

As a result, many projects have a *test suite*, a separate program that invokes the project's software in ways that have been known in the past to stimulate specific bugs. If the test suite succeeds in making one of these bugs happen, this is known as a *regression*, meaning that someone's change unexpectedly unfixed a previously fixed bug.

See also *http://en.wikipedia.org/wiki/Regression_testing*.

Regression testing is not a panacea. For one thing, it works best for programs with batch-style interfaces. Software that is operated primarily through graphical user interfaces is much harder to drive programmatically. Another problem is that the regression test suite framework itself can often be quite complex, with a learning curve and maintenance burden all its own. Reducing this complexity is one of the most useful things you can do, even though it may take a considerable amount of time. The easier it is to add new tests to the suite, the more developers will do so, and the fewer bugs will survive to release. Any effort spent making tests easier to write will be paid back manyfold over the lifetime of the project.

Many projects have a *"Don't break the build!"* rule, meaning: don't commit a change that makes the software unable to compile or run. Being the person who broke the build is usually cause for mild embarrassment and ribbing. Projects with regression test suites often have a corollary rule: don't commit any change that causes tests to fail. Such failures are easiest to spot if there are automatic nightly runs of the entire test suite, with the results mailed out to the development list or to a dedicated test-results mailing list; that's another example of a worthwhile automation.

Most volunteer developers are willing to take the extra time to write regression tests, when the test system is comprehensible and easy to work with. Accompanying changes with tests is understood to be the responsible thing to do, and it's also an easy opportunity for collaboration: often two developers will divide up the work for a bug fix, with one writing the fix itself, and the other writing the test. The latter developer may often end up with more work, and since writing a test is already less satisfying than actually fixing the bug, it is imperative that the test suite not make the experience more painful than it has to be.

Some projects go even further, requiring that a new test accompany *every* bug fix or new feature. Whether this is a good idea or not depends on many factors: the nature of the software, the makeup of the development team, and the difficulty of writing new tests. The CVS (*http://www.cvshome.org/*) project has long had such a rule. It is a good policy in theory, since CVS is version control software and therefore very risk-averse about the possibility of munging or mishandling the user's data. The problem in practice is that CVS's regression test suite is a single huge shell script (amusingly named *sanity.sh*), hard to read and hard to modify or extend. The difficulty of adding new tests, combined with the requirement that patches be accompanied by new tests, means that CVS effectively discourages patches. When I used to work on CVS, I sometimes saw people start on and even complete a patch to CVS's own code, but give up when told of the requirement to add a new test to *sanity.sh*.

It is normal to spend more time writing a new regression test than on fixing the original bug. But CVS carried this phenomenon to an extreme: one might spend hours trying to design one's test properly, and still get it wrong, because there are just too many unpredictable complexities involved in changing a 35,000-line Bourne shell script. Even longtime CVS developers often grumbled when they had to add a new test.

This situation was due to a failure on all our parts to consider the automation ratio. It is true that switching to a real test framework—whether custom-built or off-the-shelf—would have been a major effort.[2] But neglecting to do so has cost the project much more, over the years. How many bug fixes and new features are *not* in CVS today, because of the impediment of an awkward test suite? We cannot know the exact

---

2   Note that there would be no need to convert all the existing tests to the new framework; the two could happily exist side by side, with old tests converted over only as they needed to be changed.

number, but it is surely many times greater than the number of bug fixes or new features the developers might forgo in order to develop a new test system (or integrate an off-the-shelf system). That task would only take a finite amount of time, while the penalty of using the current test suite will continue forever if nothing is done.

The point is not that having strict requirements to write tests is bad, nor that writing your test system as a Bourne shell script is necessarily bad. It might work fine, depending on how you design it and what it needs to test. The point is simply that when the test system becomes a significant impediment to development, something must be done. The same is true for any routine process that turns into a barrier or a bottleneck.

Treat Every User as a Potential Volunteer

Each interaction with a user is an opportunity to get a new volunteer. When a user takes the time to post to one of the project's mailing lists, or to file a bug report, he has already tagged himself as having more potential for involvement than most users (from whom the project will never hear at all). Follow up on that potential: if he described a bug, thank him for the report and ask him if he wants to try fixing it. If he wrote to say that an important question was missing from the FAQ, or that the program's documentation was deficient in some way, then freely acknowledge the problem (assuming it really exists) and ask if he's interested in writing the missing material himself. Naturally, much of the time the user will demur. But it doesn't cost much to ask, and every time you do, it reminds the other listeners in that forum that getting involved in the project is something anyone can do.

Don't limit your goals to acquiring new developers and documentation writers. For example, even training people to write good bug reports pays off in the long run, if you don't spend *too* much time per person, and if they go on to submit more bug reports in the future—which they are more likely to do if they got a constructive reaction to their first report. A constructive reaction need not be a fix for the bug, although that's always the ideal; it can also be a solicitation for more information, or even just a confirmation that the behavior *is* a bug. People want to be listened to. Secondarily, they want their bugs fixed. You may not always be able to give them the latter in a timely fashion, but you (or rather, the project as a whole) can give them the former.

A corollary of this is that developers should not express anger at people who file well-intended but vague bug reports. This is one of my personal pet peeves; I see developers do it all the time on various open source mailing lists, and the harm it does is palpable. Some hapless newbie will post a useless report:

> Hi, I can't get Scanley to run. Every time I start it up, it just errors. Is anyone else seeing this problem?

Some developer—who has seen this kind of report a thousand times, and hasn't stopped to think that the newbie has not—will respond like this:

> What are we supposed to do with so little information? Sheesh. Give us at least some details, like the version of Scanley, your operating system, and the error.

This developer has failed to see things from the user's point of view, and also failed to consider the effect such a reaction might have on all the *other* people watching the exchange. Naturally a user who has no programming experience, and no prior experience reporting bugs, will not know how to write a bug report. What is the right way to handle such a person? Educate them! And do it in such a way that they come back for more:

> Sorry you're having trouble. We'll need more information in order to figure out what's happening here. Please tell us the version of Scanley, your operating system, and the exact text of the error. The very best thing you can do is send a transcript showing the exact commands you ran, and the output they produced. See *http://www.scanley.org/how_to_report_a_bug.html* for more.

This way of responding is far more effective at extracting the needed information from the user, because it is written to the user's point of view. First, it expresses sympathy: *You had a problem; we feel your pain.* (This is not necessary in every bug report response; it depends on the severity of the problem and how upset the user seemed.) Second, instead of belittling her for not knowing how to report a bug, it tells her how, and in enough detail to be actually useful—for example, many users don't realize that "show us the error" means "show us the exact text of the error, with no omissions or abridgements." The first time you work with such a user, you need to be specific about that. Finally, it offers a pointer to much more detailed and complete instructions for reporting bugs. If you have successfully engaged with the user, she will often take the time to read that document and do what it says. This means, of course, that you have to have the document prepared in advance. It should give clear instructions about what kind of information your development team wants to see in every bug report. Ideally, it should also evolve over time in response to the particular sorts of omissions and misreports users tend to make for your project.

The Subversion project's bug reporting instructions are a fairly standard example of the form (see Appendix D). Notice how they close with an invitation to provide a patch to fix the bug. This is not because such an invitation will lead to a greater patch/report ratio—most users who are capable of fixing bugs already know that a patch would be welcome, and don't need to be told. The invitation's real purpose is to emphasize to all readers, especially those new to the project or new to free software in general, that the project runs on volunteer contributions. In a sense, the project's current developers are no more responsible for fixing the bug than is the person who reported it. This is an important point that many new users will not be familiar with. Once they realize it, they're more likely to help make the fix happen, if not by contributing code then by providing a more thorough reproduction recipe, or by offering to test fixes that other people post. The goal is to make every user realize that there is no *innate* difference between her self and the people who work on the project—that it's a question of how much time and effort one puts in, not a question of who one is.

The admonition against responding angrily does not apply to rude users. Occasionally people post bug reports or complaints that, regardless of their informational content, show a sneering contempt at the project for some failing. Often such people are alternately insulting and flattering, such as the person who posted this to a Subversion mailing list:

> Why is it that after almost 6 days there still aren't any binaries posted for the windows platform?!? It's the same story every time and it's pretty frustrating. Why aren't these things automated so that they could be available immediately?? When you post an "RC" build, I think the idea is that you want users to test the build, but yet you don't provide any way of doing so. Why even have a soak period if you provide no means of testing??

Initial response to this rather inflammatory post was surprisingly restrained: people pointed out that the project had a published policy of not providing official binaries, and said, with varying degrees of annoyance, that he ought to volunteer to produce them himself if they were so important to him. Believe it or not, his next post started with these lines:

> First of all, let me say that I think Subversion is awesome and I really appreciate the efforts of everyone involved. [...]

...and then he went on to berate the project *again* for not providing binaries, while still not volunteering to do anything about it. After that, about 50 people just jumped all over him, and I can't say I really minded. The "zero-tolerance" policy toward rudeness advocated in "Nip Rudeness in the Bud" in Chapter 2 applies to people with whom the project has (or would like to have) a sustained interaction. But when someone makes it clear from the start that he is going to be a fountain of bile, there is no point making him feel welcome.

Such situations are fortunately quite rare, and they are noticeably rarer in projects that make an effort to engage users constructively and courteously from their very first interaction.

Share Management Tasks as Well as Technical Tasks

Share the management burden as well as the technical burden of running the project. As a project becomes more complex, more and more of the work is about managing people and information flow. There is no reason not to share that burden, and sharing it does not necessarily require a top-down hierarchy either—what happens in practice tends to be more of a peer-to-peer network topology than a military-style command structure.

Sometimes management roles are formalized, and sometimes they happen spontaneously. In the Subversion project, we have a patch manager, a translation manager, documentation managers, issue managers (albeit unofficial), and a release manager. Some of these roles we made a conscious decision to initiate, others just happened by themselves; as the project grows, I expect more roles to be added. Below we'll examine these roles, and a couple of others, in detail (except for release manager, which is covered in "Release manager" in Chapter 7 and in "Dictatorship by Release Owner" earlier in this chapter).

As you read the role descriptions, notice that none of them requires exclusive control over the domain in question. The issue manager does not prevent other people from making changes in the issues database, the FAQ manager does not insist on being the only person to edit the FAQ, and so on. These roles are all about responsibility without monopoly. An important part of each domain manager's job is to notice when other people are working in that domain, and train them to do the things the way the manager does, so that the multiple efforts reinforce rather than conflict. Domain managers should also document the processes by which they do their work, so that when one leaves, someone else can pick up the slack right away.

Sometimes there is a conflict: two or more people want the same role. There is no one right way to handle this. You could suggest that each volunteer post a proposal (an "application") and have all the committers vote on which is best. But this is cumbersome and potentially awkward. I find that a better technique is just to ask the multiple candidates to settle it among themselves. They usually do, and are more satisfied with the result than if a decision had been imposed on them from the outside.

Patch Manager

In a free software project that receives a lot of patches, keeping track of which patches have arrived and what has been decided about them can be a nightmare, especially if done in a decentralized way. Most patches arrive as posts to the project's development mailing list (though some may appear first in the issue tracker, or on external web sites), and there are a number of different routes a patch can take after arrival.

Sometimes someone reviews the patch, finds problems, and bounces it back to the original author for cleanup. This usually leads to an iterative process—all visible on the mailing list—in which the original author posts revised versions of the patch until the reviewer has nothing more to criticize. It is not always easy to tell when this process is done: if the reviewer commits the patch, then clearly the cycle is complete. But if she does not, it might be because she simply didn't have time, or doesn't have commit access herself and couldn't rope any of the other developers into doing it.

Another frequent response to a patch is a freewheeling discussion, not necessarily about the patch itself, but about whether the concept behind the patch is good. For example, the patch may fix a bug, but the project prefers to fix that bug in another way, as part of solving a more general class of problems. Often this is not known in advance, and it is the patch that stimulates the discovery.

Occasionally, a posted patch is met with utter silence. Usually this is due to no developer having time *at that moment* to review the patch, so each hopes that someone else will do it. Since there's no particular limit to how long each person waits for someone else to pick up the ball, and meanwhile other priorities are always coming up, it's very easy for a patch to slip through the cracks without any single person intending for that to happen. The project might miss out on a useful patch this way, and there are other harmful side effects as well: it is discouraging to the author, who invested work in the patch, and it makes the project as a whole look a bit out of touch, especially to others considering writing patches.

The patch manager's job is to make sure that patches don't "slip through the cracks." This is done by following every patch through to some sort of stable state. The patch manager watches every mailing list thread that results from a patch posting. If it ends in a commit of the patch, he does nothing. If it goes into a review/revise iteration, ending with a final version of the patch but no commit, he files an issue pointing to the final version, and to the mailing list thread around it, so that there is a permanent record for developers to follow up on later. If the patch addresses an existing issue, he annotates that issue with the relevant information, instead of opening a new issue.

When a patch gets no reaction at all, the patch manager waits a few days, then follows up asking if anyone is going to review it. This usually gets a reaction: a developer may explain that she doesn't think the patch should be applied, and give the reasons why, or she may review it, in which case one of the previously-described paths is taken. If there is still no response, the patch manager may or may not file an issue for the patch, at his discretion, but at least the original submitter got *some* reaction.

Having a patch manager has saved the Subversion development team a lot of time and mental energy. Without a designated person to take responsibility, every developer would constantly have to worry "If I don't have time to respond to this patch right now, can I count on someone else doing it? Should I try to keep an eye on it? But if other people are also keeping an eye on it, for the same reasons, then we'd have needlessly duplicated effort." The patch manager removes the second-guessing from the situation. Each developer can make the decision that is right for her at the moment she first sees the patch. If she wants to follow up with a review, she can do that—the patch manager will adjust his behavior accordingly. If she wants to ignore the patch completely, that's fine too; the patch manager will make sure it isn't forgotten.

Because this system works only if people can depend on the patch manager being there without fail, the role should be held formally. In Subversion, we advertised for it on the development and users mailing lists, got several volunteers, and took the first one who replied. When that person had to step down (see "Transitions" later in this chapter), we did the same thing again. We've never tried having multiple people share the role, because of the communications overhead that would be required between them; but perhaps at very high volumes of patch submission, a multi-headed patch manager might make sense.

Translation Manager

In software projects, "translation" can refer to two very different things. It can mean translating the software's documentation into other languages, or it can mean translating the software itself—that is, having the program display errors and help messages in the user's preferred language. Both are complex tasks, but once the right infrastructure is in place, they are largely separable from other development. Because the tasks are similar in some ways, it may make sense (depending on your project) to have a single translation manager handle both, or it may be better to have two different managers.

In the Subversion project, we have one translation manager handle both. He does not actually write the translations himself, of course—he may help out on one or two, but as of this writing, he would need to speak 10 languages (12 counting dialects) in order to work on all of them! Instead, he manages teams of volunteer translators: he helps them coordinate among each other, and he coordinates between the teams and the rest of the project.

Part of the reason the translation manager is necessary is that translators are a different demographic from developers. They sometimes have little or no experience working in a version control repository or, indeed, with working as part of a distributed volunteer team at all. But in other respects they are often the best kind of volunteer: people with specific domain knowledge who saw a need and chose to get involved. They are usually willing to learn, and enthusiastic to get to work. All they need is someone to tell them how. The translation manager makes sure that the translations happen in a way that does not interfere unnecessarily with regular development. He also serves as a sort of representative of the translators as a unified body, whenever the developers must be informed of technical changes required to support the translation effort.

Thus, the position's most important skills are diplomatic, not technical. For example, in Subversion we have a policy that all translations should have at least two people working on them, because otherwise there is no way for the text to be reviewed. When a new volunteer shows up offering to translate Subversion to, say, Malagasy, the translation manager has to either hook him up with someone who posted six months ago expressing interest in doing a Malagasy translation, or else politely ask the volunteer to go find *another* Malagasy translator to work with as a partner. Once enough people are available, the manager sets them up with the proper kind of commit access, informs them of the project's conventions (such as how to write log messages), and then keeps an eye out to make sure they adhere to those conventions.

Conversations between the translation manager and the developers, or between the translation manager and translation teams, are usually held in the project's original language—that is, the language from which all the translations are being made. For most free software projects, this is English, but it doesn't matter what it is as long as the project agrees on it. (English is probably best for projects that want to attract a broad international development community, though.)

Conversations *within* a particular translation team usually happen in their shared language, however, and one of the other tasks of the translation manager is to set up a dedicated mailing list for each team. That way the translators can discuss their work freely, without distracting people on the project's main lists, most of whom would not be able to understand the translation language anyway.

Internationalization Versus Localization

Internationalization (I18N) and *localization* (L10N) both refer to the process of adapting a program to work in linguistic and cultural environments other than the one for which it was originally written. The terms are often treated as interchangeable, but in fact they are not quite the same thing. As *http://en.wikipedia.org/wiki/G11n* writes:

> The distinction between them is subtle but important: Internationalization is the adaptation of products for *potential* use virtually everywhere, while localization is the addition of special features for use in a *specific* locale.

For example, changing your software to losslessly handle Unicode (*http://en.wikipedia.org/wiki/Unicode*) text encodings is an internationalization move, since it's not about a particular language, but rather about accepting text from any of a number of languages. On the other hand, making your software print all error messages in Slovenian, when it detects that it is running in a Slovenian environment, is a localization move.

Thus, the translation manager's task is principally about localization, not internationalization.

Documentation Manager

Keeping software documentation up-to-date is a never-ending task. Every new feature or enhancement that goes into the code has the potential to cause a change in the documentation. Also, once the project's documentation reaches a certain level of completeness, you will find that a lot of the patches people send in are for the documentation, not for the code. This is because there are many more people competent to fix bugs in prose than in code: all users are readers, but only a few are programmers.

Documentation patches are usually much easier to review and apply than code patches. There is little or no testing to be done, and the quality of the change can be evaluated quickly just by review. Since the quantity is high, but the review burden fairly low, the ratio of administrative overhead to productive work is greater for documentation patches than for code patches. Furthermore, most of the patches will probably need some sort of adjustment, in order to maintain a consistent authorial voice in the documentation. In many cases, patches will overlap with or affect other patches, and need to be adjusted with respect to each other before being committed.

Given the exigencies of handling documentation patches, and the fact that the code base needs to be constantly monitored so the documentation can be kept up-to-date, it makes sense to have one person, or a small team, dedicated to the task. They can keep a record of exactly where and how the documentation lags behind the software, and they can have practiced procedures for handling large quantities of patches in an integrated way.

Of course, this does not preclude other people in the project from applying documentation patches on the fly, especially small ones, as time permits. And the same patch manager (see "Patch Manager" earlier in this chapter) can track both code and documentation patches, filing them wherever the development and documentation teams want them, respectively. (If the total quantity of patches ever exceeds one human's capacity to track, though, switching to separate patch managers for code and documentation is probably a good first step.) The point of a documentation team is to have people who think of themselves as responsible for keeping the documentation organized, up-to-date, and consistent with itself. In practice, this means knowing the documentation intimately, watching the code base, watching the changes *others* commit to the documentation, watching for incoming documentation patches, and using all these information sources to do whatever is necessary to keep the documentation healthy.

Issue Manager

The number of issues in a project's bug tracker grows in proportion to the number of people using the software. Therefore, even as you fix bugs and ship an increasingly robust program, you should still expect the number of open issues to grow essentially without bound. The frequency of duplicate issues will also increase, as will the frequency of incomplete or poorly described issues.

Issue managers help alleviate these problems by watching what goes into the database, and periodically sweeping through it looking for specific problems. Their most common action is probably to fix up incoming issues, either because the reporter didn't set some of the form fields correctly, or because the issue is a duplicate of one already in the database. Obviously, the more familiar an issue manager is with the project's bug database, the more efficiently she will be able to detect duplicate issues—this is one of the main advantages of having a few people specialize in the bug database, instead of everyone trying to do it ad hoc. When the group tries to do it in a decentralized manner, no single individual acquires a deep expertise in the content of the database.

Issue managers can also help map between issues and individual developers. When there are a lot of bug reports coming in, not every developer may read the issue notification mailing list with equal attention. However, if someone who knows the development team is keeping an eye on all incoming issues, then she can discreetly direct certain developers' attention to specific bugs when appropriate. Of course, this has to be done with a sensitivity to everything else going on in development, and to the recipient's desires and temperament. Therefore, it is often best for issue managers to be developers themselves.

Depending on how your project uses the issue tracker, issue managers can also shape the database to reflect the project's priorities. For example, in Subversion we schedule issues into specific future releases, so that when someone asks, "When will bug X be fixed?" we can say, "Two releases from now," even if we can't give an exact date. The releases are represented in the issue tracker as target milestones, a field available in IssueZilla.[3] As a rule, every Subversion release has one major new feature and a list of specific bug fixes. We assign the appropriate target milestone to all the issues planned for that release (including the new feature—it gets an issue too), so that people can view the bug database through the lens of release scheduling. These targets rarely remain static, however. As new bugs come in, priorities sometimes get shifted around, and issues must be moved from one milestone to another so that each release remains manageable. This, again, is best done by people who have an overall sense of what's in the database, and how various issues relate to each other.

Another thing issue managers do is notice when issues become obsolete. Sometimes a bug is fixed accidentally as part of an unrelated change to the software, or sometimes the project changes its mind about whether a certain behavior is buggy. Finding obsoleted issues is not easy: the only way to do it systematically is by making a sweep over all the issues in the database. Full sweeps become less and less feasible over time, however, as the number of issues grows. After a certain point, the only way to keep the database sane is to use a divide-and-conquer approach: categorize issues immediately on arrival and direct them to the appropriate developer's or team's attention. The recipient then takes charge of the issue for the rest of its lifetime, shepherding it to resolution or oblivion as necessary. When the database is that

---

3   IssueZilla is the issue tracker we use; it is a descendant of BugZilla.

large, the issue manager becomes more of an overall coordinator, spending less time looking at each issue herself and more time getting it into the right person's hands.

FAQ Manager

FAQ maintenance is a surprisingly difficult problem. Unlike most other documents in a project, whose content is planned out in advance by the authors, a FAQ is a wholly reactive document (see Chapter 2). No matter how big it gets, you still never know what the next addition will be. And because it is always added to piecemeal, it is very easy for the document as a whole to become incoherent and disorganized, and even to contain duplicate or semi-duplicate entries. Even when it does not have any obvious problems like that, there are often unnoticed interdependencies between items—links that should be made but aren't—because the related items were added a year apart.

The role of an FAQ manager is twofold. First, he maintains the overall quality of the FAQ by staying familiar with at least the topics of all the questions in it, so that when people add new items that are duplicates of, or related to, existing items, the appropriate adjustments can be made. Second, he watches the project mailing lists and other forums for recurring problems or questions, and recruits volunteers to write new FAQ entries based on this input. This latter task can be quite complex: one must be able to follow a thread, recognize the core questions raised in it, post a proposed FAQ entry, incorporate comments from others (since it's impossible for the FAQ manager to be an expert in every topic covered by the FAQ), and sense when the process is finished so the item can at last be added.

The FAQ manager usually also becomes the default expert in FAQ formatting. There are a lot of little details involved in keeping a FAQ in shape (see "Treat all resources like archives" in Chapter 6); when random people edit the FAQ, they will sometimes forget some of these details. That's okay, as long as the FAQ manager is there to clean up after them.

Various free software is available to help with the process of FAQ maintenance. It's fine to use it, as long as it doesn't compromise the quality of the FAQ, but beware of over-automation. Some projects try to fully automate the process of FAQ maintenance, allowing everyone to contribute and edit FAQ items in a manner similar to a wiki (see "Wikis" in Chapter 3). I've seen this happen particularly with Faq-O-Matic (*http://faqomatic.sourceforge.net/*), though it may be that the cases I saw were simply abuses that went beyond what Faq-O-Matic was originally intended for. In any case, while complete decentralization of FAQ maintenance does reduce the workload for the project, it also results in a poorer FAQ. There's no one person with a broad view of the entire FAQ, no one to notice when certain items need updating or become obsolete entirely, and no one keeping watch for interdependencies between items. The result is an FAQ that often fails to provide users what they were looking for, and in the worst cases misleads them. Use whatever tools you need to to maintain your project's FAQ, but never let the convenience of the tools seduce you into compromising the quality of the FAQ.

See Sean Michael Kerner's article, "The FAQs on FAQs," at *http://osdir.com/Article1722.phtml*, for descriptions and evaluations of open source FAQ maintenance tools.

Transitions

From time to time, a volunteer in a position of ongoing responsibility (e.g., patch manager, translation manager, etc.) will become unable to perform the duties of the position. It may be because the job turned out to be more work than he anticipated, or it may be due to completely external factors: marriage, a new baby, a new employer, or whatever.

When a volunteer gets swamped like this, he usually doesn't notice it right away. It happens by slow degrees, and there's no point at which he consciously realizes that he can no longer fulfill the duties of the role. Instead, the rest of the project just doesn't hear much from him for a while. Then there will suddenly be a flurry of activity, as he feels guilty for neglecting the project for so long and sets aside a night to catch up. Then you won't hear from him for a while longer, and then there might or might not be another flurry. But there's rarely an unsolicited formal resignation. The volunteer was doing the job in his spare time, so resigning would mean openly acknowledging to himself that his spare time is permanently reduced. People are often reluctant to do that.

Therefore, it's up to you and the others in the project to notice what's happening—or rather, not happening—and to ask the volunteer what's going on. The inquiry should be friendly and 100% guilt-free. Your purpose is to find out a piece of information, not to make the person feel bad. Generally, the inquiry should be visible to the rest of the project, but if you know of some special reason why a private inquiry would be better, that's fine too. The main reason to do it publicly is so that if the volunteer responds by saying that he won't be able to do the job anymore, there's a context established for your *next* public post: a request for a new volunteer to fill that role.

Sometimes, a volunteer is unable to do the job he's taken on, but is either unaware or unwilling to admit that fact. Of course, anyone may have trouble at first, especially if the responsibility is complex. However, if someone just isn't working out in the task they've taken on, even after everyone else has given all the help and suggestions they can, then the only solution is for him to step aside and let someone new have a try. And if the person doesn't see this himself, he'll need to be told. There's basically only one way to handle this, I think, but it's a multistep process, and each step is important.

First, make sure you're not crazy. Privately talk to others in the project to see if they agree that the problem is as serious as you think it is. Even if you're already positive, this serves the purpose of letting others know that you're considering asking the person to step aside. Usually no one will object to that—they'll just be happy you're taking on the awkward task, so they don't have to!

Next, *privately* contact the volunteer in question and tell him, kindly but directly, about the problems you see. Be specific, giving as many examples as possible. Make sure to point out how people had tried to help, but that the problems persisted without improving. You should expect this email to take a long time to write, but with this sort of message, if you don't back up what you're saying, you shouldn't say it at all. Say that you would like to find a new volunteer to fill the role, but also point out that there are many other ways to contribute to the project. At this stage, don't say that you've talked to others about it; nobody likes to be told that people were conspiring behind his back.

There are a few different ways things can go after that. The most likely reaction is that he'll agree with you, or at any rate not want to argue, and be willing to step down. In that case, suggest that he make the announcement himself, and then you can follow up with a post seeking a replacement.

Or, he may agree that there have been problems, but ask for a little more time (or for one more chance, in the case of discrete-task roles like release manager). How you react to that is a judgement call, but whatever you do, don't agree to it just because you feel like you can't refuse such a reasonable request. That would prolong the agony, not lessen it. There is often a very good reason to refuse the request, namely, that there have already been plenty of chances, and that's how things got to where they are now. Here's how I put it in a mail to someone who was filling the release manager role but was not really suited for it:

```
> If you wish to replace me with some one else, I will gracefully
> pass on the role to who comes next.  I have one request, which
> I hope is not unreasonable.  I would like to attempt one more
>  release in an effort to prove myself.
```

```
I totally understand the desire (been there myself!), but in
this case, we shouldn't do the "one more try" thing.

This isn't the first or second release, it's the sixth or
seventh... And for all of those, I know you've been dissatisfied
with the results too (because we've talked about it before).  So
we've effectively already been down the one-more-try route.
Eventually, one of the tries has to be the last one... I think
[this past release] should be it.
```

In the worst case, the volunteer may disagree outright. Then you have to accept that things are going to be awkward and plow ahead anyway. Now is the time to say that you talked to other people about it (but still don't say who until you have their permission, since those conversations were confidential), and that you don't think it's good for the project to continue as things are. Be insistent, but never threatening. Keep in mind that with most roles, the transition really happens the moment someone new starts doing the job, *not* the moment the old person stops doing it. For example, if the contention is over the role of, say, issue manager, at any point you and other influential people in the project can solicit for a new issue manager. It's not actually necessary that the person who was previously doing it stop doing it, as long as he does not sabotage (deliberately or otherwise) the efforts of the new volunteer.

Which leads to a tempting thought: instead of asking the person to resign, why not just frame it as a matter of getting him some help? Why not just have two issue managers, or patch managers, or whatever the role is?

Although that may sound nice in theory, it is generally not a good idea. What makes the manager roles work—what makes them useful, in fact—is their centralization. Those things that can be done in a decentralized fashion are usually already being done that way. Having two people fill one managerial role introduces communications overhead between those two people, as well as the potential for slippery displacement of responsibility ("I thought you brought the first aid kit!" "Me? No, I thought *you* brought the first aid kit!"). Of course, there are exceptions. Sometimes two people work extremely well together, or the nature of the role is such that it can easily be spread across multiple people. But these are not likely to be of much use when you see someone flailing in a role he is not suited for. If he'd appreciated the problem in the first place, he would have sought such help before now. In any case, it would be disrespectful to let someone waste time continuing to do a job no one will pay attention to.

The most important factor in asking someone to step down is privacy: giving him the space to make a decision without feeling like others are watching and waiting. I once made the mistake—an obvious mistake, in retrospect—of mailing all three parties at once in order to ask Subversion's release manager to step aside in favor of two other volunteers. I'd already talked to the two new people privately, and knew that they were willing to take on the responsibility. So I thought, naively and somewhat insensitively, that I'd save some time and hassle by sending one mail to all of them to initiate the transition. I assumed that the current release manager was already fully aware of the problems and would see the reasonableness of my point immediately.

I was wrong. The current release manager was very offended, and rightly so. It's one thing to be asked to hand off the job; it's another thing to be asked that *in front of* the people you'll hand it off to. Once I got it through my head why he was offended, I apologized. He eventually did step aside gracefully, and continues to be involved with the project today. But his feelings were hurt, and needless to say, this was not the most auspicious of beginnings for the new volunteers either.

Committers

As the only formally distinct class of people found in all open source projects, committers deserve special attention here. Committers are an unavoidable concession to discrimination in a system which is otherwise as non-discriminatory as possible. But "discrimination" is not meant as a pejorative here. The function committers perform is utterly necessary, and I do not think a project could succeed without it. Quality control requires, well, control. There are always many people who feel competent to make changes to a program, and some smaller number who actually are. The project cannot rely on people's own judgement; it must impose standards and grant commit access only to those who meet them.[4] On the other hand, having people who can commit changes directly working side-by-side with people who cannot sets up an obvious power dynamic. That dynamic must be managed so that it does not harm the project.

---

4   Note that commit access means something a bit different in decentralized version control systems, where anyone can set up a repository that is linked into the project, and give themselves commit access to that repository. Nevertheless, the *concept* of commit access still applies: "commit access" is shorthand for "the right to make changes to the code that will ship in the group's next release of the software." In centralized version control systems, this means having direct commit access; in decentralized ones, it means having one's changes pulled into the main distribution by default. It is the same idea either way; the mechanics by which it is realized are not terribly important.

In "Who Votes?" in Chapter 4, we already discussed the mechanics of considering new committers. Here we will look at the standards by which potential new committers should be judged, and how this process should be presented to the larger community.

Choosing Committers

In the Subversion project, we choose committers primarily on the Hippocratic Principle: *first, do no harm.* Our main criterion is not technical skill or even knowledge of the code, but merely that the committer show good judgement. Judgement can mean simply knowing what not to take on. A person might post only small patches, fixing fairly simple problems in the code; but if the patches apply cleanly, do not contain bugs, and are mostly in accord with the project's log message and coding conventions, and there are enough patches to show a clear pattern, then an existing committer will usually propose that person for commit access. If at least three people say yes, and no one objects, then the offer is made. True, we might have no evidence that the person is able to solve complex problems in all areas of the code base, but that does not matter: the person has made it clear that she is capable of at least judging her own abilities. Technical skills can be learned (and taught), but judgment, for the most part, cannot. Therefore, it is the one thing you want to make sure a person has before you give her commit access.

When a new committer proposal does provoke a discussion, it is usually not about technical ability, but rather about the person's behavior on the mailing lists or in IRC. Sometimes someone shows technical skill and an ability to work within the project's formal guidelines, yet is also consistently belligerent or uncooperative in public forums. That's a serious concern; if the person doesn't seem to shape up over time, even in response to hints, then we won't add her as a committer no matter how skilled she is. In a volunteer group, social skills, or the ability to "play well in the sandbox," are as important as raw technical ability. Because everything is under version control, the penalty for adding a committer you shouldn't have is not so much the problems it could cause in the code (review would spot those quickly anyway), but that it might eventually force the project to revoke the person's commit access— an action that is never pleasant and can sometimes be confrontational.

Many projects insist that the potential committer demonstrate a certain level of technical expertise and persistence, by submitting some number of non-trivial patches— that is, not only do these projects want to know that the person will do no harm, they want to know that she is likely to do good across the code base. This is fine, but be careful that it doesn't start to turn committership into a matter of membership in an exclusive club. The question to keep in everyone's mind should be "What will bring the best results for the code?" not "Will we devalue the social status associated with committership by admitting this person?" The point of commit access is not to reinforce people's self-worth, it's to allow good changes to enter the code with a minimum of fuss. If you have 100 committers, 10 of whom make large changes on a regular basis, and the other 90 of whom just fix typos and small bugs a few times a year, that's still better than having only the 10.

Revoking Commit Access

The first thing to be said about revoking commit access is: try not to be in that situation in the first place. Depending on whose access is being revoked, and why, the discussions around such an action can be very divisive. Even when not divisive, they will be a time-consuming distraction from productive work.

However, if you must do it, the discussion should be had privately among the same people who would be in a position to vote for *granting* that person whatever flavor of commit access they currently have. The person herself should not be included. This contradicts the usual injunction against secrecy, but in this case, it's necessary. First, no one would be able to speak freely otherwise. Second, if the motion fails, you don't necessarily want the person to know it was ever considered, because that could open up questions ("Who was on my side? Who was against me?") that lead to the worst sort of factionalism. In certain rare circumstances, the group may want someone to know that revocation of commit access is or was being considered, as a warning, but this openness should be a decision the group makes. No one should ever, on his own initiative, reveal information from a discussion and ballot that others assumed were secret.

Once someone's access is revoked, that fact is unavoidably public (see "Avoid Mystery" later in this chapter), so try to be as tactful as you can in how it is presented to the outside world.

Partial Commit Access

Some projects offer gradations of commit access. For example, there might be contributors whose commit access gives them free rein in the documentation, but who do not commit to the code itself. Common areas for partial commit access include documentation, translations, binding code to other programming languages, specification files for packaging (e.g., RedHat RPM spec files, etc.), and other places where a mistake will not result in a problem for the core project.

Since commit access is not only about committing, but about being part of an electorate (see "Who Votes?" in Chapter 4), the question naturally arises: what can the partial committers vote on? There is no one right answer; it depends on what sorts of partial commit domains your project has. In Subversion we've kept things fairly simple: a partial committer can vote on matters confined exclusively to that committer's domain, and not on anything else. Importantly, we do have a mechanism for casting advisory votes (essentially, the committer writes "+0" or "+1 (non-binding)" instead of just "+1" on the ballot). There's no reason to silence people entirely just because their vote isn't formally binding.

Full committers can vote on anything, just as they can commit anywhere, and only full committers vote on adding new committers of any kind. In practice, though, the ability to add new partial committers is usually delegated: any full committer can "sponsor" a new partial committer, and partial committers in a domain can often essentially choose new committers for that same domain (this is especially helpful in making translation work run smoothly).

Your project may need a slightly different arrangement, depending on the nature of the work, but the same general principles apply to all projects. Each committer should be able to vote on matters that fall within the scope of her commit access, and not on matters outside that, and votes on procedural questions should default to the full committers, unless there's some reason (as decided by the full committers) to widen the electorate.

Regarding enforcement of partial commit access: it's often best *not* to have the version control system enforce partial commit domains, even if it can. See "Authorization" in Chapter 3 for the reasons why.

Dormant Committers

Some projects automatically remove people's commit access if they go a certain amount of time (say, a year) without committing anything. I think this is usually unhelpful and even counterproductive, for two reasons.

First, it may tempt some people into committing acceptable but unnecessary changes, just to prevent their commit access from expiring. Second, it doesn't really serve any purpose. If the main criterion for granting commit access is good judgement, then why assume someone's judgement would deteriorate just because he's away from the project for a while? Even if he completely vanishes for years, not looking at the code or following development discussions, when he reappears he'll *know* how out of touch he is, and act accordingly. You trusted his judgement before, so why not trust it always? If high school diplomas do not expire, then commit access certainly shouldn't.

Sometimes a committer may ask to be removed, or to be explicitly marked as dormant in the list of committers (see the following section for more about that list). In these cases, the project should accede to the person's wishes, of course.

Avoid Mystery

Although the discussions around adding any particular new committer must be confidential, the rules and procedures themselves need not be secret. In fact, it's best to publish them, so people realize that the committers are not some mysterious Star Chamber, closed off to mere mortals, but that anyone can join simply by posting good patches and knowing how to handle herself in the community. In the Subversion project, we put this information right in the developer guidelines document, since the people most likely to be interested in how commit access is granted are those thinking of contributing code to the project.

In addition to publishing the procedures, publish the actual *list* of committers. The traditional place for this is a file called *MAINTAINERS* or *COMMITTERS* in the top level of the project's source code tree. It should list all the full committers first, followed by the various partial commit domains and the members of each domain. Each person should be listed by name and email address, though the address can be encoded to prevent spam (see "Address hiding in archives" in Chapter 3) if the person prefers that.

Since the distinction between full commit and partial commit access is obvious and well defined, it is proper for the list to make that distinction too. Beyond that, the list should not try to indicate the informal distinctions that inevitably arise in a project, such as who is particularly influential and how. It is a public record, not an acknowledgments file. List committers either in alphabetical order, or in the order in which they arrived.

Credit

Credit is the primary currency of the free software world. Whatever people may say about their motivations for participating in a project, I don't know any developers who would be happy doing all their work anonymously, or under someone else's name. There are tangible reasons for this: one's reputation in a project roughly governs how much influence one has, and participation in an open source project can also indirectly have monetary value, because some employers now look for it on resumés. There are also intangible reasons, perhaps even more powerful: people simply want to be appreciated, and instinctively look for signs that their work was recognized by others.

The promise of credit is therefore one of best motivators the project has. When small contributions are acknowledged, people come back to do more.

One of the most important features of collaborative development software (see Chapter 3) is that it keeps accurate records of who did what, when. Wherever possible, use these existing mechanisms to make sure that credit is distributed accurately, and be specific about the nature of the contribution. Don't just write "Thanks to J. Random <jrandom@example.com>" if instead you can write "Thanks to J. Random <jrandom@example.com> for the bug report and reproduction recipe" in a log message.

In Subversion, we have an informal but consistent policy of crediting the reporter of a bug in either the issue filed, if there is one, or the log message of the commit that fixes the bug, if not. A quick survey of Subversion commit logs up to commit number 14525 shows that about 10% of commits give credit to someone by name and email address, usually the person who reported or analyzed the bug fixed by that commit. Note that this person is different from the developer who actually made the commit, whose name is already recorded automatically by the version control system. Of the 80-odd full and partial committers Subversion has today, 55 were credited in the commit logs (usually multiple times) before they became committers themselves. This does not, of course, prove that being credited was a factor in their continued involvement, but it at least sets up an atmosphere in which people know they can count on their contributions being acknowledged.

It's important to distinguish between routine acknowledgment and special thanks. When discussing a particular piece of code, or some other contribution someone made, it is fine to acknowledge their work. For example, saying "Daniel's recent changes to the delta code mean we can now implement feature X" simultaneously helps people identify which changes you're talking about and acknowledges Daniel's work. On the other hand, posting solely to thank Daniel for the delta code changes serves no immediate practical purpose. It doesn't add any information, since the version control system and other mechanisms have already recorded the fact that he made the changes. Thanking everyone for everything would be distracting and ultimately information-free, since thanks are effective largely by how much they stand out from the default, background level of favorable comment going on all the time. This doesn't mean, of course, that you should never thank people. Just make sure to do it in ways that tend not to lead to credit inflation. Following these guidelines will help:

- The more ephemeral the forum, the more free you should feel to express thanks there. For example, thanking someone for their bug fix in passing during an IRC conversation is fine, as is an aside in an email devoted mainly to other topics. But don't post an email solely to thank someone, unless it's for a truly unusual feat. Likewise, don't clutter the project's web pages with expressions of gratitude. Once you start that, it'll never be clear when or where to stop. And *never* put thanks into comments in the code; that would only be a distraction from the primary purpose of comments, which is to help the reader understand the code.

• The less involved someone is in the project, the more appropriate it is to thank her for something she did. This may sound counterintuitive, but it fits with the attitude that expressing thanks is something you do when someone contributes even more than you thought she would. Thus, to constantly thank regular contributors for doing what they normally do would be to express a lower expectation of them than they have of themselves. If anything, you want to aim for the opposite effect!

There are occasional exceptions to this rule. It's acceptable to thank someone for fulfilling his expected role when that role involves temporary, intense efforts from time to time. The canonical example is the release manager, who goes into high gear around the time of each release, but otherwise lies dormant (dormant as a release manager, in any case—he may also be an active developer, but that's a different matter).

• As with criticism and crediting, gratitude should be specific. Don't thank people just for being great, even if they are. Thank them for something they did that was out of the ordinary, and for bonus points, say exactly why what they did was so great.

In general, there is always a tension between making sure that people's individual contributions are recognized, and making sure the project is a group effort rather than a collection of individual glories. Just remain aware of this tension and try to err on the side of group, and things won't get out of hand.

Forks

In "Forkability" in Chapter 4, we saw how the *potential* to fork has important effects on how projects are governed. But what happens when a fork actually occurs? How should you handle it, and what effects can you expect it to have? Conversely, when should you *initiate* a fork?

The answers depend on what kind of fork it is. Some forks are due to amicable but irreconcilable disagreements about the direction of the project; perhaps more are due to both technical disagreements and interpersonal conflicts. Of course, it's not always possible to tell the difference between the two, as technical arguments may involve personal elements as well. What all forks have in common is that one group of developers (or sometimes even just one developer) has decided that the costs of working with some or all of the others now outweigh the benefits.

Once a project forks, there is no definitive answer to the question of which fork is the "true" or "original" project. People will colloquially talk of fork F coming out of project P, as though P is continuing unchanged down some natural path while F diverges into new territory, but this is, in effect, a declaration of how that particular observer feels about it. It is fundamentally a matter of perception: when a large enough percentage of observers agree, the assertion starts to become true. It is not the case that there is an objective truth from the outset, one that we are only imperfectly able to perceive at first. Rather, the perceptions *are* the objective truth, since ultimately a project—or a fork—is an entity that exists only in people's minds anyway.

If those initiating the fork feel that they are sprouting a new branch off the main project, the perception question is resolved immediately and easily. Everyone, both developers and users, will treat the fork as a new project, with a new name (perhaps based on the old name, but easily distinguishable from it), a separate web site, and a separate philosophy or goal. Things get messier, however, when both sides feel they are the legitimate guardians of the original project and therefore have the right to continue using the original name. If there is some organization with trademark rights to the name, or legal control over the domain or web pages, that usually resolves the issue by fiat: that organization will decide who is the project and who is the fork, because it holds all the cards in a public relations war. Naturally, things rarely get that far: since everyone already knows what the power dynamics are, they will avoid fighting a battle whose outcome is known in advance, and just jump straight to the end.

Fortunately, in most cases there is little doubt as to which is the project and which is the fork, because a fork is, in essence, a vote of confidence. If more than half of the developers are in favor of whatever course the fork proposes to take, usually there is no need to fork—the project can simply go that way itself, unless it is run as a dictatorship with a particularly stubborn dictator. On the other hand, if fewer than half of the developers are in favor, the fork is a clearly minority rebellion, and both courtesy and common sense indicate that it should think of itself as the divergent branch rather than the main line.

Handling a Fork

If someone threatens a fork in your project, keep calm and remember your long-term goals. The mere *existence* of a fork isn't what hurts a project; rather, it's the loss of developers and users. Your real aim, therefore, is not to squelch the fork, but to minimize these harmful effects. You may be mad, you may feel that the fork was unjust and uncalled for, but expressing that publicly can only alienate undecided developers. Instead, don't force people to make exclusive choices, and be as cooperative as is practicable with the fork. To start with, don't remove someone's commit access in your project just because she decided to work on the fork. Work on the fork doesn't mean that person has suddenly lost her competence to work on the original project; committers before should remain committers afterward. Beyond that, you should express your desire to remain as compatible as possible with the fork, and say that you hope developers will port changes between the two whenever appropriate. If you have administrative access to the project's servers, publicly offer the forkers infrastructure help at startup time. For example, offer them a complete, deep-history copy of the version control repository, if there's no other way for them to get it, so that they don't have to start off without historical data (this may not be necessary depending on the version control system). Ask them if there's anything else they need, and provide it if you can. Bend over backward to show that you are not standing in the way, and that you want the fork to succeed or fail on its own merits and nothing else.

The reason to do all this—and do it publicly—is not to actually help the fork, but to persuade developers that your side is a safe bet, by appearing as non-vindictive as possible. In war it sometimes makes sense (strategic sense, if not human sense) to force people to choose sides, but in free software it almost never does. In fact, after a fork some developers often openly work on both projects, and do their best to keep the two compatible. These developers help keep the lines of communication open after the fork. They allow your project to benefit from interesting new features in the fork (yes, the fork may have things you want), and also increase the chances of a merger down the road.

Sometimes a fork becomes so successful that, even though it was regarded even by its own instigators as a fork at the outset, it becomes the version everybody prefers, and eventually supplants the original by popular demand. A famous instance of this was the GCC/EGCS fork. The GNU C Compiler, or more recently, the GNU Compiler Collection (GCC) is the most popular open source native-code compiler, and also one of the most portable compilers in the world. Due to disagreements between the GCC's official maintainers and Cygnus Software,[5] one of GCC's most active developer groups, Cygnus created a fork of GCC called *EGCS*. The fork was deliberately non-adversarial: the EGCS developers did not, at any point, try to portray their version of GCC as a new

---

5   Now part of RedHat (*http://www.redhat.com/*).

official version. Instead, they concentrated on making EGCS as good as possible, incorporating patches at a faster rate than the official GCC maintainers. EGCS gained in popularity, and eventually some major operating system distributors decided to package EGCS as their default compiler instead of GCC. At this point, it became clear to the GCC maintainers that holding on to the "GCC" name while everyone switched to the EGCS fork would burden everyone with a needless name change, yet do nothing to prevent the switchover. So GCC adopted the EGCS codebase, and there is once again a single GCC, but greatly improved because of the fork.

This example shows why you cannot always regard a fork as an unadulteratedly bad thing. A fork may be painful and unwelcome at the time, but you cannot necessarily know whether it will succeed. Therefore, you and the rest of the project should keep an eye on it, and be prepared not only to absorb features and code where possible, but in the most extreme case, to even join the fork if it gains the bulk of the project's mindshare. Of course, you will often be able to predict a fork's likelihood of success by seeing who joins it. If the fork is started by the project's biggest complainer and joined by a handful of disgruntled developers who weren't behaving constructively anyway, they've essentially solved a problem for you by forking, and you probably don't need to worry about the fork taking momentum away from the original project. But if you see influential and respected developers supporting the fork, you should ask yourself why. Perhaps the project was being overly restrictive, and the best solution is to adopt into the mainline project some or all of the actions contemplated by the fork—in essence, to avoid the fork by becoming it.

Initiating a Fork

All the advice here assumes that you are forking as a last resort. Exhaust all other possibilities before starting a fork. Forking almost always means losing developers, with only an uncertain promise of gaining new ones later. It also means starting out with competition for users' attention: everyone who's about to download the software has to ask themselves: "Hmm, do I want that one or the other one?" Whichever one you are, the situation is messy, because a question has been introduced that wasn't there before. Some people maintain that forks are healthy for the software ecosystem as a whole, by a standard natural selection argument: the fittest will survive, which means that, in the end, everyone gets better software. This may be true from the ecosystem's point of view, but it's not true from the point of view of any individual project. Most forks do not succeed, and most projects are not happy to be forked.

A corollary is that you should not use the threat of a fork as an extremist debating technique—"Do things my way or I'll fork the project!"—because everyone is aware that a fork that fails to attract developers away from the original project is unlikely to survive long. All observers—not just developers, but users and operating system packagers too—will make their own judgement about which side to choose. You should therefore appear extremely reluctant to fork, so that if you finally do it, you can credibly claim it was the only route left.

Do not neglect to take *all* factors into account in evaluating the potential success of your fork. For example, if many of the developers on a project have the same employer, then even if they are disgruntled and privately in favor of a fork, they are unlikely to say so out loud if they know that their employer is against it. Many free software programmers like to think that having a free license on the code means no one company can dominate development. It is true that the license is, in an ultimate sense, a guarantor of freedom—if others want badly enough to fork the project, and have the resources to do so, they can. But in practice, some projects' development teams are mostly funded by one entity, and there is no point pretending that the entity's support doesn't matter. If it is opposed to the fork, its developers are unlikely to take part, even if they secretly want to.

If you still conclude that you must fork, line up support privately first, then announce the fork in a non-hostile tone. Even if you are angry at, or disappointed with, the current maintainers, don't say that in the message. Just dispassionately state what led you to the decision to fork, and that you mean no ill will toward the project from which you're forking. Assuming that you do consider it a fork (as opposed to an emergency preservation of the original project), emphasize that you're forking the code and not the name, and choose a name that does not conflict with the project's name. You can use a name that contains or refers to the original name, as long as it does not open the door to identity confusion. Of course it's fine to explain prominently on the fork's home page that it descends from the original program, and even that it hopes to supplant it. Just don't make users' lives harder by forcing them to untangle an identity dispute.

Finally, you can get things started on the right foot by automatically granting all committers of the original project commit access to the fork, including even those who openly disagreed with the need for a fork. Even if they never use the access, your message is clear: there are disagreements here, but no enemies, and you welcome code contributions from any competent source.

## CHAPTER 9

Licenses, Copyrights, and Patents

The license you select probably won't have a major impact on the adoption of your project, as long as the license is open source. Users generally choose software based on quality and features, not on the details of the license. Nevertheless, you still need a basic understanding of free software licensing issues, both to ensure that the project's license is compatible with its goals, and to be able to discuss licensing decisions with other people. Please note, however, that I am not a lawyer, and that nothing in this chapter should be construed as formal legal advice. For that, you'll need to hire a lawyer or be one.

Terminology

In any discussion of open source licensing, the first thing that becomes apparent is that there seem to be many different words for the same thing: *free software*, *open source*, *FOSS*, *F/OSS*, and *FLOSS*. Let's start by sorting those out, along with a few other terms.

Free software

Software that can be freely shared and modified, including in source code form. The term was first coined by Richard Stallman, who codified it in the GNU General Public License (GPL), and who founded the Free Software Foundation (*http://www.fsf.org/*) to promote the concept.

Although "free software" covers almost exactly the same range of software as "open source," the FSF, among others, prefers the former term because it emphasizes the idea of freedom, and the concept of freely redistributable software as primarily a social movement rather than a technical one. The FSF acknowledges that the term is ambiguous—it could mean "free" as in "zero-cost," instead of "free" as in "freedom"—but feels that it's still the best term, all things considered, and that the other possibilities in English have their own ambiguities. (Throughout this book, "free" is used in the "freedom" sense, not the "zero-cost" sense.)

Open source software

Free software under another name. But the different name reflects an important philosophical difference: "open source" was coined by the Open Source Initiative (*http://www.opensource.org/*) as a deliberate alternative to "free software," in order to make such software a more palatable choice for corporations, by presenting it as a development methodology rather than a political movement. They may also have wanted to overcome another stigma: that anything "free" must be low quality.

While any license that is free is also open source, and vice versa (with a few minor exceptions), people tend to pick one term and stick with it. In general, those who prefer "free software" are more likely to have a philosophical or moral stance on the issue, while those who prefer "open source" either don't view it as a matter of freedom, or are not interested in advertising the fact that they do. See "Free Versus Open Source" in Chapter 1 for a more detailed history of this schism.

The Free Software Foundation has an excellent—utterly unobjective, but nuanced and quite fair—exegesis of the two terms, at *http://www.fsf.org/licensing/essays/free-software-for-freedom.html*. The Open Source Initiative's take on it is spread across two pages: *http://www.opensource.org/advocacy/case_for_hackers.php#marketing* and *http://www.opensource.org/advocacy/free-notfree.php*.

FOSS, F/OSS, FLOSS

Where there are two of anything, there will soon be three, and that is exactly what is happening with terms for free software. The academic world, perhaps wanting precision and inclusiveness over elegance, seems to have settled on FOSS, or sometimes F/OSS, standing for Free/Open Source Software. Another variant gaining momentum is FLOSS, which stands for Free/Libre Open Source Software ("libre" is familiar in many languages and does not suffer from the ambiguities of "free"; see *http://en.wikipedia.org/wiki/FLOSS* for more).

All these terms mean essentially the same thing: software that can be modified and redistributed by everyone, sometimes—but not always—with the requirement that derivative works be freely redistributable under the same terms.

DFSG-compliant

Compliant with the Debian Free Software Guidelines (*http://www.debian.org/ social_contract#guidelines*). This is a widely used test for whether a given license is truly open source (free, libre, etc.). The Debian Project's mission is to maintain an entirely free operating system, such that someone installing it need never doubt that she has the right to modify and redistribute any or all of the system. The Debian Free Software Guidelines are the requirements that a software package's license must meet in order to be included in Debian. Because the Debian Project spent a good deal of time thinking about how to construct such a test, the guidelines they came up with have proven very robust (see *http://en.wikipedia. org/wiki/DFSG*), and as far as I'm aware, no serious objection to them has been raised either by the Free Software Foundation or the Open Source Initiative. If you know that a given license is DFSG-compliant, you know that it guarantees all the important freedoms (such as forkability even against the original author's wishes) required to sustain the dynamics of an open source project. All of the licenses discussed in this chapter are DFSG-compliant.

OSI-approved

Approved by the Open Source Initiative. This is another widely used test of whether a license permits all the necessary freedoms. The OSI's definition of open source software is based on the Debian Free Software Guidelines, and any license that meets one definition almost always meets the other. There have been a few exceptions over the years, but only involving niche licenses and none of any relevance here. Unlike the Debian Project, the OSI maintains a list of all licenses it has ever approved, at *http://www.opensource.org/licenses/*, so that being "OSI-approved" is an unambiguous state: a license either is or isn't on the list.

The Free Software Foundation also maintains a list of licenses at *http://www.fsf. org/licensing/licenses/license-list.html*. The FSF categorizes licenses not only by whether they are free, but whether they are compatible with the GNU General Public License. GPL compatibility is an important topic, covered in "The GPL and License Compatibility" later in this chapter.

Proprietary, closed-source

The opposite of "free" or "open source." It means software distributed under traditional, royalty-based licensing terms, where users pay per copy, or under any other terms sufficiently restrictive to prevent open source dynamics from operating. Even software distributed at no charge can still be proprietary, if its license does not permit free redistribution and modification.

Generally "proprietary" and "closed-source" are synonyms. However, "closed-source" additionally implies that the source code cannot even be seen. Since the source code cannot be seen with most proprietary software, this is normally a distinction without a difference. However, occasionally someone releases proprietary software under a license that allows others to view the source code. Confusingly, they sometimes call this "open source" or "nearly open source," etc., but that's misleading. The *visibility* of the source code is not the issue; the important question is what you're allowed to do with it. Thus, the difference between proprietary and closed-source is mostly irrelevant, and the two can be treated as synonyms.

Sometimes *commercial* is used as a synonym for "proprietary," but properly speaking, the two are not the same thing. Free software can be commercial software. After all, free software can be sold, as long as the buyers are not restricted from giving away copies themselves. It can be commercialized in other ways as well, for example by selling support, services, and certification. There are multimillion dollar companies built on free software today, so it is clearly neither inherently anti-commercial nor anti-corporate. On the other hand, it *is* anti-proprietary by its nature, and this is the key way in which it differs from traditional per-copy license models.

Public domain

Having no copyright holder, meaning that there is no one who has the right to restrict copying of the work. Being in the public domain is not the same as having no author. Everything has an author, and even if a work's author or authors choose to put it in the public domain, that doesn't change the fact that they wrote it.

When a work is in the public domain, material from it can be incorporated into a copyrighted work, and thereafter *that copy* of the material is covered under the same copyright as the whole work. But this does not affect the availability of the original work, which remains in the public domain. Thus, releasing something into the public domain is technically one way to make it "free," according to the guidelines of most free software certifying organizations. However, there are usually good reasons to use a license instead of just releasing into the public domain: even with free software, certain restrictions can be useful, not only to the copyright holder but even to recipients as well, as the next section makes clear.

Copyleft

A license that uses copyright law to achieve a result opposite to traditional copyright. Depending on whom you ask, this means either licenses that permit the freedoms under discussion here, or, more narrowly, licenses that not only permit those freedoms but *enforce* them, by stipulating that the freedoms must travel with the work. The Free Software Foundation uses the second definition exclusively; elsewhere, it's a toss-up: a lot of people use the term the same way the FSF does, but others—including some who write for mainstream media—tend to use the first definition. It's not clear that everyone using the term is aware that there's a distinction to be made.

The canonical example of the narrower, stricter definition is the GNU General Public License, which stipulates that any derivative works must also be licensed under the GPL; see "The GPL and License Compatibility" later in this chapter.

Aspects of Licenses

Although there are many different free software licenses available, in the important respects they all say the same things: that anyone can modify the code, that anyone can redistribute it both in original and modified form, and that the copyright holders and authors provide no warranties whatsoever (avoiding liability is especially important given that people might run modified versions without even knowing it). The differences between licenses boil down to a few oft-recurring issues:

Compatibility with proprietary licenses

Some free licenses allow the covered code to be used in proprietary programs. This does not affect the licensing terms of the proprietary program: it is still as proprietary as ever, it just happens to contain some code from a non-proprietary source. The Apache License, X Consortium License, BSD-style license, and the MIT-style license are all examples of proprietary-compatible licenses.

Compatibility with other free licenses

Most free licenses are compatible with each other, meaning that code under one license can be combined with code under another, and the result distributed under either license without violating the terms of the other. The major exception to this is the GNU General Public License, which requires that any work using GPLed code be itself distributed under the GPL, and without adding any further restrictions beyond what the GPL requires. The GPL is compatible with some free licenses, but not with others. This is discussed in more detail in "The GPL and License Compatibility" later in this chapter.

Enforcement of crediting

Some free licenses stipulate that any use of the covered code be accompanied by a notice, whose placement and display is usually specified, giving credit to the authors or copyright holders of the code. These licenses are often still proprietary-compatible: they do not necessarily demand that the derivative work be free, merely that credit be given to the free code.

Protection of trademark

A variant of credit enforcement. Trademark-protecting licenses specify that the name of the original software (or its copyright holders, or their institution, etc.) may *not* be used by derivative works without prior written permission. Although credit enforcement insists that a certain name be used, and trademark protection insists that it not be used, they are both expressions of the same desire: that the original code's reputation be preserved and transmitted, but not tarnished by association.

Protection of "artistic integrity"

Some licenses (the Artistic License, used for the most popular implementation of the Perl programming language, and Donald Knuth's TeX license, for example) require that modification and redistribution be done in a manner that distinguishes clearly between the pristine original version of the code and any modifications. They permit essentially the same freedoms as other free licenses, but impose certain requirements that make the integrity of the original code easy to verify. These licenses have not caught on much beyond the specific programs they were made for, and will not be discussed in this chapter; they are mentioned here only for the sake of completeness.

Most of these stipulations are not mutually exclusive, and some licenses include several. The common thread among them is that they place demands on the recipient in exchange for the recipient's right to use and/or redistribute the code. For example, some projects want their name and reputation to be transmitted along with the code, and this is worth imposing the extra burden of a credit or trademark clause; depending on its onerousness, that burden may result in some users choosing a package with a less demanding license.

The GPL and License Compatibility

By far the sharpest dividing line in licensing is that between proprietary-incompatible and proprietary-compatible licenses, that is, between the GNU General Public License and everything else. Because the primary goal of the GPL's authors is the promotion of free software, they deliberately crafted the license to make it impossible to mix GPLed code into proprietary programs. Specifically, among the GPL's requirements (see *http:// www.fsf.org/licensing/licenses/gpl.html* for its full text) are these two:

- Any derivative work—that is, any work containing a non-trivial amount of GPLed code—must itself be distributed under the GPL.

- No additional restrictions may be placed on the redistribution of either the original work or a derivative work. (The exact language is: "You may not impose any further restrictions on the recipients' exercise of the rights granted herein.")

With these conditions, the GPL succeeds in making freedom contagious. Once a program is copyrighted under the GPL, its terms of redistribution are *viral*—they are passed on to anything else the code gets incorporated into, making it effectively impossible to use GPLed code in closed-source programs. However, these same clauses also make the GPL incompatible with certain other free licenses. The usual way this happens is that the other license imposes a requirement—for example, a credit clause requiring the original authors to be mentioned in some way—that is incompatible with the GPL's "You may not impose any further restrictions..." language. From the point of view of the Free Software Foundation, these second-order consequences are desirable, or at least not regrettable. The GPL not only keeps your software free, but effectively makes your software an agent in pushing *other* software to enforce freedom as well.

The question of whether or not this is a good way to promote free software is one of the most persistent holy wars on the Internet (see "Avoid Holy Wars" in Chapter 6), and we won't investigate it here. What's important for our purposes is that GPL compatibility is an important issue when choosing a license. The GPL is by far the most popular open source license; at *http://freshmeat.net/stats/#license*, it is at 68%, and the next highest license is at 6%. If you want your code to be able to be mixed freely with GPLed code—and there's a lot of GPLed code out there—then you should pick a GPL-compatible license. Most of the GPL-compatible open source licenses are also proprietary-compatible: that is, code under such a license can be used in a GPLed program, and it can be used in a proprietary program. Of course, the *results* of these mixings would not be compatible with each other, since one would be under the GPL and the other would be under a closed-source license. But that concern applies only to the derivative works, not to the code you distribute in the first place.

Fortunately, the Free Software Foundation maintains a list showing which licenses are compatible with the GPL at *http://www.gnu.org/licenses/license-list.html*. All licenses discussed in this chapter are present on that list, on one side or the other.

Choosing a License

When choosing a license to apply to your project, if at all possible use an existing license instead of making up a new one. There are two reasons why existing licenses are better:

Familiarity
> If you use one of the three or four most popular licenses, people won't feel they have to read the legalese in order to use your code, because they'll have already done so for that license a long time ago.

Quality
> Unless you have a team of lawyers at your disposal, you are unlikely to come up with a legally solid license. The licenses mentioned here are the products of much thought and experience; unless your project has truly unusual needs, it is unlikely you would do better.

To apply one of these licenses to your project, see "How to Apply a License to Your Software" in Chapter 2.

The MIT/X Window System License

If your goal is that your code be accessible by the greatest possible number of developers and derivative works, and you do not mind the code being used in proprietary programs, choose the MIT/X Window System license (so named because it is the license under which the Massachusetts Institute of Technology released the original X Window System code). This license's basic message is "You are free to use this code however you want." It is taken from *http://www.opensource.org/licenses/mit-license.php*; is compatible with the GNU GPL; and is short, simple, and easy to understand:

```
Copyright (c) <year> <copyright holders>

Permission is hereby granted, free of charge, to any person obtaining
a copy of this software and associated documentation files (the
"Software"), to deal in the Software without restriction, including
without limitation the rights to use, copy, modify, merge, publish,
distribute, sublicense, and/or sell copies of the Software, and to
permit persons to whom the Software is furnished to do so, subject to
the following conditions:

The above copyright notice and this permission notice shall be
included in all copies or substantial portions of the Software.

THE SOFTWARE IS PROVIDED "AS IS", WITHOUT WARRANTY OF ANY KIND,
EXPRESS OR IMPLIED, INCLUDING BUT NOT LIMITED TO THE WARRANTIES OF
MERCHANTABILITY, FITNESS FOR A PARTICULAR PURPOSE AND
NONINFRINGEMENT. IN NO EVENT SHALL THE AUTHORS OR COPYRIGHT HOLDERS BE
```

LIABLE FOR ANY CLAIM, DAMAGES OR OTHER LIABILITY, WHETHER IN AN ACTION
OF CONTRACT, TORT OR OTHERWISE, ARISING FROM, OUT OF OR IN CONNECTION
WITH THE SOFTWARE OR THE USE OR OTHER DEALINGS IN THE SOFTWARE.

The GNU General Public License

If you prefer that your project's code not be used in proprietary programs, or if you
at least don't care whether or not it can be used in proprietary programs, choose the
GNU General Public License (*http://www.fsf.org/licensing/licenses/gpl.html*). The GPL is
probably the most widely used free software license in the world today; this instant
recognizability is itself one of the GPL's major advantages.

When writing a code library that is meant mainly to be used as part of other programs, consider carefully whether the restrictions imposed by the GPL are in line
with your project's goals. In some cases—for example, when you're trying to unseat a
competing, proprietary library that does the same thing—it may make more strategic sense to license your code in such a way that it can be mixed into proprietary
programs, even though you would otherwise not wish this. The Free Software Foundation even fashioned an alternative to the GPL for such circumstances: the *GNU
Library GPL*, later renamed to the *GNU Lesser GPL* (most people just use the acro-
nym *LGPL,* in any case). The LGPL has looser restrictions than the GPL, and can be
mixed more easily with non-free code. However, it's also a bit complex and takes
some time to understand, so if you're not going to use the GPL, I recommend just
using the MIT/X-style license.

Is the GPL free or not free?

One consequence of choosing the GPL is the possibility—small, but not infinitely
small—of finding yourself or your project embroiled in a dispute about whether or
not the GPL is truly "free," given that it places some restrictions on what you can do
with the code—namely, the restriction that the code cannot be distributed under any
other license. For some people, the existence of this restriction means the GPL is
"less free" than more permissive licenses such as the MIT/X license. Where this argument usually goes, of course, is that since "more free" must be better than "less free"
(after all, who's not in favor of freedom?), it follows that those licenses are better than
the GPL.

This debate is another popular holy war (see "Avoid Holy Wars" in Chapter 6). Avoid
participating in it, at least in project forums. Don't attempt to prove that the GPL is
less free, as free, or more free than other licenses. Instead, emphasize the specific reasons your project chose the GPL. If the recognizability of license was a reason, say
that. If the enforcement of a free license on derivative works was also a reason, say

that too, but refuse to be drawn into discussion about whether this makes the code more or less "free." Freedom is a complex topic, and there is little point talking about it if terminology is going to be used as a stalking horse for substance.

Since this is a book and not a mailing list thread, however, I will admit that I've never understood the "GPL is not free" argument. The only restriction the GPL imposes is that it prevents people from imposing *further* restrictions. To say that this results in less freedom has always seemed to me like saying that outlawing slavery reduces freedom, because it prevents some people from owning slaves.

(Oh, and if you do get drawn into a debate about it, don't raise the stakes by making inflammatory analogies.)

What About The BSD License?

A fair amount of open source software is distributed under a *BSD license* (or sometimes a *BSD-style license*). The original BSD license was used for the Berkeley Software Distribution, in which the University of California released important portions of a Unix implementation. This license (the exact text may be seen in section 2.2.2 of *http://www.xfree86.org/3.3.6/COPYRIGHT2.html#6*) was similar in spirit to the MIT/X license, except for one clause:

> All advertising materials mentioning features or use of this software must display the following acknowledgement: This product includes software developed by the University of California, Lawrence Berkeley Laboratory.

The presence of that clause not only made the original BSD license GPL-incompatible, it also set a dangerous precedent: as other organizations put similar advertising clauses into *their* free software—substituting their own organization's name in place of "the University of California, Lawrence Berkeley Laboratory"—software redistributors faced an ever-increasing burden in what they were required to display. Fortunately, many of the projects that used this license became aware of the problem, and simply dropped the advertising clause. In 1999, even the University of California did so.

The result is the revised BSD license, which is simply the original BSD license with the advertising clause removed. However, this history makes the phrase "BSD license" a bit ambiguous: does it refer to the original, or the revised version? This is why I prefer the MIT/X license, which is essentially equivalent, and which does not suffer from any ambiguity. However, there is perhaps one reason to prefer the revised BSD license to the MIT/X license, which is that the BSD includes this clause:

> Neither the name of the <ORGANIZATION> nor the names of its contributors may be used to endorse or promote products derived from this software without specific prior written permission.

It's not clear that without such a clause, a recipient of the software would have had the right to use the licensor's name anyway, but the clause removes any possible doubt. For organizations worried about trademark control, therefore, the revised BSD license may be slightly preferable to MIT/X. In general, however, a liberal copyright license does not imply that recipients have any right to use or dilute your trademarks—copyright law and trademark law are two different beasts.

If you wish to use the revised BSD license, a template is available at *http://www. opensource.org/licenses/bsd-license.php*.

Copyright Assignment and Ownership

Most projects have a single legal entity own the copyright on the entire code base. This is done for various reasons. If the terms of the copyright ever need to be defended or enforced in court, it's much easier if a single entity has the right to do so; otherwise, all of the contributors would have to cooperate, and some might not have time or even be reachable when the issue arises. Also, if the code is the target of a copyright infringement suit, you wouldn't want the individual developers to be personally exposed to liability.

Remember that centralized ownership of the copyright does not make the code any less free. Open source licenses do not give the copyright holder the right to retroactively proprietize all copies of the code. Even if the copyright-holding entity suddenly turned around and started distributing all the code under a restrictive license, it wouldn't cause a problem for the public project. The other developers would simply start a fork based on the latest free copy of the code, and continue as if nothing had happened. Because they know they can do this, most developers do not object when asked to assign copyright to some sponsoring organization.

Different organizations apply different amounts of rigor to the task of collecting copyright assignments. For most, simply getting an informal statement from a contributor on the public list is enough—something to the effect of "I hereby assign copyright in this code to the project, to be licensed under the same terms as the rest of the code." At least one lawyer I've talked to says that's really enough, presumably because it happens in a context where copyright assignment is normal and expected anyway, and because it represents a bona fide effort on the project's part to ascertain the developer's true intentions. On the other hand, the Free Software Foundation goes to the opposite extreme: they require contributors to physically sign and mail in a piece of paper containing a formal statement of copyright assignment, sometimes for just one contribution, sometimes for current and future contributions. If the developer is employed, the FSF asks that the employer sign it too.

The FSF's paranoia is understandable. If someone violates the terms of the GPL by incorporating some of their software into a proprietary program, the FSF will need to fight that in court, and they want their copyrights to be as airtight as possible when that happens. Since the FSF is copyright holder for a lot of popular software, they view this as a real possibility. Whether your organization needs to be similarly scrupulous is something only you can decide, in consultation with lawyers.

Dual Licensing Schemes

Some projects try to fund themselves by using a dual licensing scheme, in which proprietary derivative works may pay the copyright holder for the right to use the code, but the code still remains free for use by open source projects. This tends to work better with code libraries than with standalone applications, naturally. The exact terms differ from case to case. Often the license for the free side is the GNU GPL, since it already bars others from incorporating the covered code into their proprietary product without permission from the copyright holder, but sometimes it is a custom license that has the same effect. An example of the former is the MySQL license, described at *http://www.mysql.com/company/legal/licensing/*; an example of the latter is Sleepycat Software's licensing strategy, described at *http://www.sleepycat.com/download/licensinginfo.shtml*.

You might be wondering: how can the copyright holder offer proprietary licensing for a mandatory fee if the terms of the GNU GPL stipulate that the code must be available under less restrictive terms? The answer is that the GPL's terms are something the copyright holder imposes on everyone else; the owner is therefore free to decide *not* to apply those terms to itself. A good way to think of it is to imagine that the copyright owner has an infinite number of copies of the software stored in a bucket. Each time it takes one out of the bucket to send into the world, it can decide what license to put on it: GPL, proprietary, or something else. Its right to do this is not tied to the GPL or any other open source license; it is simply a power granted by copyright law.

The attractiveness of dual licensing is that, at its best, it provides a way for a free software project to get a reliable income stream. Unfortunately, it can also interfere with the normal dynamics of open source projects. The problem is that any volunteer who makes a code contribution is now contributing to two distinct entities: the free version of the code and the proprietary version. While the contributor will be comfortable contributing to the free version, since that's the norm in open source projects, she may feel funny about contributing to someone else's semi-proprietary revenue stream. The awkwardness is exacerbated by the fact that in dual licensing, the copyright owner really needs to gather formal, signed copyright assignments from all contributors, in order to protect itself from a disgruntled contributor later claiming a percentage of royalties from the proprietary stream. The process of collecting these assignment papers means that contributors are starkly confronted with the fact that they are doing work that makes money for someone else.

Not all volunteers will be bothered by this; after all, their contributions go into the open source edition as well, and that may be where their main interest lies. Nevertheless, dual licensing is an instance of the copyright holder assigning itself a special right that others in the project do not have, and is thus bound to raise tensions at some point, at least with some volunteers.

What seems to happen in practice is that companies based on dual licensed software do not have truly egalitarian development communities. They get small-scale bug fixes and cleanup patches from external sources, but end up doing most of the hard work with internal resources. For example, Zack Urlocker, vice president of marketing at MySQL, told me that the company generally ends up hiring the most active volunteers anyway. Thus, although the product itself is open source, licensed under the GPL, its development is more or less controlled by the company, albeit with the (extremely unlikely) possibility that someone truly dissatisfied with the company's handling of the software could fork the project. To what degree this threat preemptively shapes the company's policies I don't know, but at any rate, MySQL does not seem to be having acceptance problems either in the open source world or beyond.

Patents

Software patents are the lightning rod issue of the moment in free software, because they pose the only real threat against which the free software community cannot defend itself. Copyright and trademark problems can always be gotten around. If part of your code looks like it may infringe on someone else's copyright, you can just rewrite that part. If it turns out someone has a trademark on your project's name, at the very worst, you can just rename the project. Although changing names would be a temporary inconvenience, it wouldn't matter in the long run, since the code itself would still do what it always did.

But a patent is a blanket injunction against implementing a certain idea. It doesn't matter who writes the code, nor even what programming language is used. Once someone has accused a free software project of infringing a patent, the project must either stop implementing that particular feature, or face an expensive and time-consuming lawsuit. Since the instigators of such lawsuits are usually corporations with deep pockets—that's who has the resources and inclination to acquire patents in the first place—most free software projects cannot afford the latter possibility, and must capitulate immediately even if they think it highly likely that the patent would be unenforceable in court. To avoid getting into such a situation in the first place, free software projects are starting to code defensively, avoiding patented algorithms in advance even when they are the best or only available solution to a programming problem.[1]

Surveys and anecdotal evidence show that not only the vast majority of open source programmers, but a majority of *all* programmers, think that software patents should be abolished entirely.[2] Open source programmers tend to feel particularly strongly about it, and may refuse to work on projects that are too closely associated with the collection or enforcement of software patents. If your organization collects software patents, then make it clear, in a public and irrevocable way, that the patents would never be enforced on open source projects, and that they are only to be used as a defense in case some other party initiates an infringement suit against your organization. This is not only the right thing to do, it's also good open source public relations.

Unfortunately, collecting patents for defensive purposes is a rational action. The current patent system, at least in the United States, is by its nature an arms race: if your competitors have acquired a lot of patents, then your best defense is to acquire a lot of patents yourself, so that if you're ever hit with a patent infringement suit you can respond with a similar threat—then the two parties usually sit down and work out a cross-licensing deal so that neither of them has to pay anything, except to their intellectual property lawyers, of course.

The harm done to free software by software patents is more insidious than just direct threats to code development, however. Software patents encourage an atmosphere of secrecy among firmware designers, who justifiably worry that by publishing details of

---

1   Sun Microsystems and IBM have also made at least a gesture at the problem from the other direction, by freeing large numbers of software patents—1600 and 500 respectively—for use by the open source community. I am not a lawyer and thus can't evaluate the real utility of these grants, but even if they are all important patents, and the terms of the grants make them truly free for use by any open source project, it would still be only a drop in the bucket.

2   See *http://lpf.ai.mit.edu/Whatsnew/survey.html* for one such survey.

their interfaces they will be giving technical help to competitors seeking to slap them with patent infringement suits. This is not just a theoretical danger; it has apparently been happening for a long time in the video card industry, for example. Many video card manufacturers are reluctant to release the detailed programming specifications needed to produce high-performance open source drivers for their cards, thus making it impossible for free operating systems to support those cards to their full potential. Why would the manufacturers do this? It doesn't make sense for them to work *against* software support; after all, compatibility with more operating systems can only mean more card sales. But it turns out that, behind the design room door, these shops are all violating one another's patents, sometimes knowingly and sometimes accidentally. The patents are so unpredictable and so potentially broad that no card manufacturer can ever be certain it's safe, even after doing a patent search. Thus, manufacturers dare not publish their full interface specifications, since that would make it much easier for competitors to figure out whether any patents are being infringed. (Of course, the nature of this situation is such that you will not find a written admission from a primary source that it is going on; I learned it through a personal communication.)

Some free software licenses have special clauses to combat, or at least discourage, software patents. The GNU GPL, for example, contains this language:

> 7. If, as a consequence of a court judgment or allegation of patent
> infringement or for any other reason (not limited to patent issues),
> conditions are imposed on you (whether by court order, agreement or
> otherwise) that contradict the conditions of this License, they do not
> excuse you from the conditions of this License. If you cannot
> distribute so as to satisfy simultaneously your obligations under this
> License and any other pertinent obligations, then as a consequence you
> may not distribute the Program at all. For example, if a patent
> license would not permit royalty-free redistribution of the Program by
> all those who receive copies directly or indirectly through you, then
> the only way you could satisfy both it and this License would be to
> refrain entirely from distribution of the Program.
>
> [...]
>
> It is not the purpose of this section to induce you to infringe any
> patents or other property right claims or to contest validity of any
> such claims; this section has the sole purpose of protecting the
> integrity of the free software distribution system, which is
> implemented by public license practices. Many people have made
> generous contributions to the wide range of software distributed
> through that system in reliance on consistent application of that

system; it is up to the author/donor to decide if he or she is willing to distribute software through any other system and a licensee cannot impose that choice.

The Apache License, Version 2.0 (*http://www.apache.org/licenses/LICENSE-2.0*) also contains anti-patent requirements. First, it stipulates that anyone distributing code under the license must implicitly include a royalty-free patent license for any patents they might hold that could apply to the code. Second, and most ingeniously, it punishes anyone who initiates a patent infringement claim on the covered work, by automatically terminating their implicit patent license the moment such a claim is made:

> 3. Grant of Patent License. Subject to the terms and conditions of this License, each Contributor hereby grants to You a perpetual, worldwide, non-exclusive, no-charge, royalty-free, irrevocable (except as stated in this section) patent license to make, have made, use, offer to sell, sell, import, and otherwise transfer the Work, where such license applies only to those patent claims licensable by such Contributor that are necessarily infringed by their Contribution(s) alone or by combination of their Contribution(s) with the Work to which such Contribution(s) was submitted. If You institute patent litigation against any entity (including a cross-claim or counterclaim in a lawsuit) alleging that the Work or a Contribution incorporated within the Work constitutes direct or contributory patent infringement, then any patent licenses granted to You under this License for that Work shall terminate as of the date such litigation is filed.

Although it is useful, both legally and politically, to build patent defenses into free software licenses this way, in the end these steps will not be enough to dispel the chilling effect that the threat of patent lawsuits has on free software. Only changes in the substance or interpretation of international patent law will do that. To learn more about the problem, and how it's being fought, go to *http://www.nosoftwarepatents.com/*. The Wikipedia article at *http://en.wikipedia.org/wiki/Software_patent* also has a lot of useful information on software patents.

Further Resources

This chapter has only been an introduction to free software licensing issues. Although I hope it contains enough information to get you started on your own open source project, any serious investigation of licensing issues will quickly exhaust what this book can provide. Here is a list of further resources on open source licensing:

- *Understanding Open Source and Free Software Licensing* by Andrew M. St. Laurent (O'Reilly Media).

  This is a full-length book on open source licensing in all its complexity, including many topics omitted from this chapter. See *http://www.oreilly.com/catalog/ osfreesoft/* for details.

- "Make Your Open Source Software GPL-Compatible. Or Else" by David A. Wheeler, at *http://www.dwheeler.com/essays/gpl-compatible.html*.

  This is a detailed and well-written article on why it is important to use a GPL-compatible license even if you don't use the GPL itself. The article also touches on many other licensing questions, and has a high density of excellent links.

- *http://creativecommons.org/*

  Creative Commons is an organization that promotes a range of more flexible and liberal copyrights than traditional copyright practice encourages. They offer licenses not just for software, but for text, art, and music as well, all accessible via a user-friendly license selector; some of the licenses are copylefts, some are non-copyleft but still free, others are simply traditional copyrights but with some restrictions relaxed. The Creative Commons web site gives extremely clear explanations of what it's about. If I had to pick one site to demonstrate the broader philosophical implications of the free software movement, this would be it.

Free Version Control Systems

CVS's shortcomings have inspired many efforts to replace it, and in the last few years many of these projects have reached usability. CVS's days as the uncontested default choice are slowly coming to an end. Following are all the other open source version control systems I was aware of as of early 2005. The only one I use on a regular basis is Subversion, that's why it's listed first. I have no recommendations for or against any of the others; a lot of information here is taken from their web sites. See also *http://en.wikipedia.org/wiki/List_of_revision_control_software*.

Subversion

Subversion was written first and foremost to be a replacement for CVS—that is, to approach version control in roughly the same way CVS does, but without the problems and feature omissions that most frequently annoy users of CVS. One of Subversion's goals is for people already accustomed to CVS to find the transition to Subversion relatively smooth. There is not space here to go into detail about Subversion's features; see its web site for more information. *[Disclaimer: I am involved in Subversion development, and it is the only one of these systems that I use on a regular basis.]*

http://subversion.tigris.org/

SVK

Although it is built on top of Subversion, SVK probably resembles Arch more than it does Subversion. SVK supports distributed (noncentralized) development, sophisticated change merging, and the ability to mirror trees from non-SVK version control systems. See the web site for details.

http://svk.elixus.org/

Arch

GNU Arch supports both distributed and centralized development. Developers commit their changes to an "archive," which may be local, and the changes can be pushed and pulled to other archives as the managers of those archives see fit. As such a methodology implies, Arch has more sophisticated merge support than CVS. Arch also allows one to easily make branches of archives to which one does not have commit access. This is only a brief summary; see the Arch web pages for details.

http://www.gnu.org/software/gnu-arch/

monotone

"monotone is a free distributed version control system. it provides a simple, single-file transactional version store, with fully disconnected operation and an efficient peer-to-peer synchronization protocol. it understands history-sensitive merging, lightweight branches, integrated code review and 3rd party testing. it uses cryptographic version naming and client-side RSA certificates. it has good internationalization support, has no external dependencies, runs on linux, solaris, OSX, and windows, and is licensed under the GNU GPL."

http://www.venge.net/monotone/

Codeville

"Why yet another version control system? All other version control systems require that you keep careful track of the relationships between branches so as not [to] have to repeatedly merge the same conflicts. Codeville is much more anarchic. It allows you to update from or commit to any repository at any time with no unnecessary re-merges.

"Codeville works by creating an identifier for each change which is done, and remembering the list of all changes which have been applied to each file and the last change which modified each line in each file. When there's a conflict, it checks to see if one of the two sides has already been applied to the other one, and if so makes the other side win automatically. When there's an actual not automatically mergeable version conflict, Codeville behaves in almost exactly the same way as CVS."

http://codeville.org/

Vesta

"Vesta is a portable SCM [Software Configuration Management] system targeted at supporting development of software systems of almost any size, from fairly small (under 10,000 source lines) to very large (10,000,000 source lines).

"Vesta is a mature system. It is the result of over 10 years of research and development at the Compaq/Digital Systems Research Center, and it was in production use by Compaq's Alpha microprocessor group for over two and a half years. The Alpha group had over 150 active developers at two sites thousands of miles apart, on the east and west coasts of the United States. The group used Vesta to manage builds with as much as 130 MB of source data, each producing 1.5 GB of derived data. The builds done at the eastern site in an average day produced about 10–15 GB of derived data, all managed by Vesta. Although Vesta was designed with software development in mind, the Alpha group demonstrated the system's flexibility by using it for hardware development, checking their hardware description language files into Vesta's source code control facility and building simulators and other derived objects with Vesta's builder. The members of the former Alpha group, now a part of Intel, are continuing to use Vesta today in a new microprocessor project."

http://www.vestasys.org/

Darcs

"David's Advanced Revision Control System is yet another replacement for CVS. It is written in Haskell, and has been used on Linux, MacOS X, FreeBSD, OpenBSD and Microsoft Windows. Darcs includes a cgi script, which can be used to view the contents of your repository."

http://abridgegame.org/darcs/

Aegis

"Aegis is a transaction-based software configuration management system. It provides a framework within which a team of developers may work on many changes to a program independently, and Aegis coordinates integrating these changes back into the master source of the program, with as little disruption as possible."

http://aegis.sourceforge.net/

CVSNT

"CVSNT is an advanced multiplatform version control system. Compatible with the industry standard CVS protocol it now supports many more features… CVSNT is Open Source, Free software licensed under the GNU General Public License."

Its feature list includes authentication via all standard CVS protocols, plus Windows-specific SSPI and Active Directory; secure transport support, via sserver or encrypted SSPI; cross platform (runs in Windows or Unix environments); NT version is fully integrated with Win32 system; MergePoint processing means no more tagging to merge; under active development.

http://cvsnt.org/

Meta-CVS

"Meta-CVS is a version control system built around CVS. Although it retains most of the features of CVS, including all of the networking support, it is more capable than CVS, and easier to use."

The features listed on Meta-CVS's web site include: directory structure versioning, improved file type handling, simpler and more user-friendly branching and merging, support for symbolic links, property lists attached to versioned data, improved third-party data importing, and easy upgrading from stock CVS.

http://users.footprints.net/~kaz/mcvs.html

OpenCM

"OpenCM is designed as a secure, high-integrity replacement for CVS. A list of the key features can be found on the features page. While not as 'feature rich' as CVS, it supports some useful things that CVS lacks. Briefly, OpenCM provides first-class support for renames and configuration, cryptographic authentication and access control, and first-class branches."

http://www.opencm.org/

Stellation

"Stellation is an advanced, extensible software configuration management system, originally developed at IBM Research. While Stellation provides all of the standard functions available in any SCM system, it is distinguished by a number of advanced features, such as task-oriented change management, consistent project versioning and lightweight branching, intended to ease the development of software systems by large groups of loosely coordinated developers."

http://www.eclipse.org/stellation/

PRCS

"PRCS, the Project Revision Control System, is the front end to a set of tools that (like CVS) provide a way to deal with sets of files and directories as an entity, preserving coherent versions of the entire set... Its purpose is similar to that of SCCS, RCS, and CVS, but (according to its authors, at least), it is much simpler than any of those systems."

http://prcs.sourceforge.net/

Bazaar

Bazaar is still under development. It will be an implementation of the GNU Arch protocol, will retain compatibility with the GNU Arch protocol as it evolves, and work with the GNU Arch community process for any protocol changes that might be required for user friendliness.

http://bazaar.canonical.com/

Bazaar-NG

Bazaar-NG (or bzr) is currently under development by Canonical (*http://canonical. com/*). It offers a choice between centralized and decentralized work within a single project. For example, when in the office, you can work on a shared central branch; for experimental changes or offline work you can make a branch on your laptop and merge back in later.

http://bazaar-ng.org/

ArX

ArX is a distributed version control system offering branching and merging features, cryptographic data integrity verification, and the ability to publish archives easily on any HTTP server.

http://www.nongnu.org/arx/

SourceJammer

"SourceJammer is a source control and versioning system written in Java. It consists of a server-side component that maintains the files and version history, and handles check-in, check-out, etc. and other commands; and a client-side component that makes requests of the server and manages the files on the client-side file system."

http://sourcejammer.org/

FastCST

"A 'modern' system that uses changesets over file revisions and distributed operation rather than centralized control. As long as you have an e-mail account you can use FastCST. For larger distribution you only need an FTP server and/or an HTTP server or use the built in 'serve' command to serve your stuff up directly. All changesets are universally unique and have tons of meta-data.... Merging is done by comparing a merged changeset against the current directory contents, rather than trying to merge it with another changeset."

http://www.zedshaw.com/projects/fastcst/index.html

GIT

GIT is a project started by Linus Torvalds to manage the Linux kernel source tree. It is very narrowly focused on the needs of kernel development, and was still under development as of this writing. It doesn't appear to have a home page yet, but check the Wikipedia page above for updates.

http://en.wikipedia.org/wiki/Git

Superversion

"Superversion is a multiuser distributed version control system based on change sets. It aims to be an industrial-strength, open source alternative to commercial solutions that is equally easy to use (or even easier) and similarly powerful. In fact, intuitive and efficient usability has been one of the top priorities in Superversion's development from the very beginning."

http://www.superversion.org/

APPENDIX B

Free Bug Trackers

No matter what bug tracker a project uses, some developers always like to complain about it. This seems to be more true of bug trackers than of any other standard development tool. I think it's because bug trackers are so visual and so interactive that it's easy to imagine the improvements one would make (if one only had the time), and to describe those improvements out loud. Take the inevitable complaints with a grain of salt—many of the trackers below are pretty good.

Throughout these listings, the word "issue" is used to refer to the items the trackers track. But remember that each system may have its own terminology, in which the corresponding term might be "artifact" or "bug" or something else.

Bugzilla

Bugzilla is very popular, actively maintained, and seems to make its users pretty happy. I've been using a modified variant of it in my work for four years now, and like it. It's not highly customizeable, but in a odd way that may be one of its features: Bugzilla installations tend to look pretty much the same wherever they are found, which means many developers are already accustomed to its interface and will feel they are in familiar territory.

http://www.bugzilla.org/

GNATS

GNU GNATS is one of the oldest open source bug trackers, and is widely used. It's biggest strengths are interface diversity (it can be used not just through a web browser, but also through email or command-line tools), and plain-text issue storage. The fact that all issue data is stored in text files on disk makes it easier to write custom tools to trawl and parse the data (for example, to generate statistical reports). GNATS can also absorb emails automatically by various means, and add them to the appropriate issues based on patterns in the email headers, which makes logging user/ developer conversations very easy.

http://www.gnu.org/software/gnats/

RT

RequestTracker's web site says "RT is an enterprise-grade ticketing system which enables a group of people to intelligently and efficiently manage tasks, issues, and requests submitted by a community of users," and that about sums it up. RT has a fairly polished web interface, and seems to have a pretty wide installed base. The interface is a bit visually complex, but that becomes less distracting as you get used to it. RT is licensed under the GNU GPL (for some reason their web site doesn't make this clear).

http://www.bestpractical.com/rt/

Trac

Trac is a bit more than a bug tracker: it's really an integrated wiki and bug tracking system. It uses a wiki linking to connect issues, files, version control changesets, and plain wiki pages. It's fairly simple to set up, and integrates with Subversion (see Appendix A).

http://trac.edgewall.com/

Roundup

Roundup is pretty easy to install (only Python 2.1 or higher is required), and simple to use. It has web, email, and command-line interfaces. The issue data templates and web interface are customizeable, as is some of its state-transition logic.

http://roundup.sourceforge.net/

Mantis

Mantis is a web-based bug tracking system, written in PHP, and using MySQL database for storage. It has the features you'd expect. Personally, I find the web interface clean, intuitive, and easy on the eyes.

http://www.mantisbt.org/

Scarab

Scarab is meant to be a highly customizable, full-featured bug tracker, offering more or less the union of the features offered by other bug trackers: data entry, queries, reports, notifications to interested parties, collaborative accumulation of comments, and dependency tracking.

It is customizable through administrative web pages. You can have multiple "modules" (projects) active in a single Scarab installation. Within a given module, you can create new issue types (defects, enhancements, tasks, support requests, etc.), and add arbitrary attributes, to tune the tracker to your project's specific requirements.

As of late 2004, Scarab was getting close to its 1.0 release.

http://scarab.tigris.org/

DBTS

The Debian Bug Tracking System is unusual in that all input and manipulation of issues is done via email: each issue gets its own dedicated email address. The DBTS scales pretty well: *http://bugs.debian.org/* has 277,741 issues, for example.

Since interaction is done via regular mail clients, an environment that is familiar and easily accessible to most people, the DBTS is good for handling high volumes of incoming reports that need quick classification and response. There are disadvantages too, of course. Developers must invest the time needed to learn the email command system, and users must write their bug reports without a web-form to guide them in choosing what information to write. There are tools available to help users send better bug reports, such as the command-line *reportbug* program or the *debbugs-el* package for Emacs. But most people won't use these tools, they'll just write email manually, and they may or may not follow the bug reporting guidelines posted by your project.

The DBTS has a read-only web interface, for viewing and querying issues.

http://www.chiark.greenend.org.uk/~ian/debbugs/

Trouble-Ticket Trackers

These are more oriented toward help desk ticket tracking than software bug tracking. You'll probably do better with a regular bug tracker, but these are listed for the sake of completeness, and because there could conceivably be unusual projects for which a trouble-ticket system might be more appropriate than a traditional bug tracker.

WebCall
> *http://myrapid.com/webcall/*

Teacup
> *http://www.altara.org/teacup.html.* (Teacup doesn't appear to be under active development anymore, but the downloads are still available. Note that it has both web and email interfaces.)

BTT

Bluetail Ticket Tracker is somewhere between a standard trouble ticket tracker and a bug tracker. It offers privacy features that are somewhat unusual among open-source bug trackers: users of the system are categorized as Staff, Friend, Customer, or Anonymous, and makes more or less data available depending on one's category. It offers some email integration, a command-line interface, and mechanisms for converting emails into tickets. It also has features for maintaining information not associated with any specific ticket, such as internal documentation or FAQs.

http://btt.sourceforge.net/

Why Should I Care What Color the Bikeshed Is?

You shouldn't; it doesn't really matter, and you have better things to spend your time on.

Poul-Henning Kamp's famous "bikeshed" post (an excerpt from which appears in Chapter 6) is an eloquent disquisition on what tends to go wrong in group discussions. It is reprinted here with his permission. The orginal URL is *http://www.freebsd. org/cgi/getmsg.cgi?fetch=506636+517178+/usr/local/www/db/text/1999/freebsd-hackers/ 19991003.freebsd-hackers.*

```
Subject: A bike shed (any colour will do) on greener grass...

From: Poul-Henning Kamp <phk@freebsd.org>

Date: Sat, 02 Oct 1999 16:14:10 +0200

Message-ID: <18238.938873650@critter.freebsd.dk>

Sender: phk@critter.freebsd.dk

Bcc: Blind Distribution List: ;

MIME-Version: 1.0


[bcc'ed to committers, hackers]
```

My last pamphlet was sufficiently well received that I was not
scared away from sending another one, and today I have the time
and inclination to do so.

I've had a little trouble with deciding on the right distribution
of this kind of stuff, this time it is bcc'ed to committers and
hackers, that is probably the best I can do. I'm not subscribed
to hackers myself but more on that later.

The thing which have triggered me this time is the "sleep(1) should
do fractional seconds" thread, which have pestered our lives for
many days now, it's probably already a couple of weeks, I can't
even be bothered to check.

To those of you who have missed this particular thread: Congratulations.

It was a proposal to make sleep(1) DTRT if given a non-integer
argument that set this particular grass-fire off. I'm not going
to say anymore about it than that, because it is a much smaller
item than one would expect from the length of the thread, and it
has already received far more attention than some of the *problems*
we have around here.

The sleep(1) saga is the most blatant example of a bike shed
discussion we have had ever in FreeBSD. The proposal was well
thought out, we would gain compatibility with OpenBSD and NetBSD,
and still be fully compatible with any code anyone ever wrote.

Yet so many objections, proposals and changes were raised and
launched that one would think the change would have plugged all

the holes in swiss cheese or changed the taste of Coca Cola or
something similar serious.

"What is it about this bike shed ?" Some of you have asked me.

It's a long story, or rather it's an old story, but it is quite
short actually. C. Northcote Parkinson wrote a book in the early
1960'ies, called "Parkinson's Law", which contains a lot of insight
into the dynamics of management.

You can find it on Amazon, and maybe also in your dads book-shelf,
it is well worth its price and the time to read it either way,
if you like Dilbert, you'll like Parkinson.

Somebody recently told me that he had read it and found that only
about 50% of it applied these days. That is pretty darn good I
would say, many of the modern management books have hit-rates a
lot lower than that, and this one is 35+ years old.

In the specific example involving the bike shed, the other vital
component is an atomic power-plant, I guess that illustrates the
age of the book.

Parkinson shows how you can go in to the board of directors and
get approval for building a multi-million or even billion dollar
atomic power plant, but if you want to build a bike shed you will
be tangled up in endless discussions.

Parkinson explains that this is because an atomic plant is so vast,
so expensive and so complicated that people cannot grasp it, and

rather than try, they fall back on the assumption that somebody else checked all the details before it got this far.   Richard P. Feynmann gives a couple of interesting, and very much to the point, examples relating to Los Alamos in his books.

A bike shed on the other hand. Anyone can build one of those over a weekend, and still have time to watch the game on TV. So no matter how well prepared, no matter how reasonable you are with your proposal, somebody will seize the chance to show that he is doing his job, that he is paying attention, that he is *here*.

In Denmark we call it "setting your fingerprint". It is about personal pride and prestige, it is about being able to point somewhere and say "There! *I* did that." It is a strong trait in politicians, but present in most people given the chance. Just think about footsteps in wet cement.

I bow my head in respect to the original proposer because he stuck to his guns through this carpet blanking from the peanut gallery, and the change is in our tree today. I would have turned my back and walked away after less than a handful of messages in that thread.

And that brings me, as I promised earlier, to why I am not subscribed to -hackers:

I un-subscribed from -hackers several years ago, because I could not keep up with the email load. Since then I have dropped off several other lists as well for the very same reason.

And I still get a lot of email. A lot of it gets routed to /dev/null
by filters: People like [omitted] will never make it onto my
screen, commits to documents in languages I don't understand
likewise, commits to ports as such. All these things and more go
the winter way without me ever even knowing about it.

But despite these sharp teeth under my mailbox I still get too much
email.

This is where the greener grass comes into the picture:

I wish we could reduce the amount of noise in our lists and I wish
we could let people build a bike shed every so often, and I don't
really care what colour they paint it.

The first of these wishes is about being civil, sensitive and
intelligent in our use of email.

If I could concisely and precisely define a set of criteria for
when one should and when one should not reply to an email so that
everybody would agree and abide by it, I would be a happy man, but
I am too wise to even attempt that.

But let me suggest a few pop-up windows I would like to see
mail-programs implement whenever people send or reply to email
to the lists they want me to subscribe to:

```
        +----------------------------------------------------------------+
        | Your email is about to be sent to several hundred thousand |
        | people, who will have to spend at least 10 seconds reading |
        | it before they can decide if it is interesting.  At least  |
```

```
| two man-weeks will be spent reading your email.  Many of  |
| the recipients will have to pay to download your email.   |
|                                                           |
| Are you absolutely sure that your email is of sufficient  |
| importance to bother all these people ?                   |
|                                                           |
|                  [YES]  [REVISE]  [CANCEL]                 |
+-----------------------------------------------------------+


+-----------------------------------------------------------+
| Warning:  You have not read all emails in this thread yet. |
| Somebody else may already have said what you are about to  |
| say in your reply.  Please read the entire thread before   |
| replying to any email in it.                               |
|                                                            |
|                       [CANCEL]                             |
+------------------------------------------------------------+


+-----------------------------------------------------------+
| Warning:  Your mail program have not even shown you the    |
| entire message yet.  Logically it follows that you cannot  |
| possibly have read it all and understood it.               |
|                                                            |
| It is not polite to reply to an email until you have       |
| read it all and thought about it.                          |
|                                                            |
| A cool off timer for this thread will prevent you from     |
| replying to any email in this thread for the next one hour |
|                                                            |
|                       [Cancel]                             |
+------------------------------------------------------------+
```

```
+----------------------------------------------------------------+
| You composed this email at a rate of more than N.NN cps       |
| It is generally not possible to think and type at a rate      |
| faster than A.AA cps, and therefore you reply is likely to |
| incoherent, badly thought out and/or emotional.                |
|                                                                |
| A cool off timer will prevent you from sending any email      |
| for the next one hour.                                         |
|                                                                |
|                        [Cancel]                               |
+----------------------------------------------------------------+
```

The second part of my wish is more emotional. Obviously, the
capacities we had manning the unfriendly fire in the sleep(1)
thread, despite their many years with the project, never cared
enough to do this tiny deed, so why are they suddenly so enflamed
by somebody else so much their junior doing it ?

I wish I knew.

I do know that reasoning will have no power to stop such "reactionaire
conservatism". It may be that these people are frustrated about
their own lack of tangible contribution lately or it may be a bad
case of "we're old and grumpy, WE know how youth should behave".

Either way it is very unproductive for the project, but I have no
suggestions for how to stop it. The best I can suggest is to refrain
from fuelling the monsters that lurk in the mailing lists: Ignore
them, don't answer them, forget they're there.

I hope we can get a stronger and broader base of contributors in
FreeBSD, and I hope we together can prevent the grumpy old men
and the [omitted] of the world from chewing them up, spitting

them out and scaring them away before they ever get a leg to the
ground.

For the people who have been lurking out there, scared away from
participating by the gargoyles: I can only apologise and encourage
you to try anyway, this is not the way I want the environment in
the project to be.

Poul-Henning

Example Instructions for Reporting Bugs

This is a lightly edited copy of the Subversion project's online instructions to new users on how to report bugs. See "Treat Every User as a Potential Volunteer" in Chapter 8 for why it is important that a project have such instructions. The original document is located at *http://svn.collab.net/repos/svn/trunk/BUGS*.

```
                    REPORTING BUGS

                    = == == == == == == ==


   This document tells how and where to report bugs.  It is not a list of

   all outstanding bugs -- we use an online issue tracker for that, see


      http://subversion.tigris.org/project_issues.html


   If you're about to report a bug, please take a look at the guidelines

   in the section "How To Report A Bug" below.
```

```
Where To Report A Bug:

= == == == == == == == == == =


    * If the bug is in Subversion itself, send mail to
      users@subversion.tigris.org.  Once it's confirmed as a bug,
      someone, possibly you, can enter it into the issue tracker at
      http://subversion.tigris.org/servlets/ProjectIssues


    * If the bug is in the APR library, please report it to both of
      these mailing lists: dev@apr.apache.org, dev@subversion.tigris.org


    * If the bug is in the Neon HTTP library, please report it to:
      neon@webdav.org, dev@subversion.tigris.org


    * If the bug is in Apache httpd 2.0, please report it to both of
      these mailing lists: dev@httpd.apache.org, dev@subversion.tigris.org
      The Apache httpd developer mailing list is high-traffic, so your
      bug report post has the possibility to be overlooked.  You may also
      file a bug report at:
      http://httpd.apache.org/bug_report.html


    * If the bug is in your rug, please give it a hug and keep it snug.


How To Report A Bug:

= == == == == == == == == == =


First, make sure it's a bug.  If Subversion does not behave the way
you expect, look in the documentation and mailing list archives for
evidence that it should behave the way you expect.  Of course, if it's
a common-sense thing, like Subversion just destroyed your data and
caused smoke to pour out of your monitor, then you can trust your
```

judgement. But if you're not sure, go ahead and ask on the users mailing list first, users@subversion.tigris.org.

Once you've established that it's a bug, the most important thing you can do is come up with a simple description and reproduction recipe. For example, if the bug, as you initially found it, involves five files over ten commits, try to make it happen with just one file and one commit. The simpler the reproduction recipe, the more likely a developer is to successfully reproduce the bug and fix it.

When you write up the reproduction recipe, don't just write a prose description of what you did to make the bug happen. Instead, give a literal transcript of the exact series of commands you ran, and their output. If there are files involved, be sure to include the names of the files, and even their content if you think it might be relevant. The very best thing is to package your reproduction recipe as a script, that helps us a lot.

   [Quick sanity check: you *are* running the most recent version of
   Subversion, right? :-) Possibly the bug has already been fixed; you
   should test your reproduction recipe against the most recent
   Subversion development tree. Also, make sure your APR tree is
   up-to-date.]

In addition to the reproduction recipe, we'll also need a complete description of the environment in which you reproduced the bug. That means:

   - Your operating system
   - The release and/or revision of Subversion
   - The compiler and configuration options you built Subversion with

- Any private modifications you made to your Subversion

- The version of Berkeley DB you're running Subversion with

- Anything else that could possibly be relevant. Err on the side
  of too much information, rather than too little.

Once you have all this, you're ready to write the report. Start out
with a clear description of what the bug is. That is, say how you
expected Subversion to behave, and contrast that with how it actually
behaved. While the bug may seem obvious to you, it may not be so
obvious to someone else, so it's best to avoid a guessing game.

Follow that with the environment description, and the reproduction
recipe. If you also want to include speculation as to the cause, and
even a patch to fix the bug, that's great! See the HACKING file for
more information about writing patches.

 Index

C

CAN/CVE numbers, 158
candidate releases, 186
canned hosting, 32, 48, 84–86
change management, 61
ChangeLog files, 180
changes and changesets, 62
CHANGES files, 179
checkouts, 62
closed-source licensing, 233
code review, 40
Codeville, 250
CollabNet, 101
commits, 61
committers, 219–223
    COMMITTERS file, 223
    dormant committers, 222
    partial commit access, 221
    qualities of, 220
    revocation of commit access, 221
    voting, and, 95
communication, 27, 121–162
    bug tracking and, 151–153
    difficult people, 139–142
    mailing lists (see mailing lists)
    publicity, 153–155
    security vulnerabilities, 155–162
        CAN/CVE numbers, 158
        fix distribution, 161
        prenotification, 160
    writing, 122–131
        content, 124
        email conventions, 123
        face, 129
        impact of good writing, 122
        rudeness, 128
        signature blocks, 130
        structure and format, 123
        tone, 126
compilation process, 182
conflicts, 64
consensus, 91
    voting and, 92
contract work, 109–113
contrib/ area, 201
COPYING files, 34, 179
copyleft, 235
copy-modify-merge model, 64

copyright, 34
    assignment of, 241
corporate funding, 99–119
    contracting, 109–113
    funder relations to open source
        community, 104–109
    impacts on open source projects, 100
    issues for funders, 100
    marketing concerns, 117–119
    motivations for, 101–103
        dual-licensing, 102
    non-programming activities, 113–117
        documentation, 116
        hosting and bandwidth, 116
        legal issues, addressing, 115
        quality assurance, 114
        usability testing, 116
    programmers, hiring of, 103
credit for participation, 223
criticism, employing toward project
    members, 198
CVS (Concurrent Version System), 64
    regression test suite, 204
CVSNT, 252

D

Darcs (David's Advanced Revision Control
    System), 251
DBTS (Debian Bug Tracking System), 259
delegation, 195–198
democracy, 90
developer documentation, 31
developer guidelines, 28
development status, 24
DFSG-compliant (Debian Free Software
    Guidelines) licensing, 233
diffs, 63
discussion threads, 133–139
    holy wars, 136
    noisy minorities, 138
    productive and unproductive, 133–134
    soft topics and debate, 135
documentation, 28–33
    automated compilation, 202
    availability, 30
    developer documentation, 31
    documentation managers, 212
    documentation patches, 212
    example output, 32

format, 30
funding of, 116
governance and, 97
screenshots, 32
downloads, 25
dual-licensing, 102, 242

E

email
content, 124
conventions, 123
signature blocks, 130
tone, 126
employing programmers, 103
contract work, 109–113

F

FAQS (Frequently Asked Questions), 31
FAQ managers, 215
FastCST, 254
features lists, 24
filtering email, 50
filtering mailing list posts, 50
forks, 88, 225–229
causes, 225
GCC/EGCS example, 227
initiating, 228
managing, 226
forward-compatible releases, 168
FOSS, F/OSS, and FLOSS licensing, 232
free software, xiii, 11
culture, 14
licensing, 231
open source software, versus, 11–14
(see also open source software), 15
Free Software Foundation (FSF), 7, 9
free software directory, 19
Frequently Asked Questions (see FAQs)
freshmeat.net, 19
funding, 99
(see also corporate funding)
donations, 102

G

GCC/EGCS fork, 227
GIT, 254
GNATS, 258
GNU General Public License (see GPL)
GNU Project, 7

governance, 87–98
Apache Software Foundation
governance documents, 98
benevolent dictators, 89
consensus, 91
democracy, 90
documentation, 97
forks, impact of, 88
funding of projects (see corporate
funding)
honest brokers, 93
polling, 96
Subversion HACKING file, 98
version control, impact of, 92
vetoes, 96
voting, 92–96
approval voting, 93
circumstances requiring, 94
voting privileges, assigning, 95
GPL (GNU General Public License), 7, 34,
235, 239
compatibility with other licensing, 236
patents and, 245

H

hacker ethic, 6
hacktivation energy, 21
headers, 53
holy wars, 136–138
honest brokers, 93
hosting, funding of, 116
hyperbole, 125

I

information management, 45–86
bug tracking software, 73–79
canned hosting (see canned hosting)
essential components, 47
mailing lists (see mailing lists)
management software, 59
real-time chat software, 79–82
version control (see version control)
web sites, 84
wikis, 82
INSTALL files, 179
installation process, 182
internationalization (118N) and localization
(L10N), 212

About the Author

In 1995, KARL FOGEL cofounded Cyclic Software, a company offering commercial CVS support. In 1999, he added support to CVS for anonymous read-only repository access, inaugurating a new standard for access to development sources in open source projects. That same year, he wrote *Open Source Development With CVS* (published by Coriolis), now in its third edition with Paraglyph Press.

Since early 2000, he has worked for CollabNet, Inc., managing the creation and development of Subversion, a version control system written from scratch by CollabNet and a team of open source volunteers and meant to replace CVS as the de facto standard among open source projects. He also participates in various other open source projects as a module maintainer, patch contributor, and documentation writer.

Colophon

MARY ANNE WEEKS MAYO was the production editor and Chris Downey was the copyeditor for *Producing Open Source Software*. Sada Preisch proofread the book. Claire Cloutier provided quality control. John Bickelhaupt wrote the index.

MIKE KOHNKE designed the cover of this book. Karen Montgomery produced the cover layout in Adobe InDesign CS using Akzidenz Grotesk and Orator fonts.

PHYLLIS MCKEE designed the interior layout and the template. This book was converted by Andrew Savikas to FrameMaker 5.5.6 with a format conversion tool created by Erik Ray, Jason McIntosh, Neil Walls, and Mike Sierra that uses Perl and XML technologies. The text font is Adobe's Meridien; the heading font is ITC Bailey.

CPSIA information can be obtained at www.ICGtesting.com
Printed in the USA
265769BV00014B/1/P